IMAGES
of America

BETHLEHEM

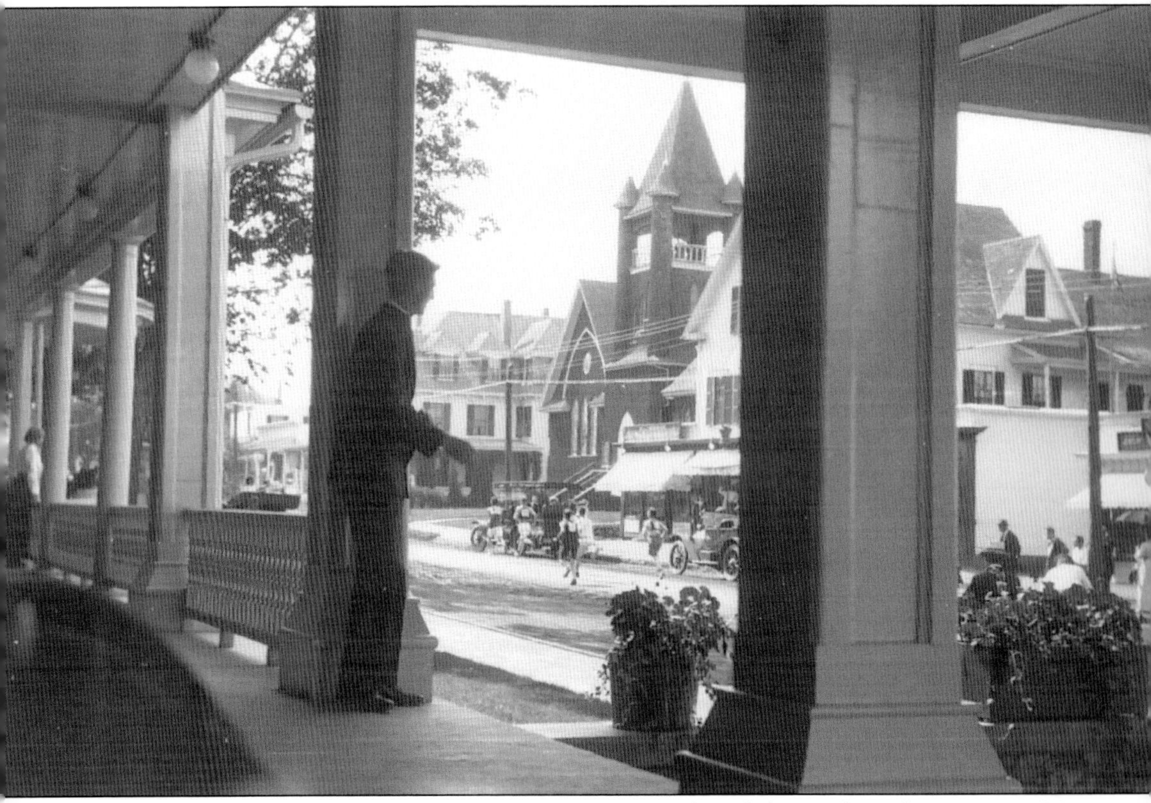

The Sinclair hotel's wide porch was a favorite spot to relax while watching the action on Main Street. (Clare Brown, Morrell Crawford photograph.)

IMAGES
of America

BETHLEHEM

Elizabeth Anne Ward

ARCADIA
PUBLISHING

ISBN 978-0-7385-0440-7

Published by Arcadia Publishing
Charleston, South Carolina

Printed in the United States of America

Library of Congress Catalog Card Number: 00-106420

For all general information, contact Arcadia Publishing:
Telephone 843-853-2070
Fax 843-853-0044
E-mail sales@arcadiapublishing.com
For customer service and orders:
Toll-free 1-888-313-2665

Visit us on the Internet at www.arcadiapublishing.com

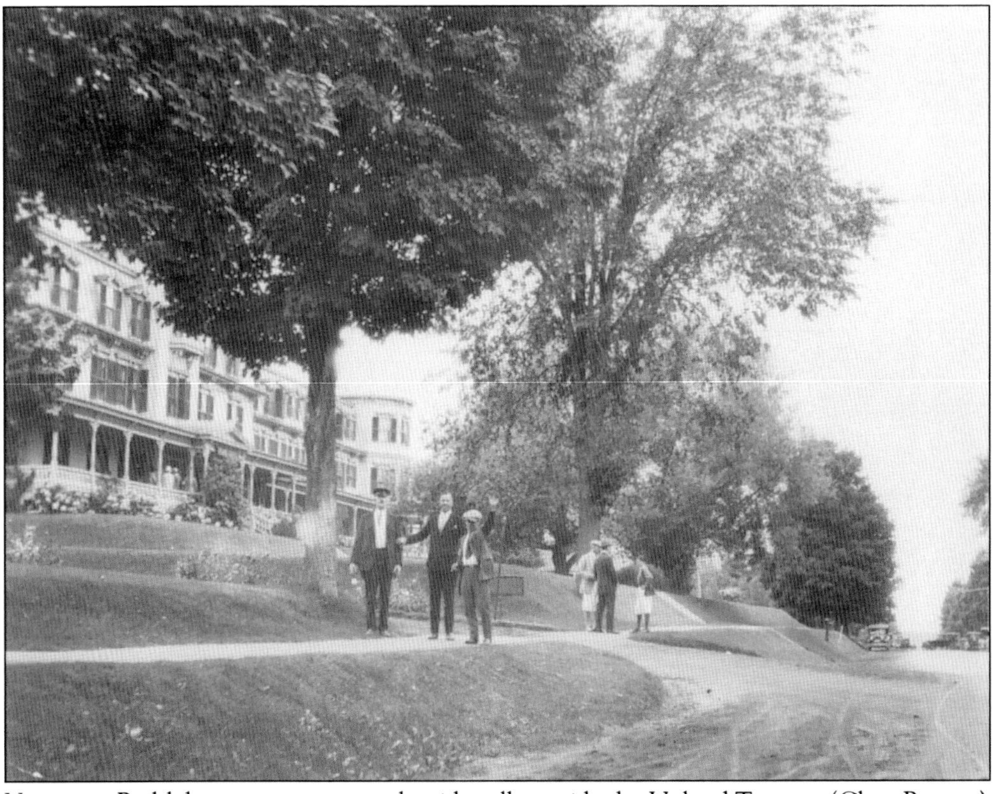

Visitors to Bethlehem congregate on the sidewalk outside the Upland Terrace. (Clare Brown.)

Contents

ACKNOWLEDGMENTS

I would like to thank all those who helped with this project, providing me with photographs and anecdotes, facts and corrections. Special thanks to Clare Brown for her proofreading, reconnaissance work, and contributions; Paul Hudson for his memories and extensive postcard collection; Kathy Parrish for her photographic skill; Philip Bell, Patsy Bonardi, Muriel Brown, Harvey and Thelma Burlock, Marilyn Carmen, Norm Chapman, Helen Cunningham, Joyce Donadio, Marilyn Johnson, Adele Fisch, Solomon Fleischman, Betty Glusky, Keith Harvey, Alice McCullock, Wayne Miller, Pat Murray, David Olson, Dick and Sharon Robie, the Sanborn family, John and Nancy Stevenson, Ruth Whitcomb, Bill and Judy Whitman, and Olive Whittier for their generous interest and contributions. Thank you to Dartmouth College Library, the Society for the Protection of New Hampshire Forests, and the Bethlehem Library for the loan of images. I would also like to express my gratitude for the support of the officers and members of the Bethlehem Heritage Society.

INTRODUCTION

For the first ten years that I lived in Bethlehem, my interests revolved around the abundant outdoor recreation opportunities that the White Mountains have to offer—hiking, camping, and cross-country skiing. Oh, I noticed and appreciated Bethlehem's fine old buildings, but I had no idea of the depth of the town's history—until I had a conversation one evening with the town librarian, Muriel Brown.

"We had 30 hotels here, you know," she told me. "On summer nights we'd take our daughter up to Main Street to watch the ladies walking up and down the sidewalks in their fur coats. The sidewalks would be filled with people. The doors to the Sinclair ballroom would be open, and you could hear the orchestra playing."

Her reminiscences fired my imagination. Her daughter is about my age, so I too could have experienced the heyday of this mountain resort town. I walked the now quiet Main Street and tried to imagine how it had looked lined with hotels, thronged with sophisticated city people, music playing, luxurious automobiles tooling back and forth, shops and restaurants bustling.

The impact of an influx of thousands on a tiny mountain community intrigued me. How did residents and visitors get along? How did exposure to worldly attitudes and opinions change the natives of this isolated village?

I cannot say that my study has been exhaustive, but I have concluded that a comfortable symbiotic relationship developed. The visitors wanted Bethlehem's clean air and beauty, its quiet atmosphere, and its proximity to the mountains. They wanted the leisure and relaxation on a scale that we today can only dream of—a whole summer spent among congenial companions enjoying healthy recreation, social opportunities, good food, and lots of rocking chair time on the wide porches.

The residents, in turn, made a living providing goods and services to the summer people. A few owned hotels; some had small lodging houses or stores; many were carpenters, tradesmen, farmers, or professionals. Others were employed by the hotels as gardeners, maintenance men, cooks, chambermaids, and wait staff. The hotel trade meant that townspeople were no longer dependent on farming or logging, and an industrial base was not necessary for employment.

Today, tourism adds billions of dollars to New Hampshire's economy. The small town of Bethlehem has contributed greatly to creating the experience that millions of visitors enjoy each year.

One

Thirty Hotels

If anything came to define Bethlehem, it was the town's astonishing number of hotels. In the 1880s, Bethlehem had 1,400 residents and 30 hotels. Several of those 30 qualified as grand hotels due to their capacity, size, and style; however, most were more modest buildings holding between 50 and 100 guests.

The architecture of the hotels varied. Many were square or rectangular boxes with mansard roofs and white clapboards. The New Arlington and the Sherman Inn are current examples of this style. A few had gambrel roofs, such as the Maplehurst. Some were farmhouses, added on to as the business grew. The Wayside Inn exemplifies this type.

Despite any similarities in structure, each hotel offered a unique experience. Bethlehem had something for everyone, for every taste and pocketbook.

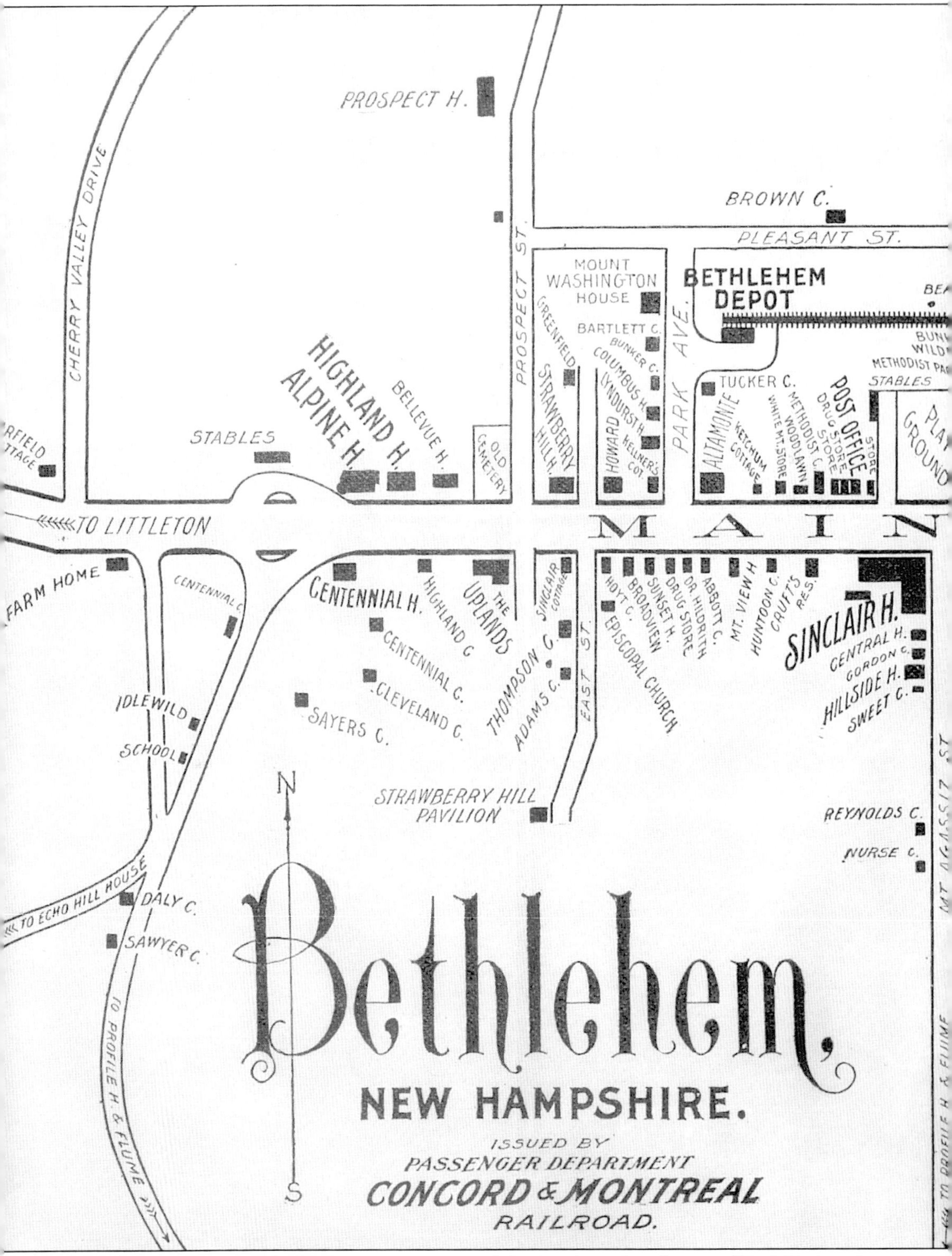

A late-1890s map of Bethlehem shows many of the hotels in this chapter. (Paul Hudson.)

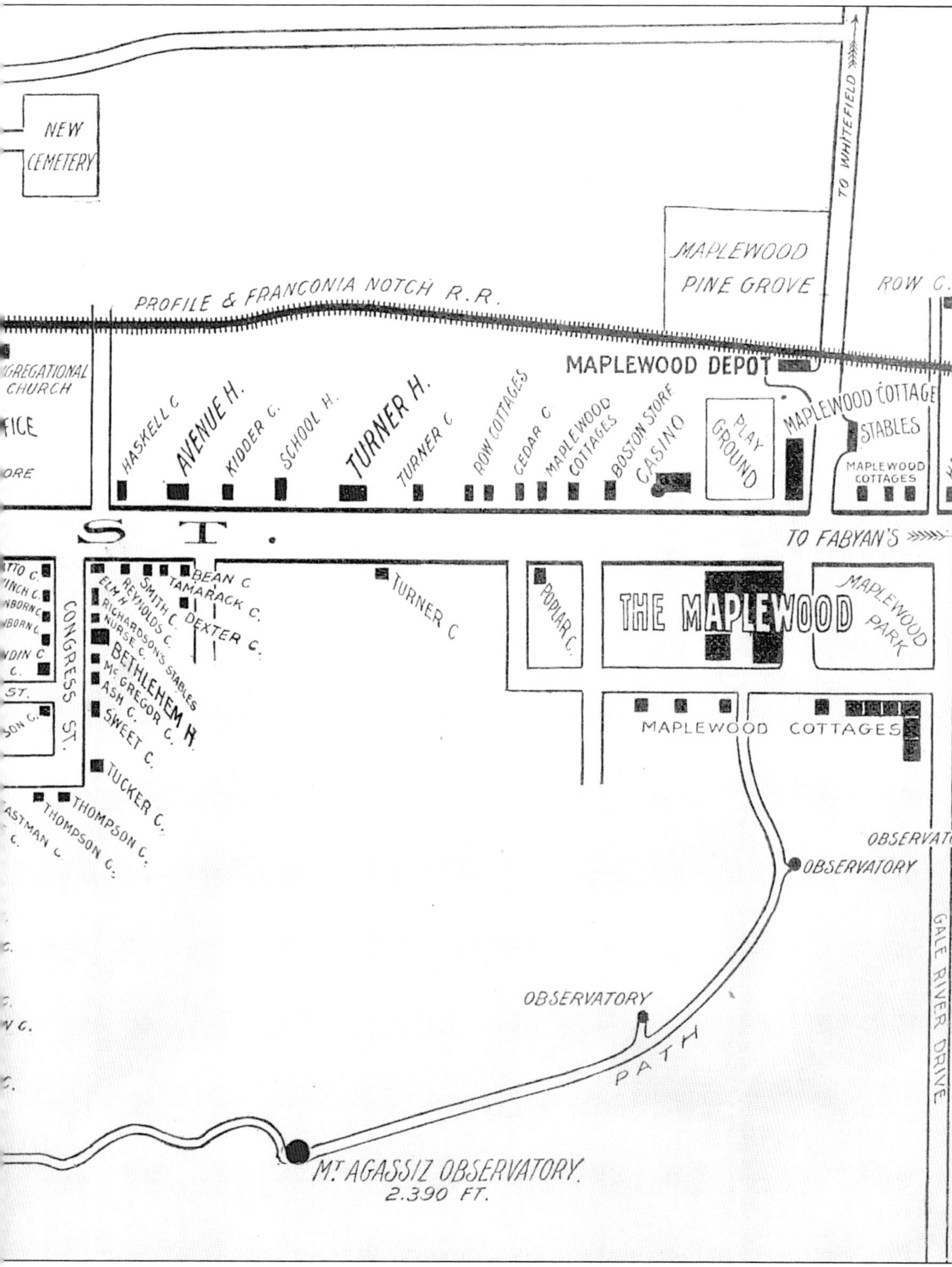
NEW CEMETERY
TO WHITEFIELD
MAPLEWOOD PINE GROVE
ROW C.
PROFILE & FRANCONIA NOTCH R.R.
MAPLEWOOD DEPOT
CHURCH
HASKELL C
AVENUE H.
KIDDER C.
SCHOOL H.
TURNER H.
TURNER C
ROW COTTAGES
CEDAR C
MAPLEWOOD COTTAGES
BOSTON STORE
CASINO
PLAY GROUND
MAPLEWOOD COTTAGE
STABLES
MAPLEWOOD COTTAGES
S T.
TO FABYAN'S
CONGRESS ST.
BEAN C
TAMARACK C.
SMITH C.
DEXTER C.
REYNOLDS C.
ELM H
RICHARDSON'S STABLES
NURSE C.
BETHLEHEM H.
McGREGOR C.
ASH C.
SWEET C.
TUCKER C.
THOMPSON C.
THOMPSON C.
TURNER C
POPLAR C.
THE MAPLEWOOD
MAPLEWOOD PARK
MAPLEWOOD COTTAGES
OBSERVATORY
OBSERVATORY
GALE RIVER DRIVE
PATH
MT AGASSIZ OBSERVATORY
2.390 FT.

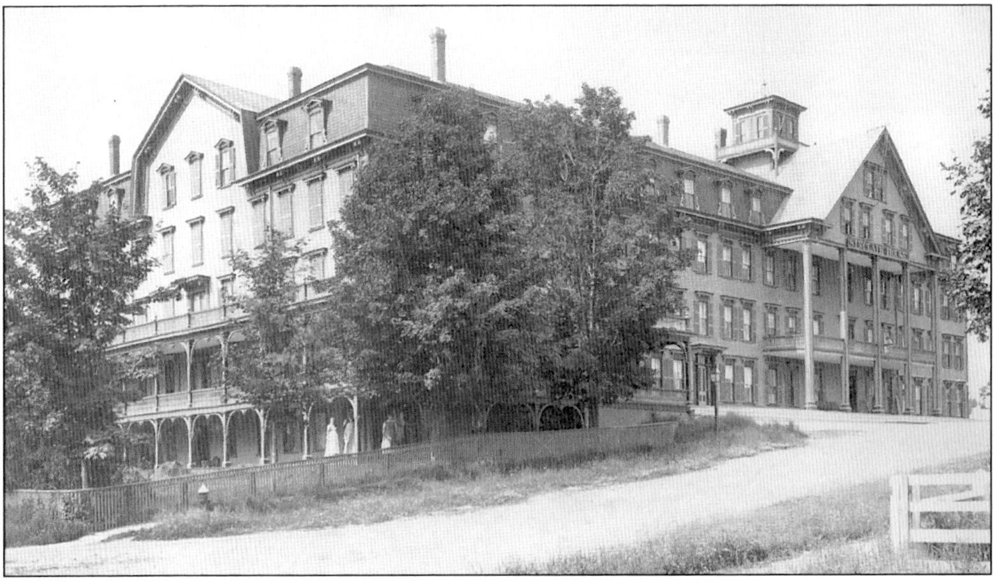

Built in 1857 as a small tavern with a few rooms for travelers, the Sinclair had a great influence on Bethlehem's development. In 1863, a carriage accident forced Gov. Henry Howard of Rhode Island to prolong his stay in the White Mountains, and he ended up at the Sinclair. Howard enjoyed his visit so much that he returned to build his own cottage and a hotel, marking the beginning of Bethlehem's fame as a resort. Eventually, the Sinclair became the second largest hotel in Bethlehem, with room for 300 guests. Famous guests included Prof. Louis Agassiz and Pres. Ulysses Grant. The Sinclair burned in 1978. (Paul Hudson.)

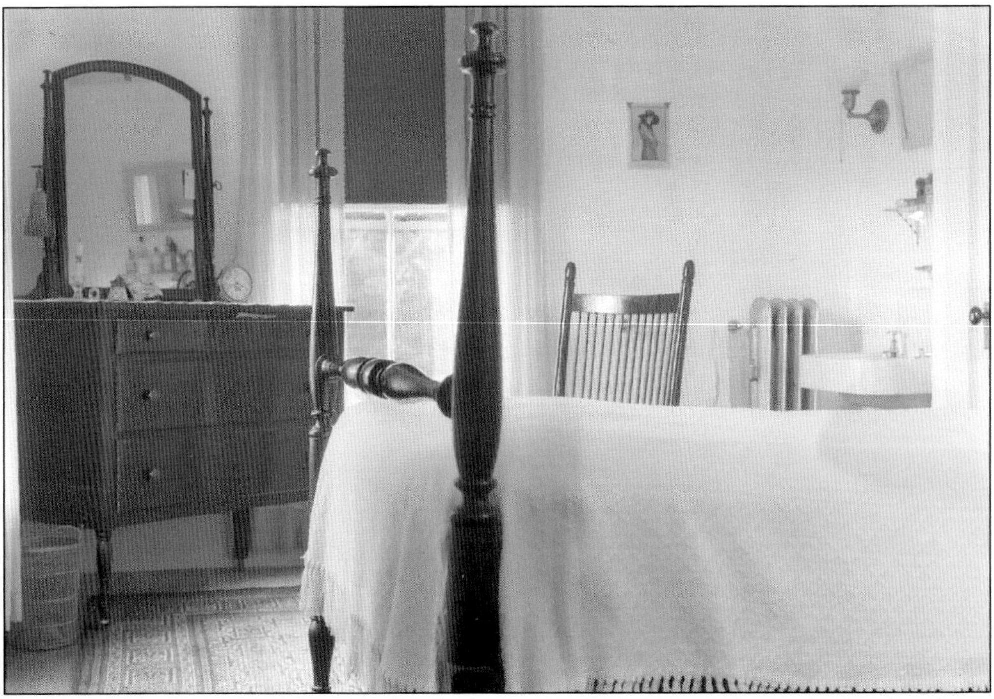

It is not known why Morrell Crawford took this picture of Room No. 141 at the Sinclair, but it is nice to see what a typical room looked like. (Clare Brown.)

MENU

Potage, Tortue Verts   Consomme a la Deslignac

Kromisky de volaille a la Bellevue

Sliced Tomatoes   *Queen Olives*

English Turbot a la Marechale   Boiled Penobscot Salmon a l' ecossaise

Cucumbers   *Potatoe Croquettes*

Boiled Philadelphia Capon, Bechamel Sauce

Leg of Mutton a l' anglaise

Filet de Bœuf a la Perigueux

Stall-fed Pigeons, Patted

Macaroni a la Milanaise

Vol au Vent a la Financiere

Apricots a la Conde

Roast Ribs of Beef, Dish Gravy

Turkey, Cranberry Sauce

Duck with Jelly

Spring Lamb, Mint Sauce

Lettuce Salad a la Parisienne   Chicken Mayonaise

Cold Ham,   Turkey,   Beef Tongue,   Corned Beef

Green Peas   Cauliflower   Stewed Tomatoes   Boiled Rice

Boiled Potatoes   Mashed Potatoes   String Beans

Bermuda Onions   Summer Squash   New Beets

Baked Indian Pudding, Cream Sauce.   Boiled Fruit Pudding, Wine Sauce

Lemon Pie   Apple Pie   Sunshine Cake   Blueberry Pie

Blanc-Mange   Ruby Under the Snow

Strawberry Ice Cream   Tipsy Charlotte   Assorted Cake

Pears   Watermelon   Bananas   Oranges   Nuts and Raisins

Coffee   Edam, Pine Apple and American Cheese   Tea

AN EXTRA CHARGE FOR DISHES NOT ON BILL-OF-FARE.

The Sinclair, Bethlehem, White Mountains, N. H., July 22, '88.

Patted stall-fed pigeons, tipsy Charlotte, and Ruby under the snow—these items, listed on a July 1888 menu at the Sinclair, evoke interesting mental pictures. Menus were printed every day for each meal, either in-house or by a local press. (Bethlehem Library.)

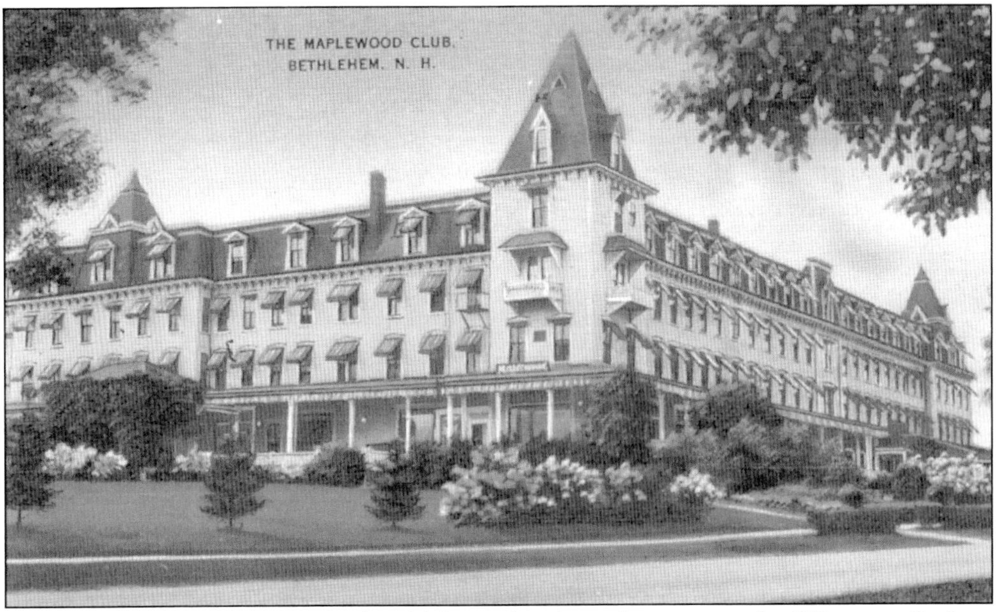

The Maplewood was the largest of Bethlehem's hotels, with a capacity for 550 guests. Built in 1876 by Isaac Cruft, the hotel gradually became a complex, consisting of the main building, an annex across the street, more than a dozen large cottages, and the Bethlehem Casino. The Maplewood was self-sufficient, with its 500-acre farm, sugar bush, post office, and train station. Guests enjoyed the beautiful grounds, an 18-hole golf course, riding stables, tennis courts, a swimming pool, and a full calendar of social events. The Maplewood burned in 1963. (Paul Hudson.)

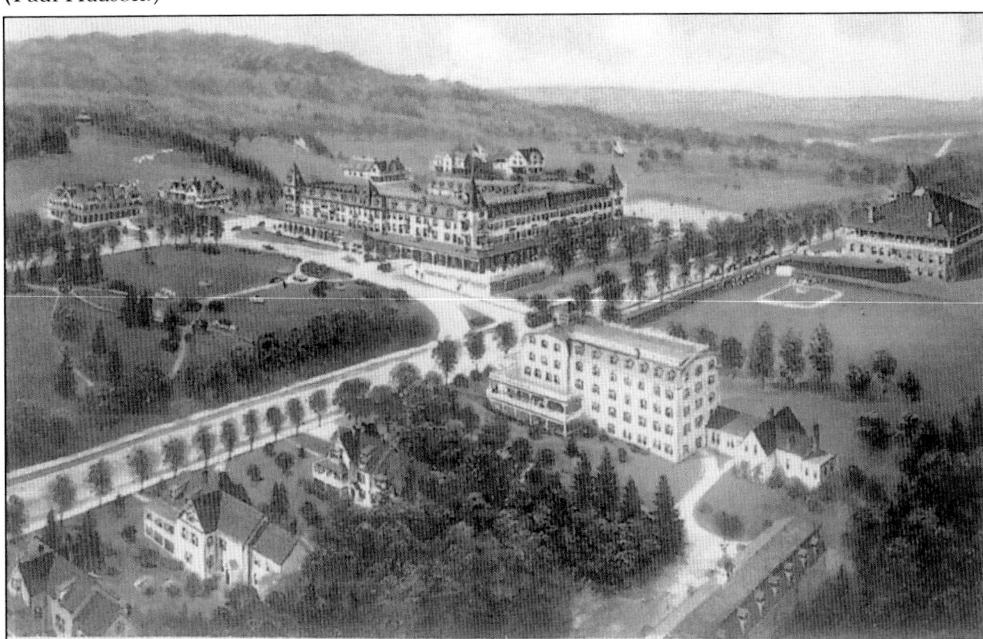

An aerial view of the Maplewood vicinity shows the size of the Maplewood complex. (Bethlehem Heritage Museum.)

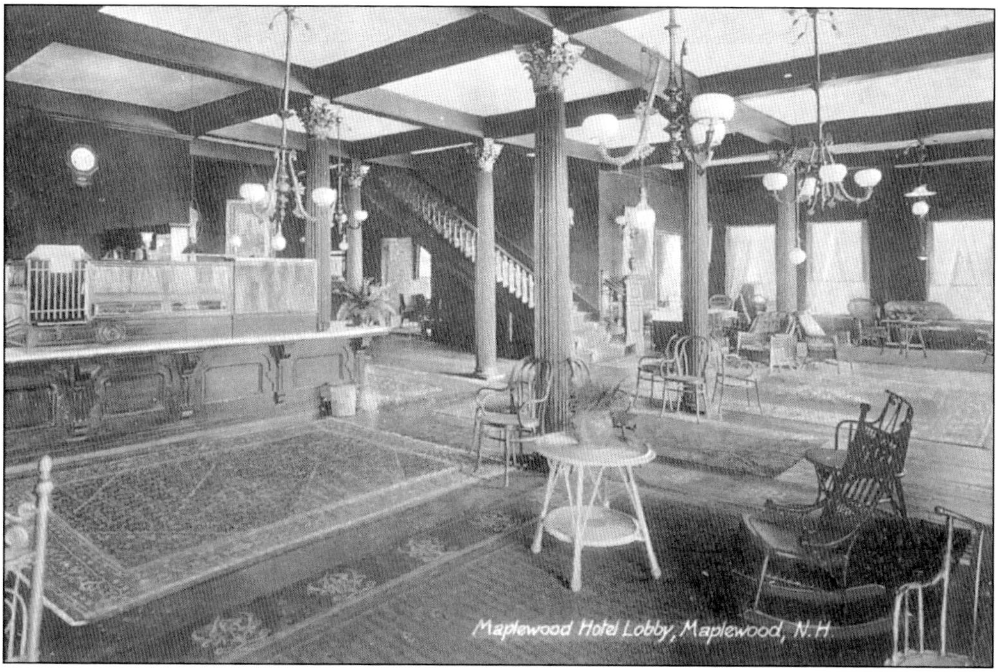

A postcard of the Maplewood lobby offers a glimpse of the hotel's elegant ambiance. (David Olson.)

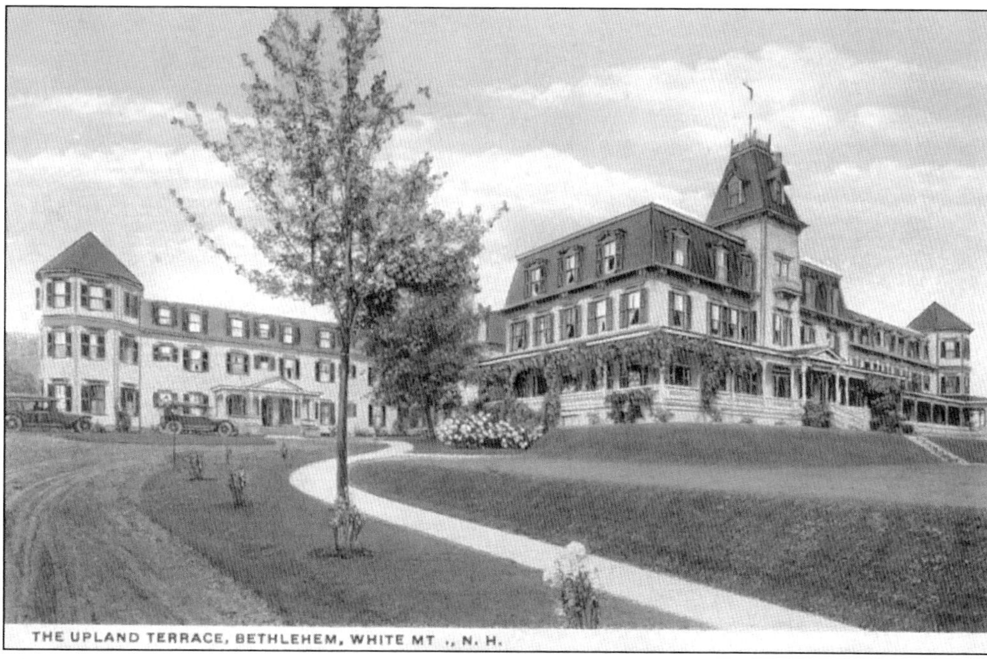

The Upland Terrace was perhaps one of Bethlehem's most attractive hotels and one of the largest, with room for 200 guests. It sat gracefully on a knoll above Main Street from 1877 to 1991, when it burned. Karl Abbott, son of the third owner, made his boyhood there the subject of his book *Open for the Season*. The Upland Terrace was last used as part of the Chase Golf and Tennis Camp. (David Olson.)

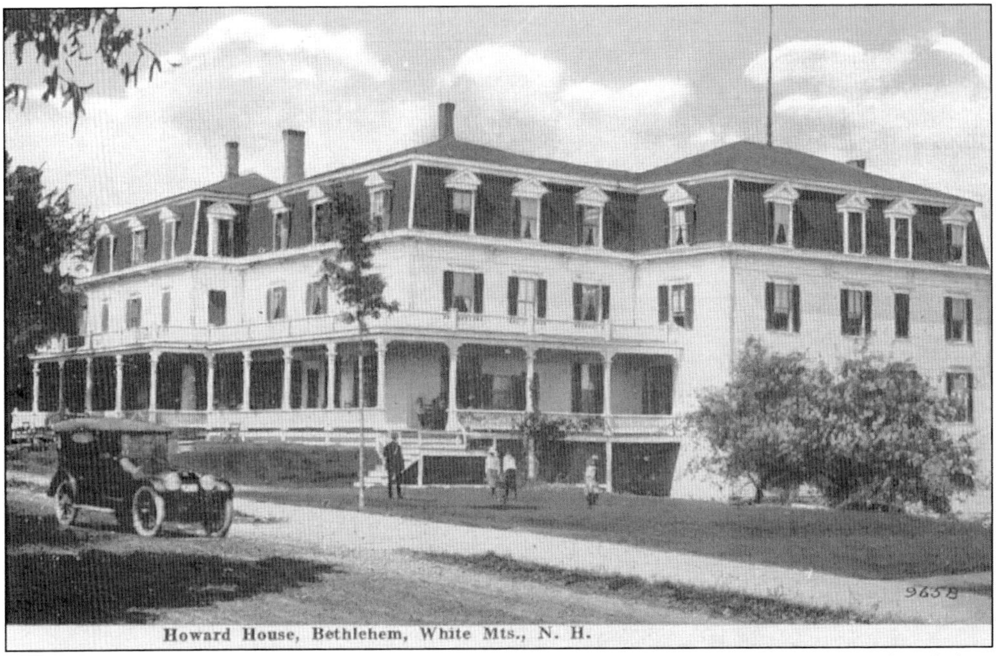

Gov. Henry Howard, whose interest sparked the tourism industry in Bethlehem, decided to dabble in tourism himself by building the Howard House in 1870. His hotel, which held 80 guests, burned down in 1874. Cyrus Bunker, who built several hotels in town, built a larger structure on the spot in 1878. The second Howard House held 250 guests. It was torn down in 1958. (Paul Hudson.)

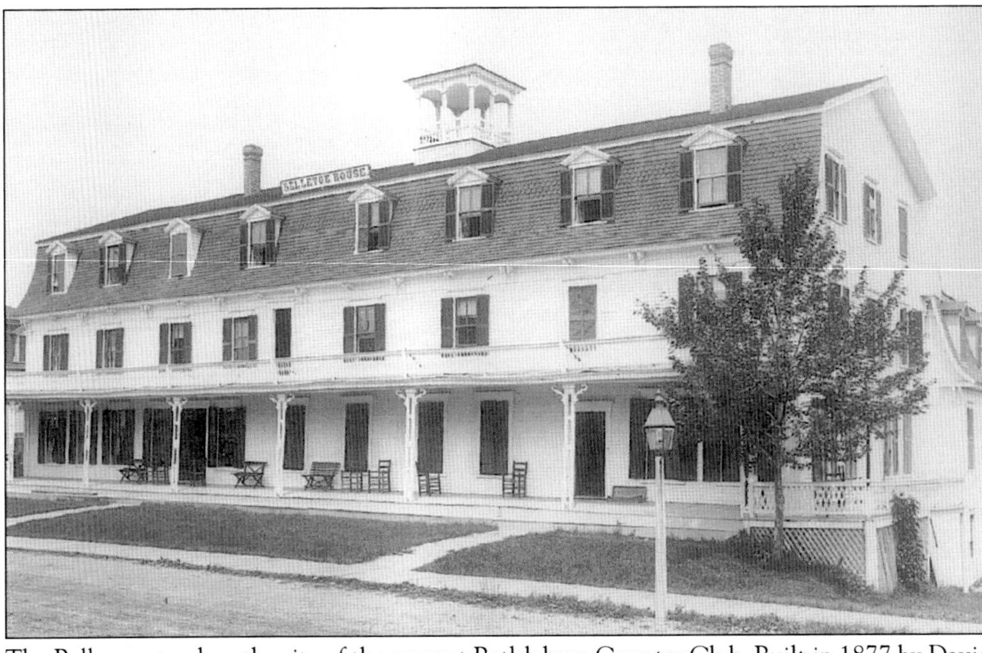

The Bellevue stood on the site of the present Bethlehem Country Club. Built in 1877 by David Phillips, it burned in 1900. It held 90 guests. (Bethlehem Heritage Museum.)

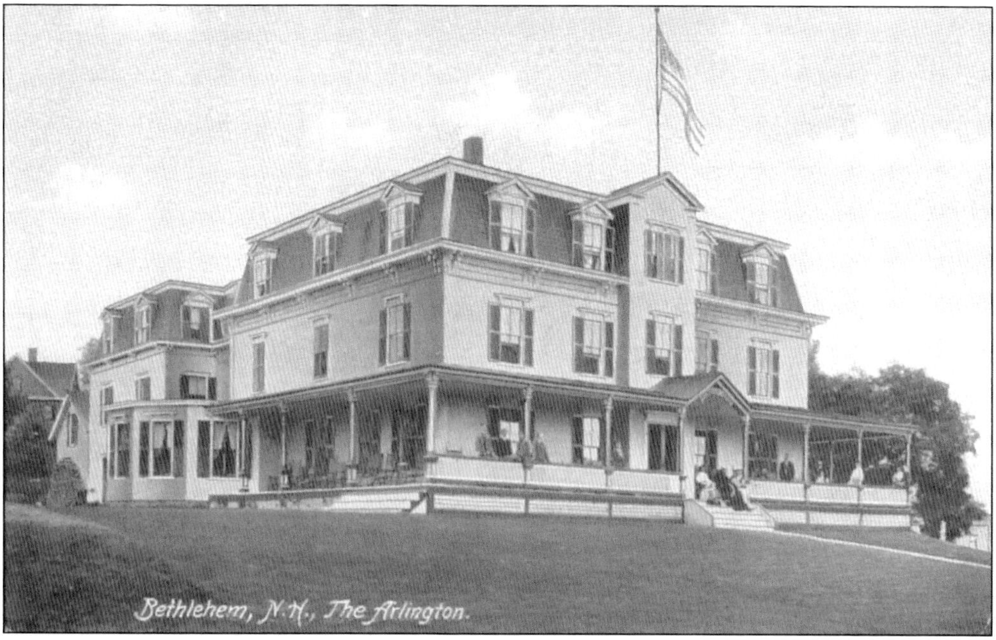

The Arlington Hotel is one of the few hotels operating in Bethlehem today. It stands on the corner of Lewis Hill Road and Main Street, across from the Bethlehem Country Club grounds. Horace Wilder, whose name appears on the old Congregational church clock, built the hotel in 1876 and named it the Centennial House. The present owner, Jolan Strulovic, offers a kosher kitchen, catering to Hassidic visitors. (Paul Hudson.)

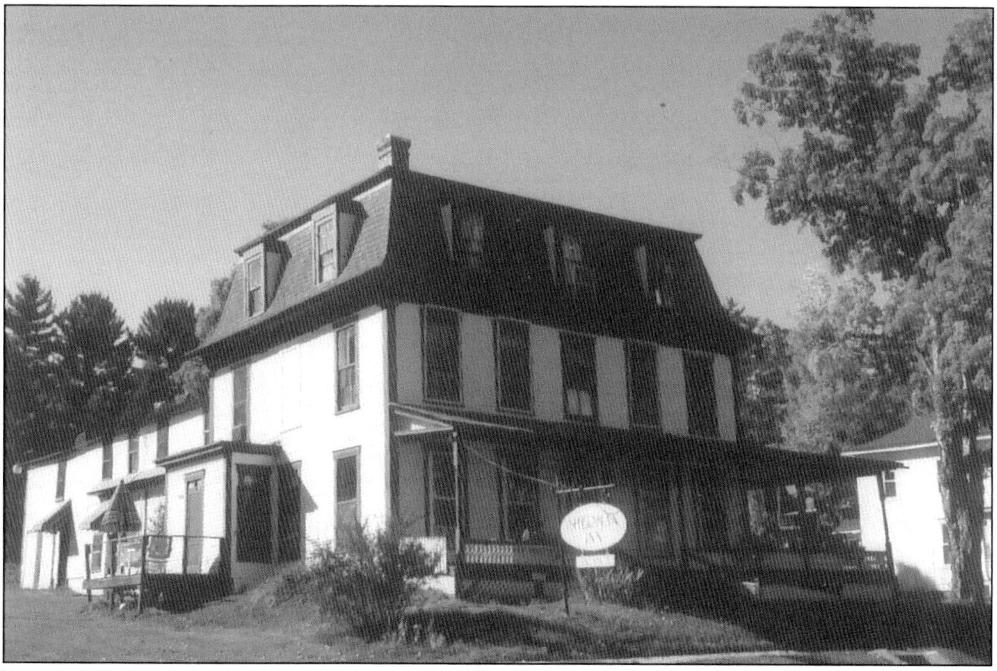

Formerly known as the Sunset House, the Sherman Inn also caters to Hassidic visitors. The mansard roof architecture and the white clapboards and green trim are very typical of early hotels. (Kathleen J. Parrish.)

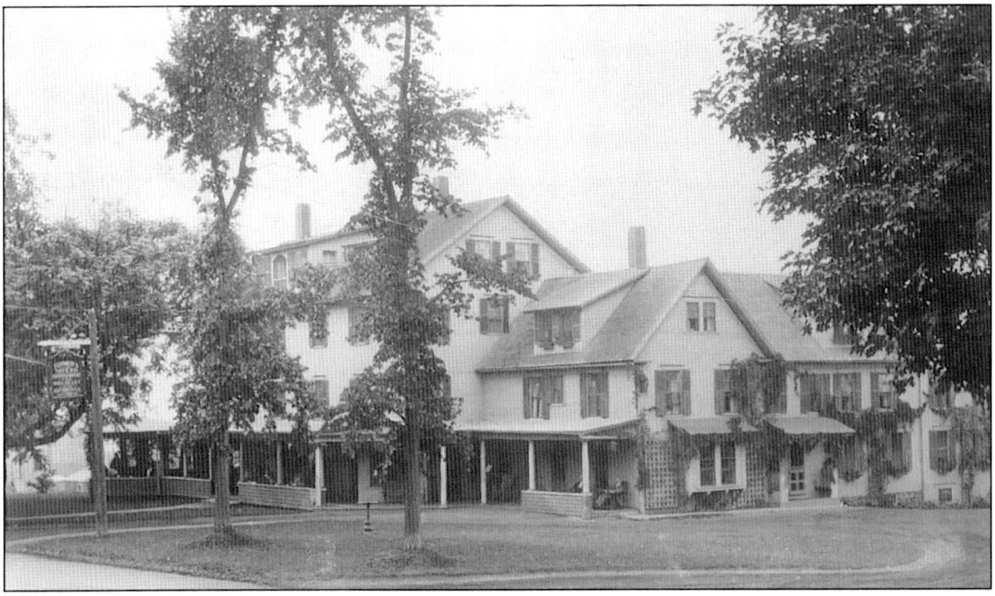

Turner's Tavern was operated from 1803 to 1945 by descendants of James Turner, the third settler to arrive in Bethlehem. The Turners were active in Bethlehem public life, serving as selectmen, on the school board, and in the state legislature. A later descendent, insurance man George Noyes, served on the governor's council and as a county commissioner. Land from the original 250 acres was donated for the Bethlehem Elementary School. Turner's Tavern is now an apartment house. (Paul Hudson.)

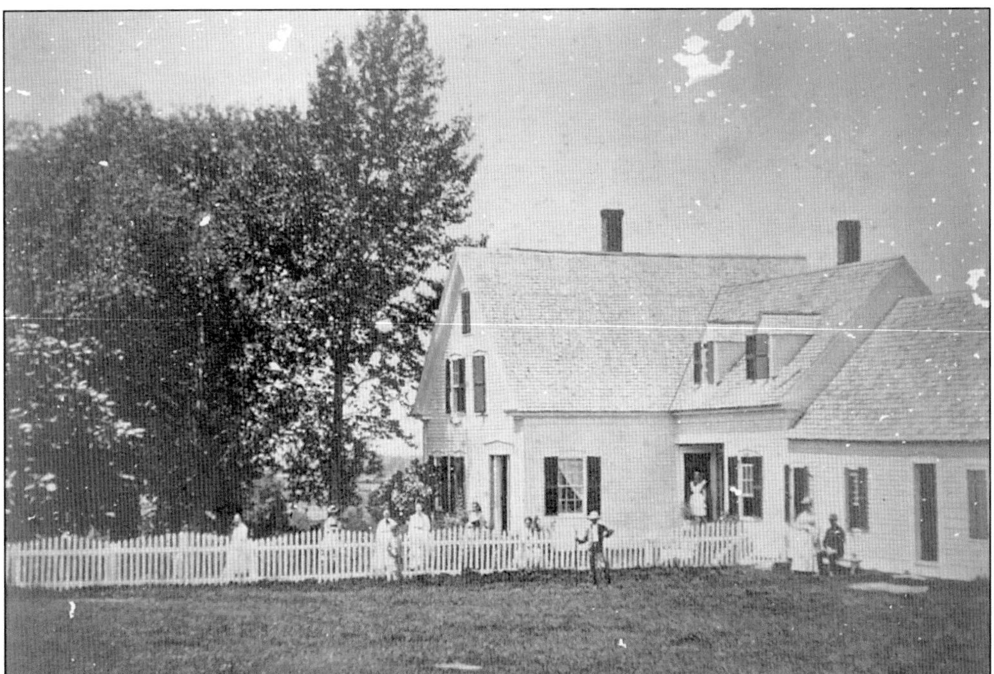

Turner's Tavern started as a farmhouse-type lodging known as the Turner House. (Marilyn Noyes Carmen.)

This 1908 picture of the Turners shows, from left to right, James N. Turner (1824–1908), James A. Turner (1888–1974), George H. Turner (1859–1924), and George Turner Noyes (1907–1992). (Marilyn Noyes Carmen.)

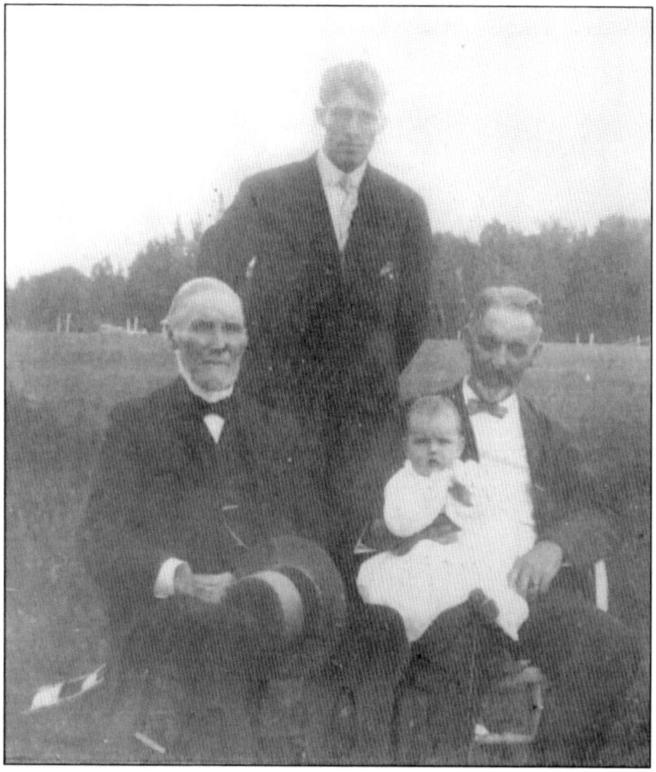

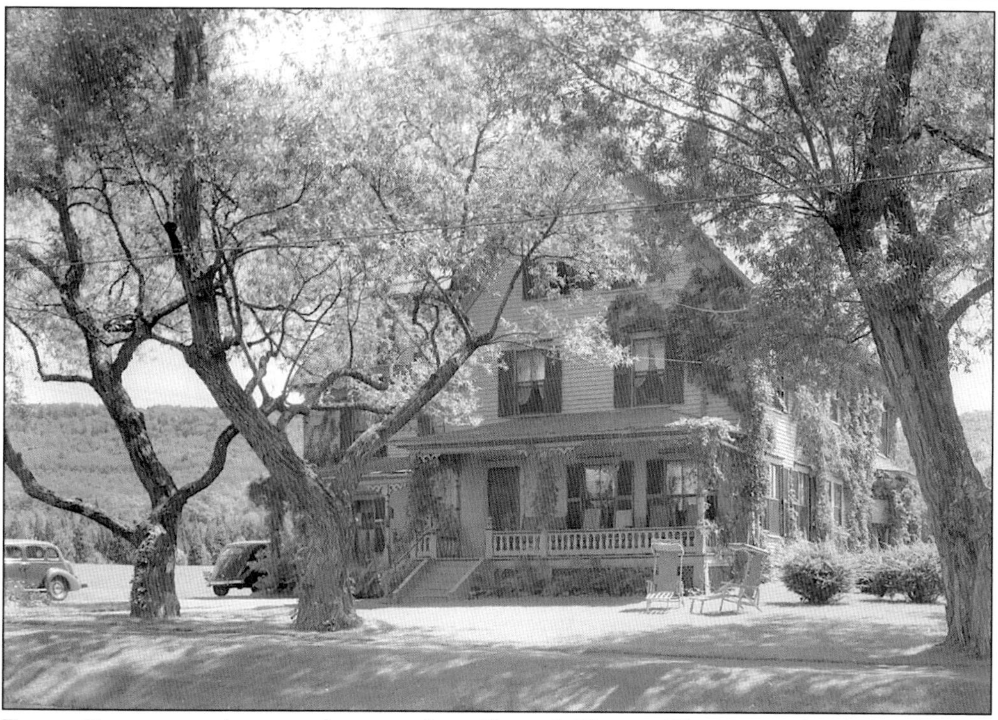

Turner Cottage stands across the street from Turner's Tavern. The Turner family lived in the cottage and often used it as an annex to the hotel. (Clare Brown.)

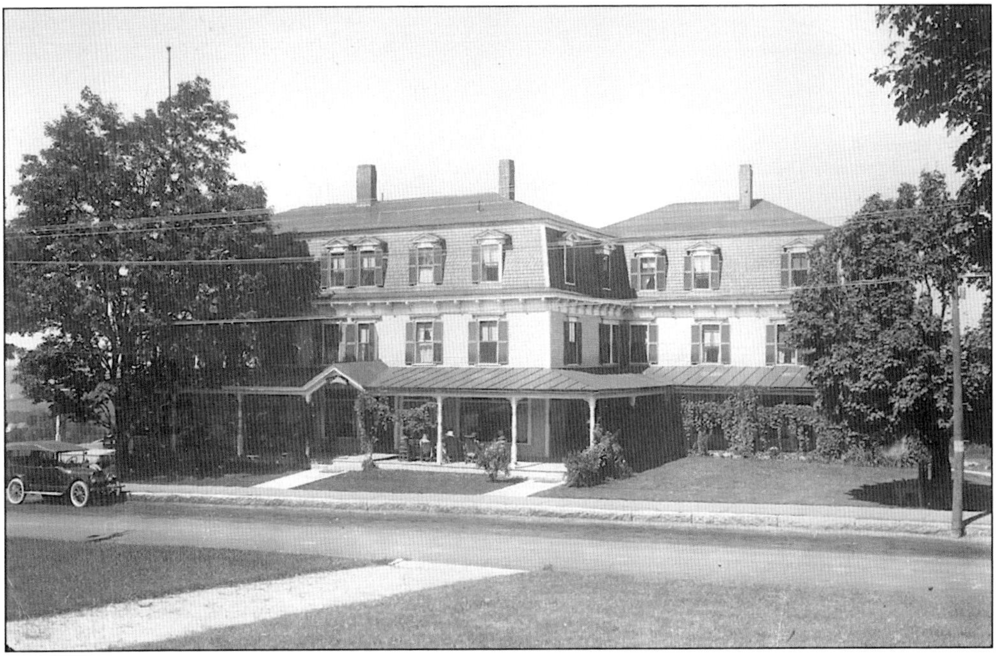

The Alpine Hotel stood on Main Street west of the Highland House and the Bethlehem Country Club. The location allowed an unrestricted view of Bethlehem's beautiful sunsets. Advertising in an 1893 issue of the *White Mountain Echo* stated, "the house is well-furnished, has a good table, is thoroughly drained and has modern water closets with the sewage carried to a considerable distance through tiled pipes." Built in 1877 by Charles Clark, the Alpine held 100 guests. A later owner purchased the Highland House, and the two hotels catered to Jewish visitors well into the 1980s. The Alpine burned in 1991. (Bethlehem Heritage Museum.)

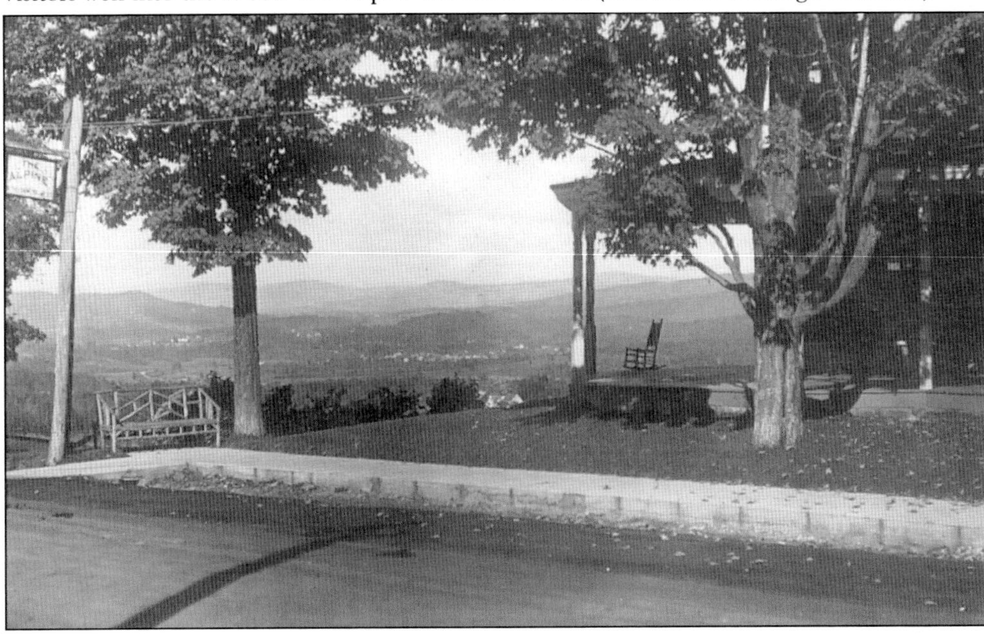

A rocking chair on the Alpine's porch effectively conveys the relaxing atmosphere and scenic beauty that attracted many people to Bethlehem. (Paul Hudson.)

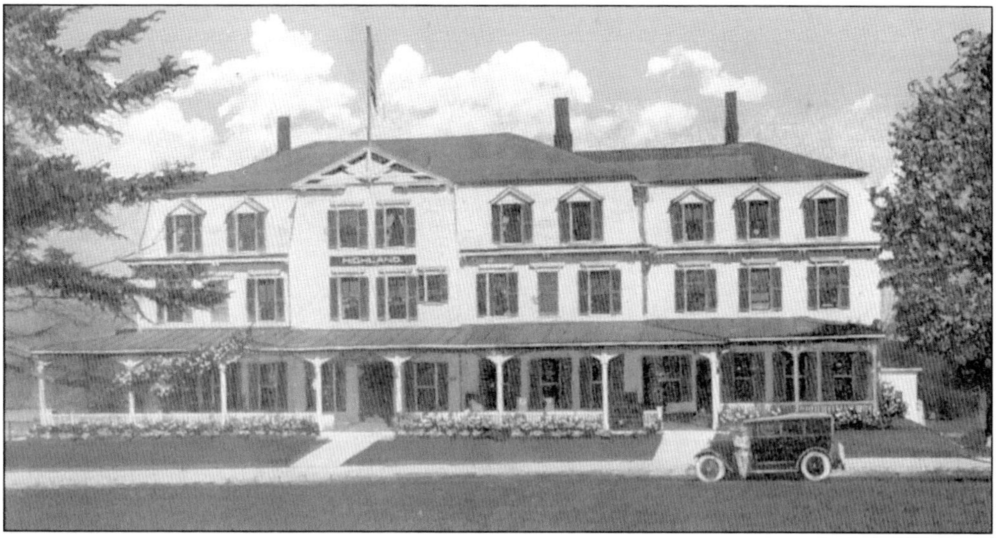

Pres. William Howard Taft once stayed at the Highland House, a 100-guest hotel on Main Street west of the Bethlehem Country Club. Advertising boasted of "spacious apartments with closets, open fireplaces, hot and cold water on every floor." Lawn tennis and croquet were popular activities. The Highland Hotel is still standing, a poor remnant of its former self. (Paul Hudson.)

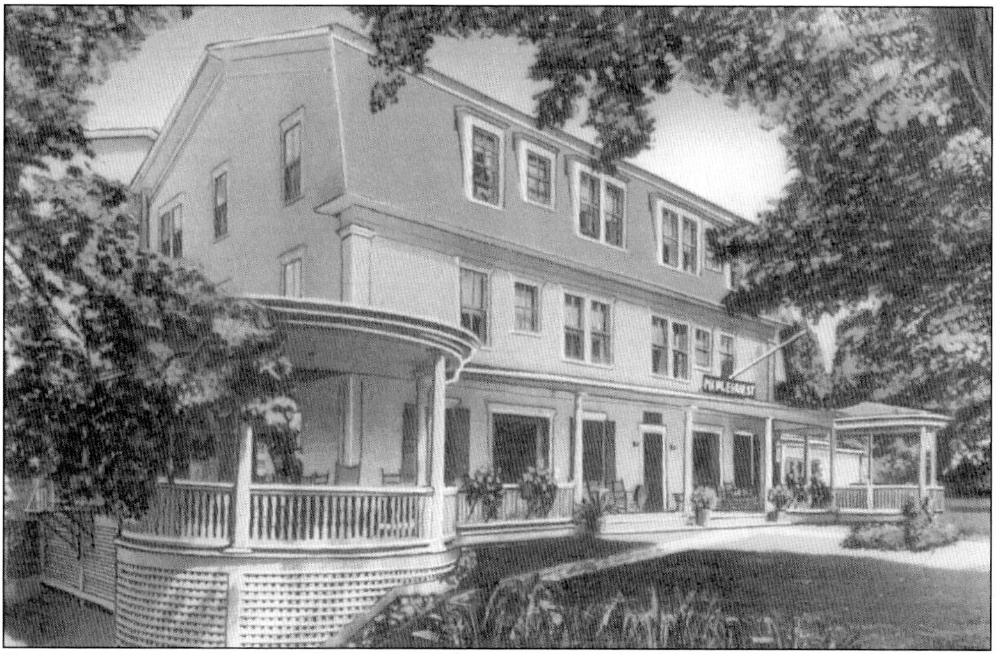

Built in 1876 under the name of Avenue House, the Maplehurst held 75 to 100 guests. An early advertisement in the *White Mountain Echo* read, "Perfectly drained and separated from the road by a fine lawn. Rooms light and airy and well warmed for the comfort of those staying in the Fall. Farm connected. Terms: transient $2.50 per day with reasonable rates for permanent guests. Good livery." Tennis, golf, and cards were popular pastimes. In later years, the Maplehurst served as part of the Chase Golf and Tennis Camp. Vacant since the early 1990s, the hotel still stands today. (Paul Hudson.)

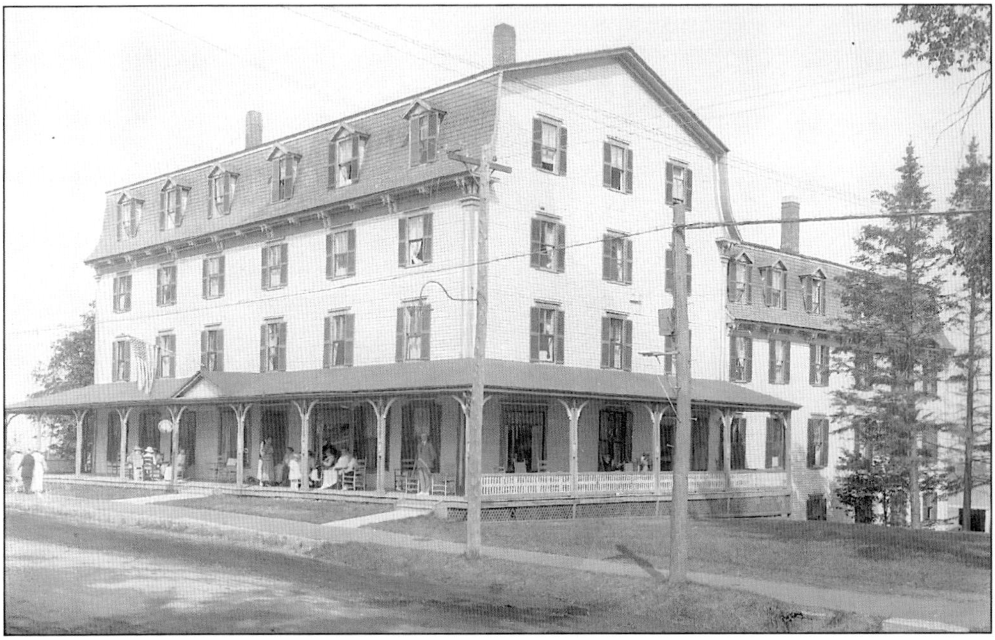

Located on Main Street near the corner of Prospect Street, the Strawberry Hill House held 100 guests. Moderately sized and priced, it was a popular hotel, a tier down from the Sinclair and Maplewood. The August 25, 1900 issue of the *White Mountain Echo* reported that "sixteen guests of the Strawberry Hill enjoyed a ride to Round Pond in Whitefield last Tuesday evening." Built in 1874, the hotel was torn down in 1965. (Paul Hudson.)

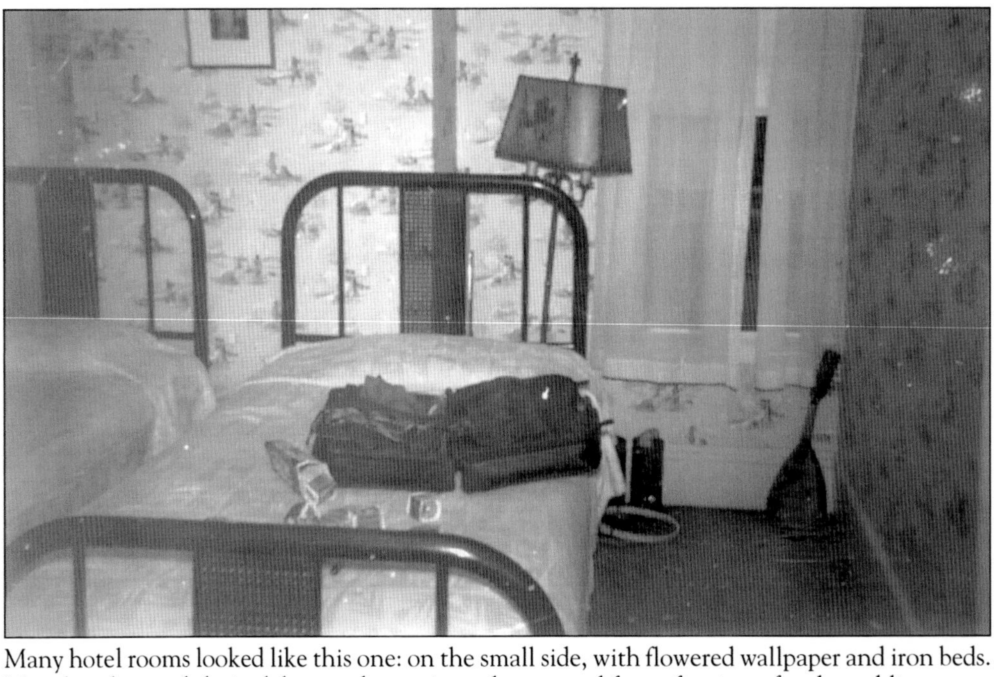

Many hotel rooms looked like this one: on the small side, with flowered wallpaper and iron beds. Most hotels saved their elaborate decorating schemes and fancy furniture for the public rooms. The reasoning was that people spent little time in their rooms, which were used for sleeping and storing clothes. (Bethlehem Heritage Museum.)

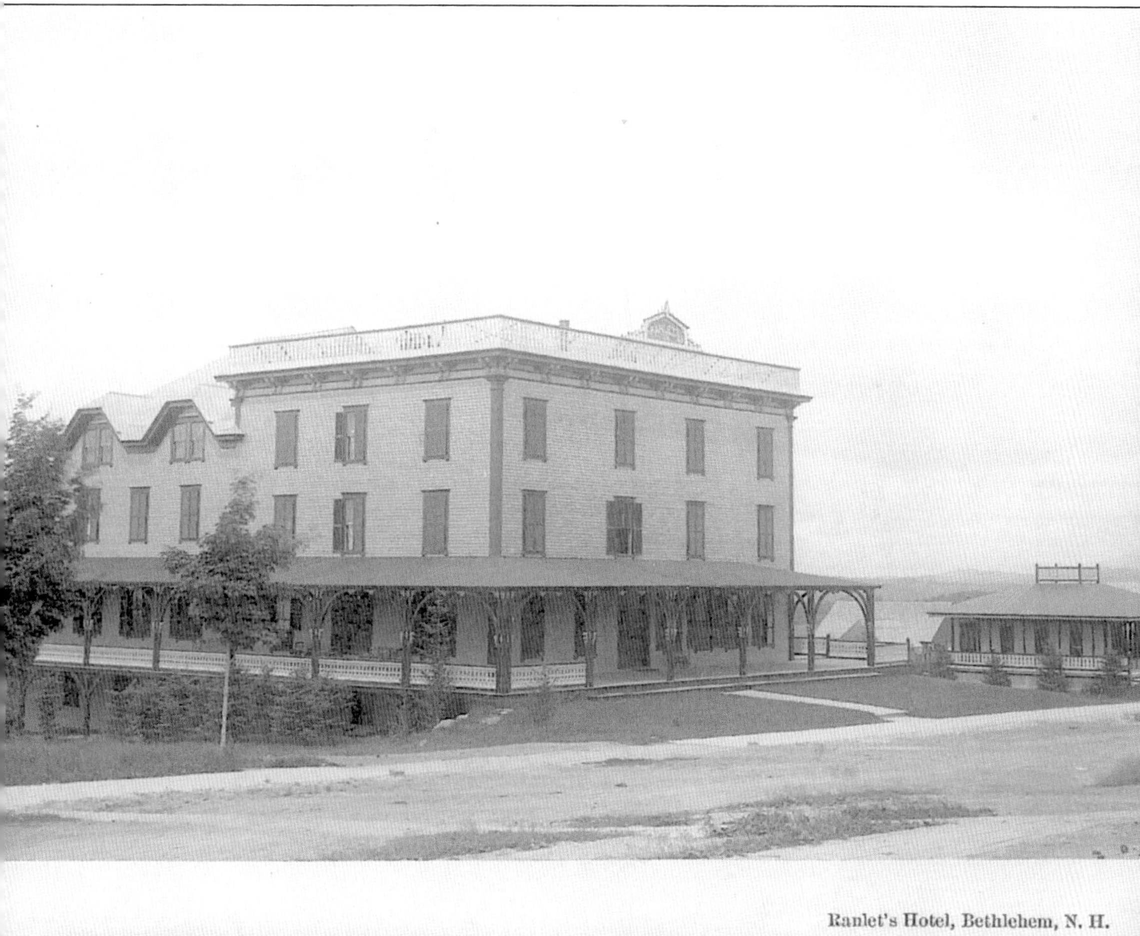

Built in 1876 by Cyrus Bunker, the Altamonte House, also known as the Park House and Ranlet's Hotel, stood on the corner of Park Avenue and Main Street. In 1916, the Altamonte had the distinction of being the first Bethlehem hotel to be owned by a Jewish person. A July 1893 issue of the *White Mountain Echo* reports that guests took a walking trip to North Woodstock—more than 25 miles away! The Altamonte was torn down in 1986. (John Stevenson.)

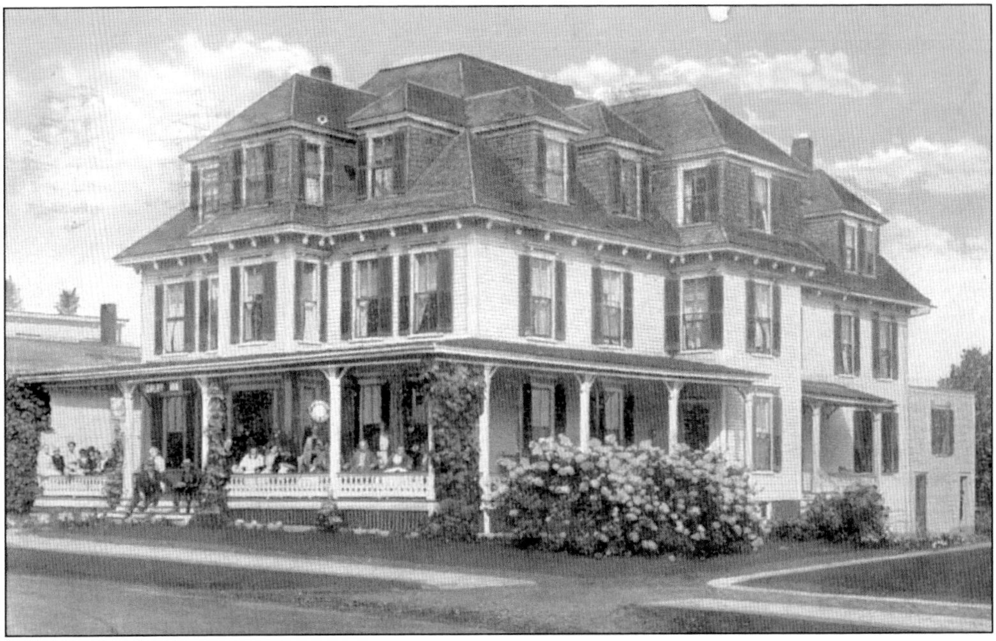

The Colby Inn had several names: Woodlawn, Bethmer, Colby, and Stage Depot. Located across from the Colonial Theater and next to the Methodist church, the Colby was one of Bethlehem's smaller hotels. A 1923 advertisement in the *White Mountain Echo* read, "Large rooms, good closets, up-to-date. Excellent cuisine; steam heat." A 1913 issue of *White Mountain Topics* reported that guests at the Bethmer entertained themselves with psychic readings and English monologues. The Colby Inn was demolished in 1982. (Paul Hudson.)

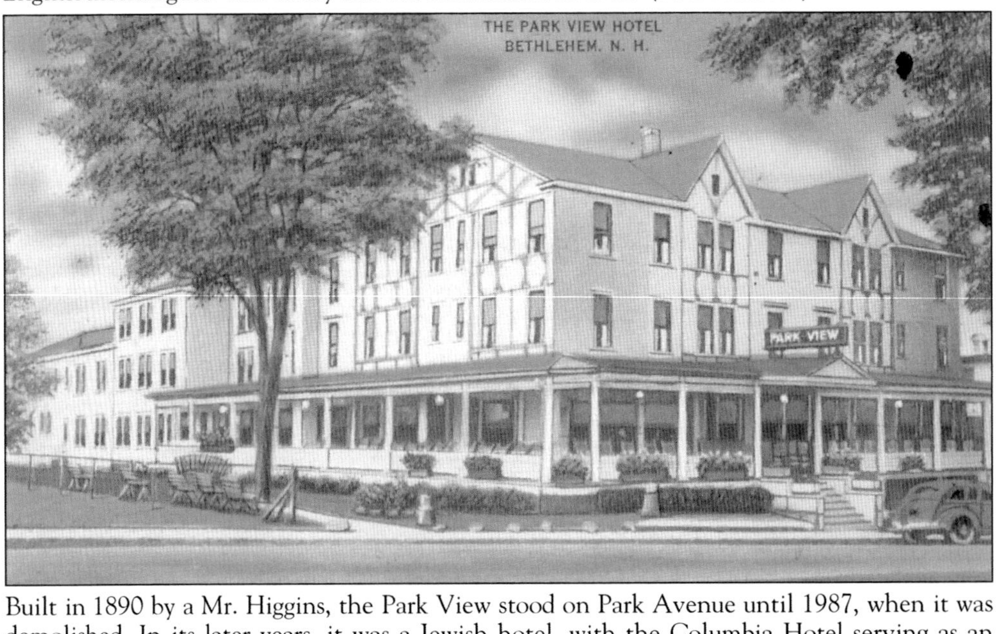

Built in 1890 by a Mr. Higgins, the Park View stood on Park Avenue until 1987, when it was demolished. In its later years, it was a Jewish hotel, with the Columbia Hotel serving as an annex. The Park View, also known as the East View and the Lyndhurst, held 125 guests. With gleaming white clapboards and green trim, plenty of shade trees and well-kept grounds, the Park View must have appeared very attractive to tired city visitors. (David Olson.)

The Park View stands forlornly awaiting its imminent demolition in 1987. (Bethlehem Heritage Museum.)

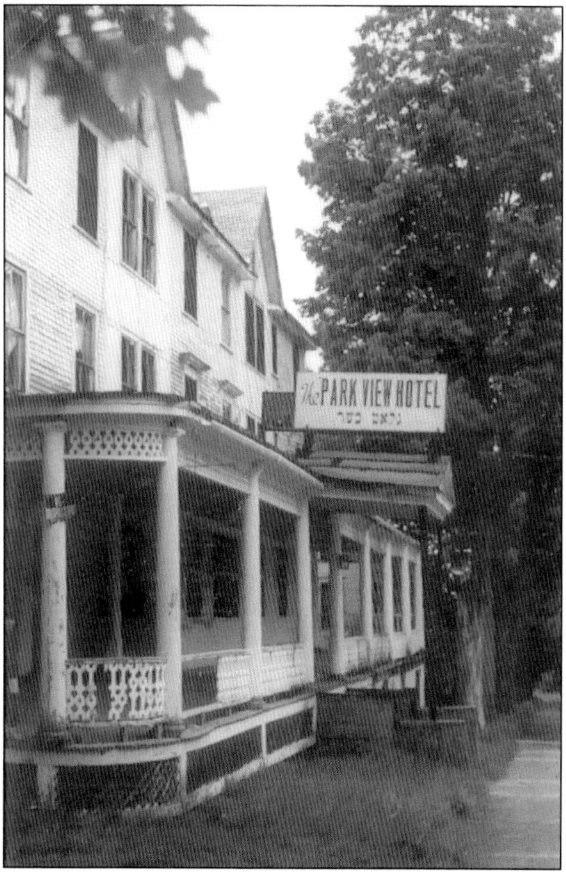

The Columbia Hotel, built in 1892 by G. Allen Noyes, was also known as Central Cottage and the Columbus Hotel. It stood on Park Avenue next to the Park View and later served as the Park View's annex. An article in the August 25, 1900 *White Mountain Echo* read, "A straw ride to Littleton was enjoyed by the young people who are summering at the Columbus, last Monday evening, under the chaperonage of the Mrs. H.V.G. Canfield." The Columbia was torn down in 1987. (Paul Hudson.)

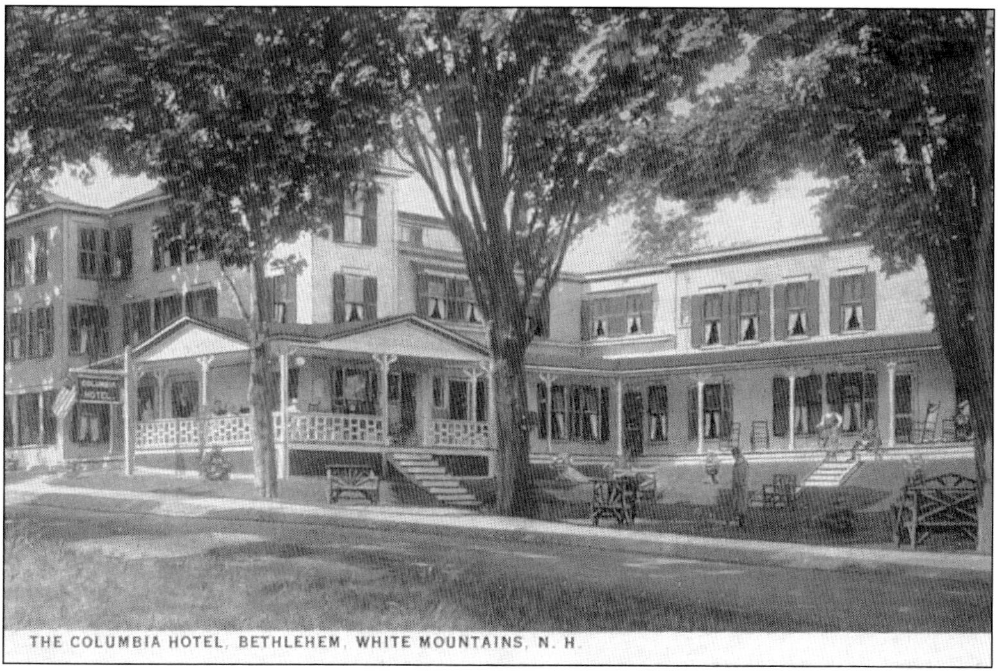

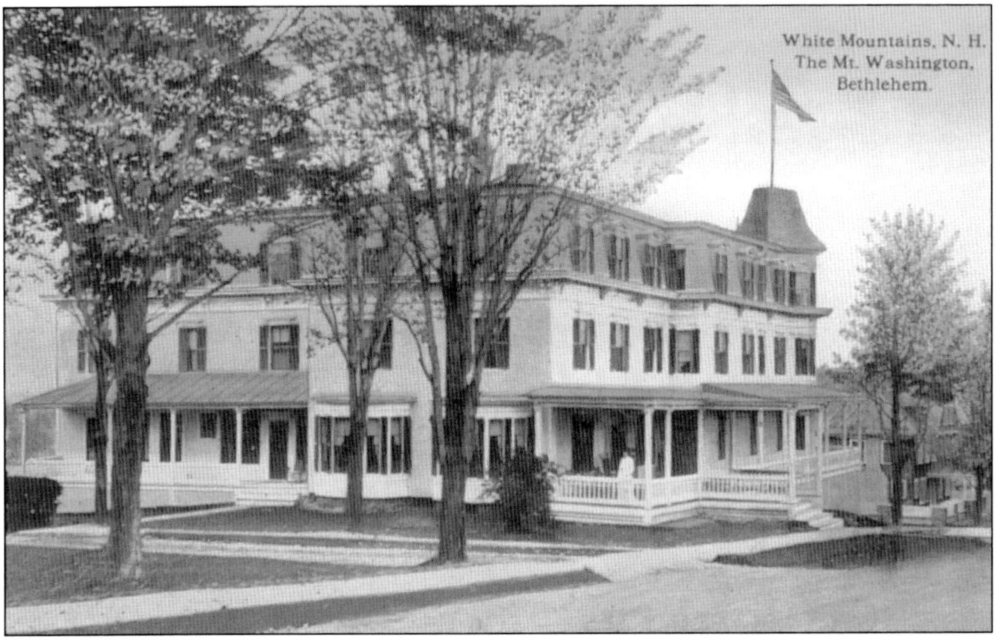

Located near the end of Park Street and across from the railroad station, the Mount Washington House boasted of a 40-peak view from the front piazza. The hotel, then named the London House, burned in 1934. In 1943, motel units were constructed on the site. This may have been one of the earliest motels. (David Olson.)

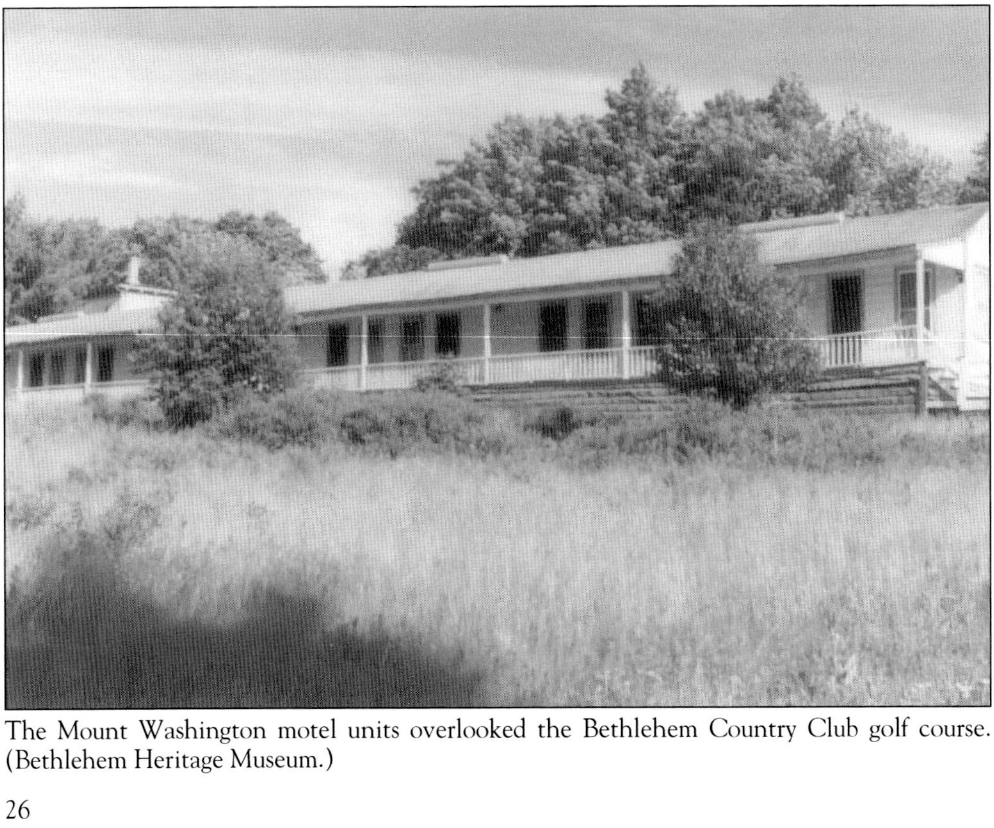

The Mount Washington motel units overlooked the Bethlehem Country Club golf course. (Bethlehem Heritage Museum.)

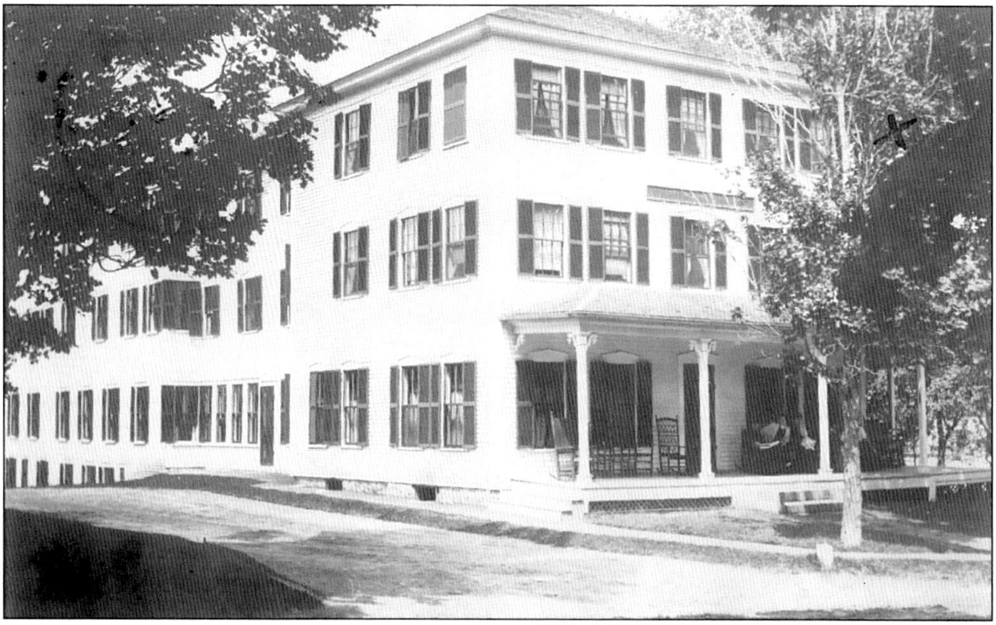

The Central House stood on Agassiz Street on the present site of the senior housing development. The first proprietor was Ambrose Blandin, who ran it as the Blandin House. Built in the 1870s, it held 75 guests. Georgianna Lewis owned the Central House and the Hillside Inn until the early 1930s. Alfred Perry and his wife operated it as the Perry House until the late 1970s. In 1954, motel units and a pool were built in back of the hotel. (Bethlehem Heritage Museum.)

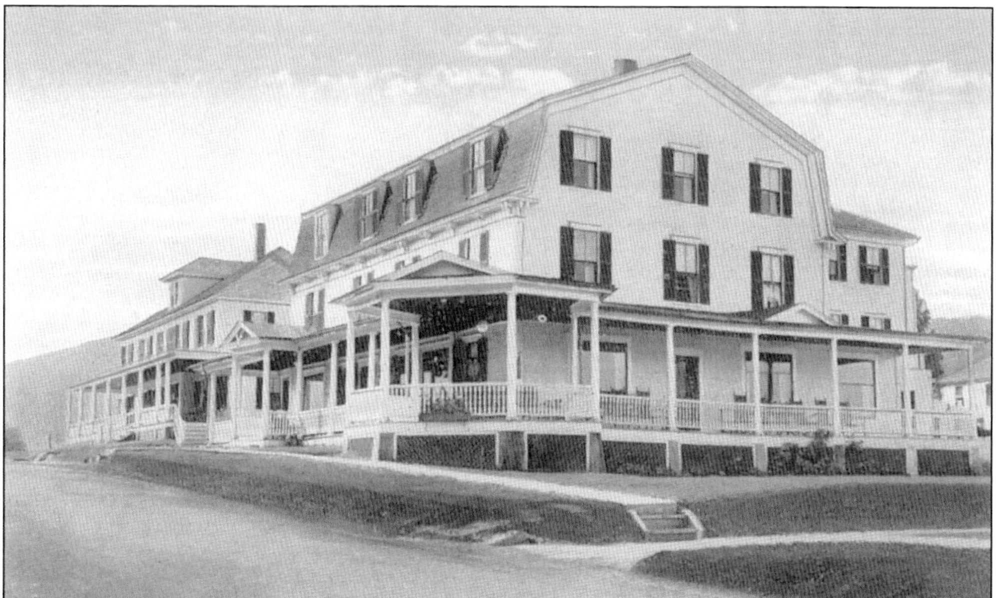

THE HILLSIDE INN, BETHLEHEM, WHITE MTS., N. H.

Built in 1874 by Deacon Davis, Hillside House also stood on Agassiz Street, not far from the Central House. In the early 1930s, the Perrys purchased Hillside House and after tearing part of it down, they used the remainder for the Perry House Theater. (David Olson.)

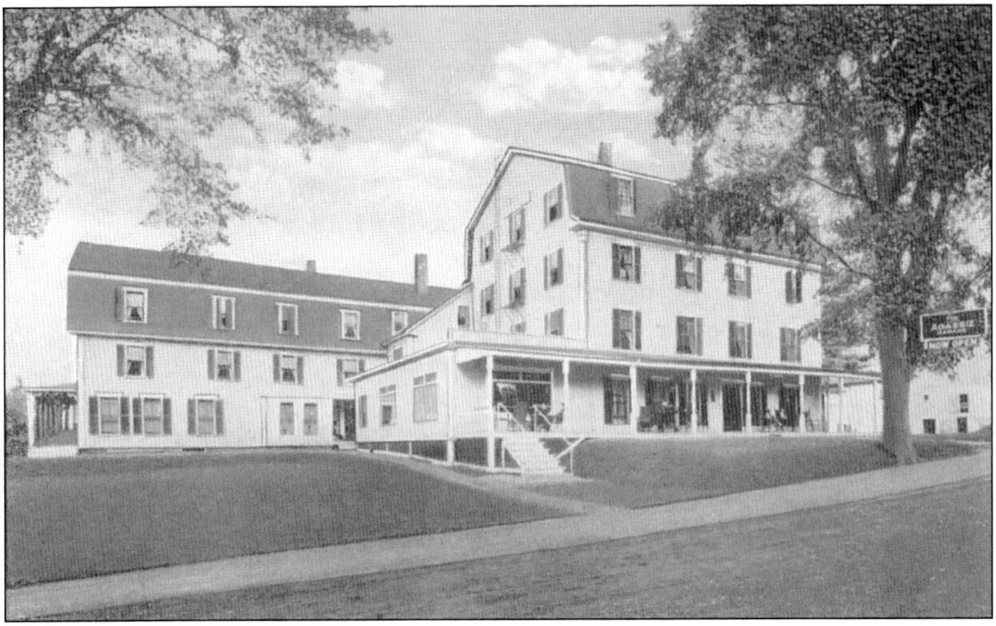

The Agassiz, later called the New Agassiz, was built in 1870 by Cyrus Bunker on the corner of Agassiz Street across from the Sinclair. A brochure from the beginning of the 20th century states that the hotel was open all year. Guests were encouraged to enjoy Bethlehem's "bracing and invigorating atmosphere," amid the "beauty and grandeur" of the mountains in winter. The hotel, which held 125 guests and featured steam heat and open fires, was touted as the "ideal headquarters for tramping parties." (Paul Hudson.)

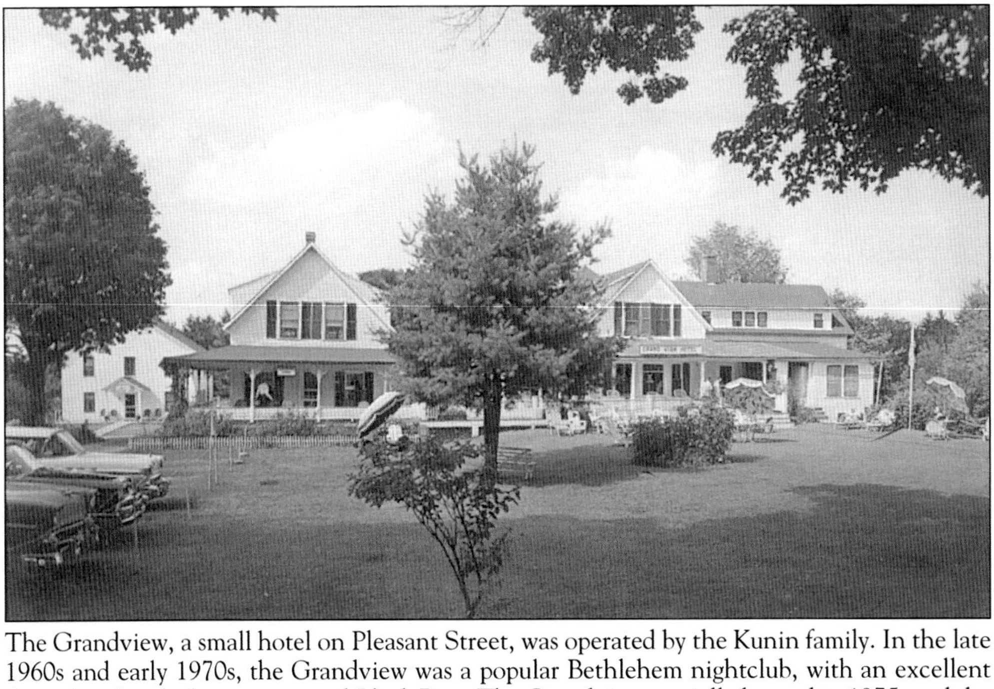

The Grandview, a small hotel on Pleasant Street, was operated by the Kunin family. In the late 1960s and early 1970s, the Grandview was a popular Bethlehem nightclub, with an excellent dance band and a bouncer named Black Bart. The Grandview partially burned in 1975, and the remaining structure was remodeled as a shared home facility. (Paul Hudson.)

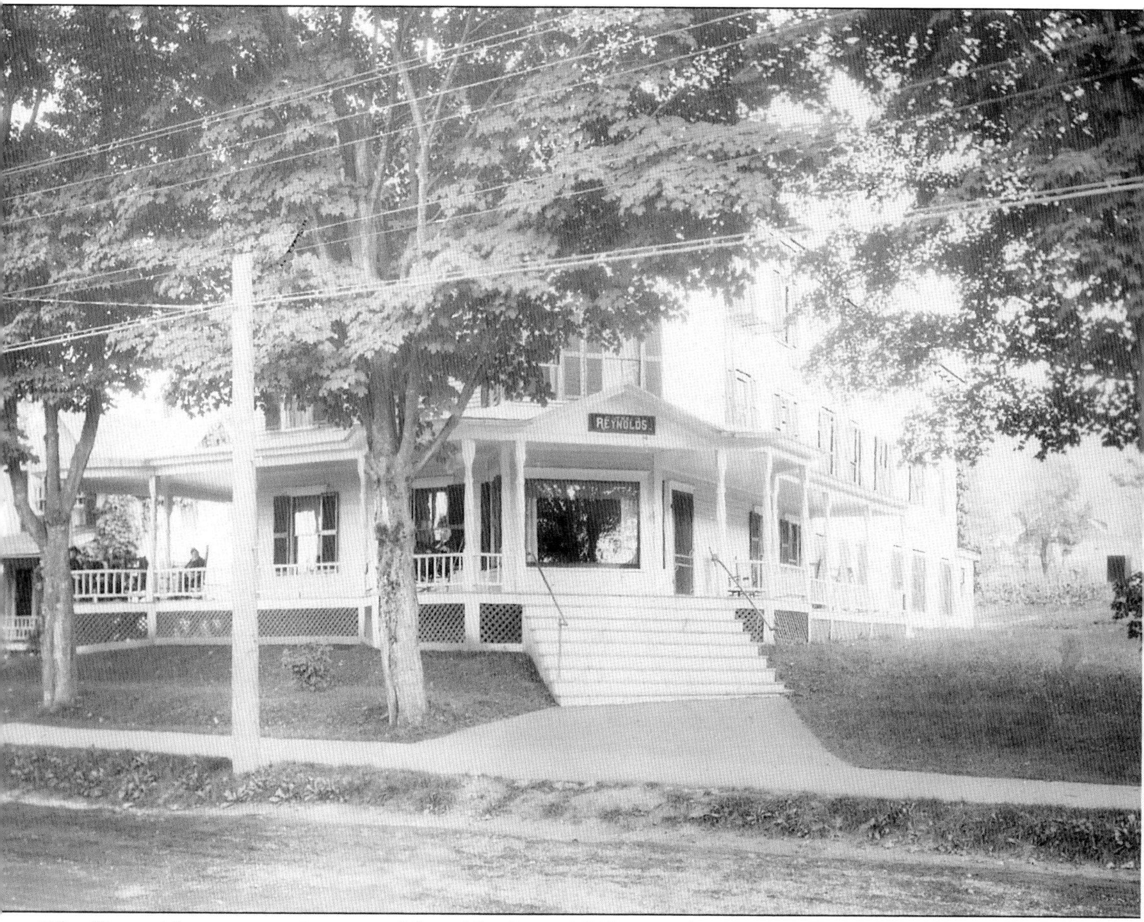

The Reynolds was a medium-sized hotel built in 1895 near the corner of Congress and Main Streets. It held 90 guests. The Elm House next door served as an annex. Both buildings were torn down in 1958. A bank now stands on the site. (Bethlehem Heritage Society.)

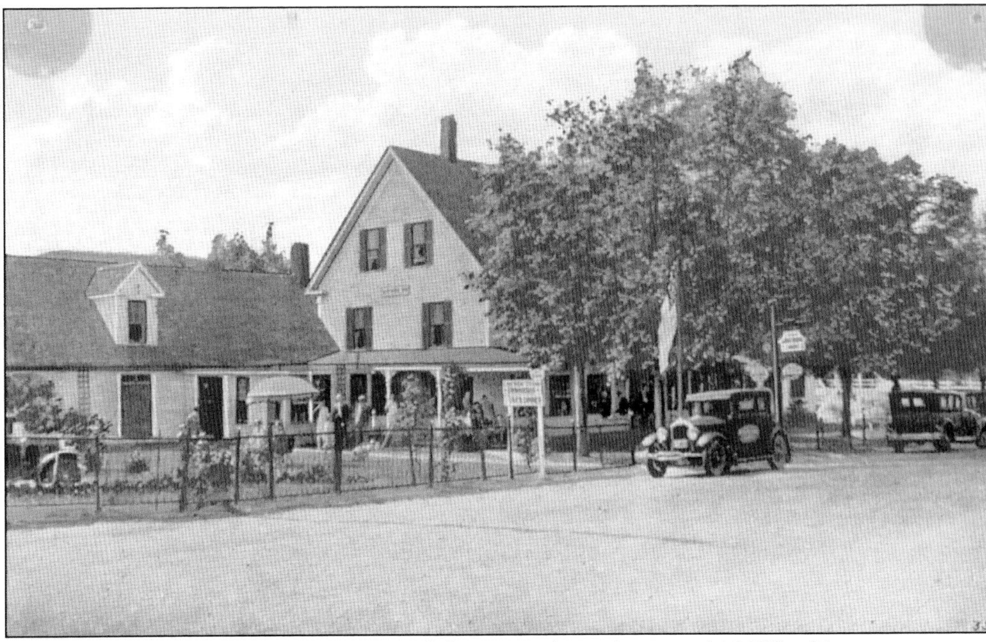

The nephew of Pres. Franklin Pierce used the Wayside Inn's original 1825 building as a summer home. In 1910, it became a lodging place for railroad workers and has operated continuously ever since. The inn is located on Route 302 in a section of Bethlehem called Pierce Bridge or Bethlehem Junction. The Pierce Bridge name came from John Pierce (no relation to the president), who built a large sawmill nearby on the Ammonoosuc River in 1847. A railroad station across the road from the Wayside—from which passengers could go on to Bethlehem, Franconia Notch, or Littleton—gave rise to the nickname Bethlehem Junction. Victor and Kathe Hofmann are the present owners of the Wayside Inn. (Paul Hudson.)

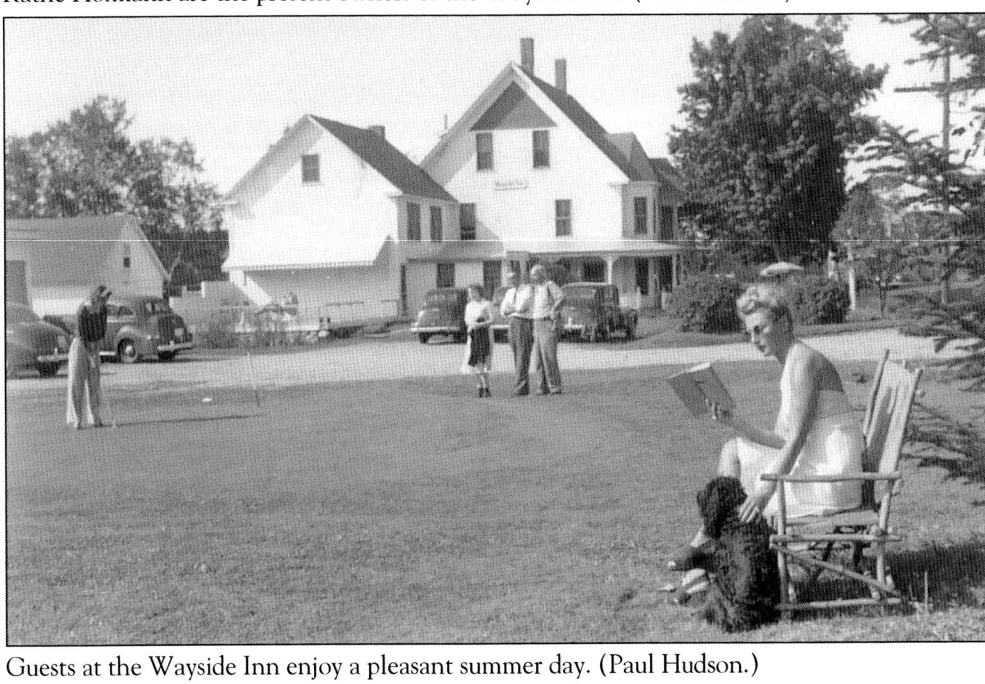

Guests at the Wayside Inn enjoy a pleasant summer day. (Paul Hudson.)

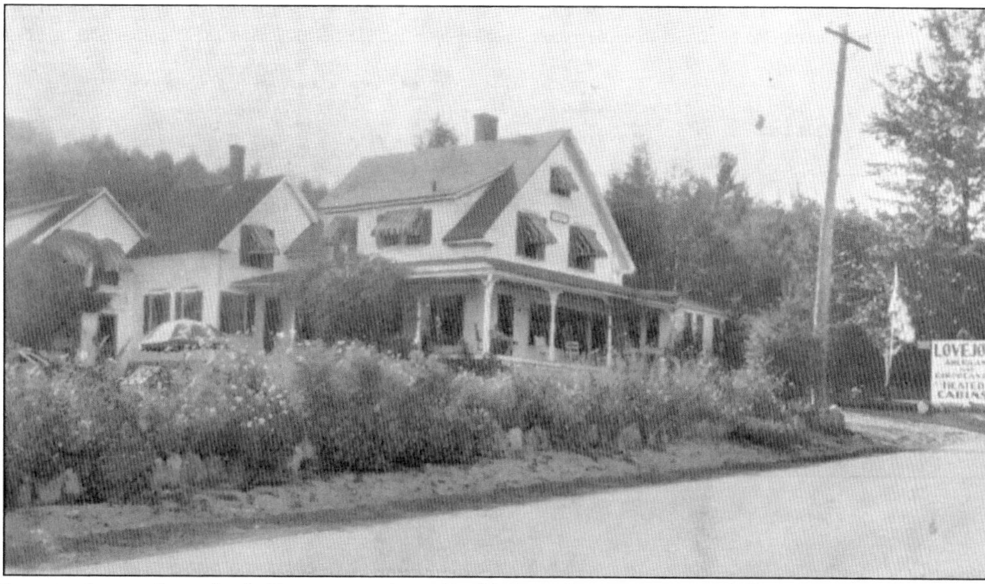

Lovejoy's stood on the hill going up from Bethlehem Junction toward the Maplewood. Besides rooms in the rambling farmhouse building, Lovejoy's offered small cabins across the road. Muriel Jobin Brown remembers picking berries and selling them to the guests. The guests also enjoyed watching Muriel and her siblings herd cows across the road to pasture. Lovejoy's promised more than steak and lobster dinners, hot water, and dancing from nine to midnight: the slogan in 1929 was "All those who Love Joy come Inn." The Lovejoys also operated Lovejoy's Log House in Southern Pines, North Carolina. After years of decay, Lovejoy's burned partially in the 1980s, and the remaining buildings were torn down. (Paul Hudson.)

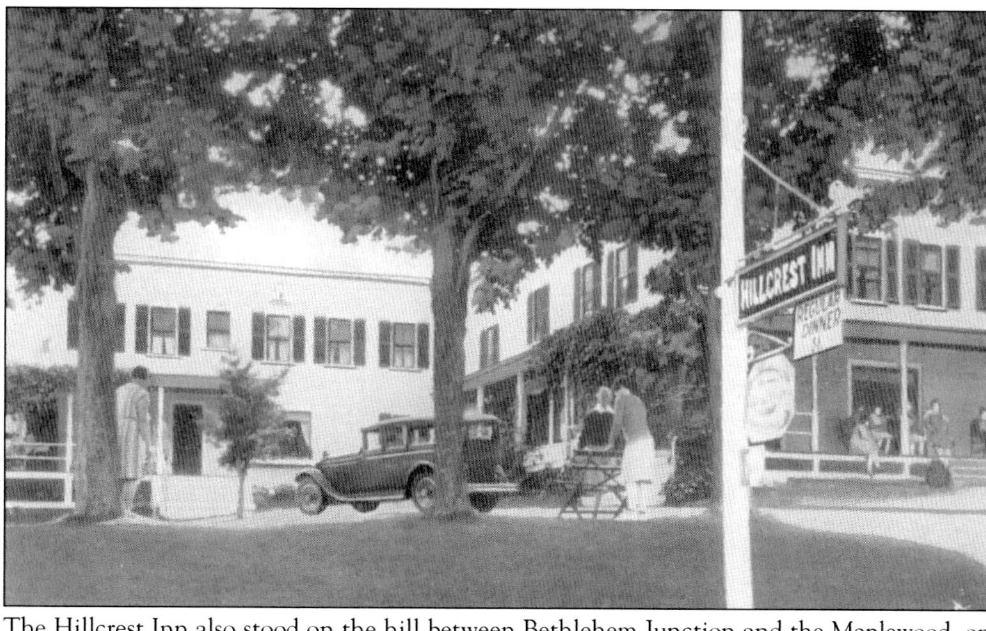

The Hillcrest Inn also stood on the hill between Bethlehem Junction and the Maplewood, on the same side of the road as Lovejoy's. Hillcrest's annex still stands and is currently the home and office of a dentist. The inn, which accommodated about 60 people, boasted views of Mount Washington and Franconia Notch. (Patricia Kezer Murray.)

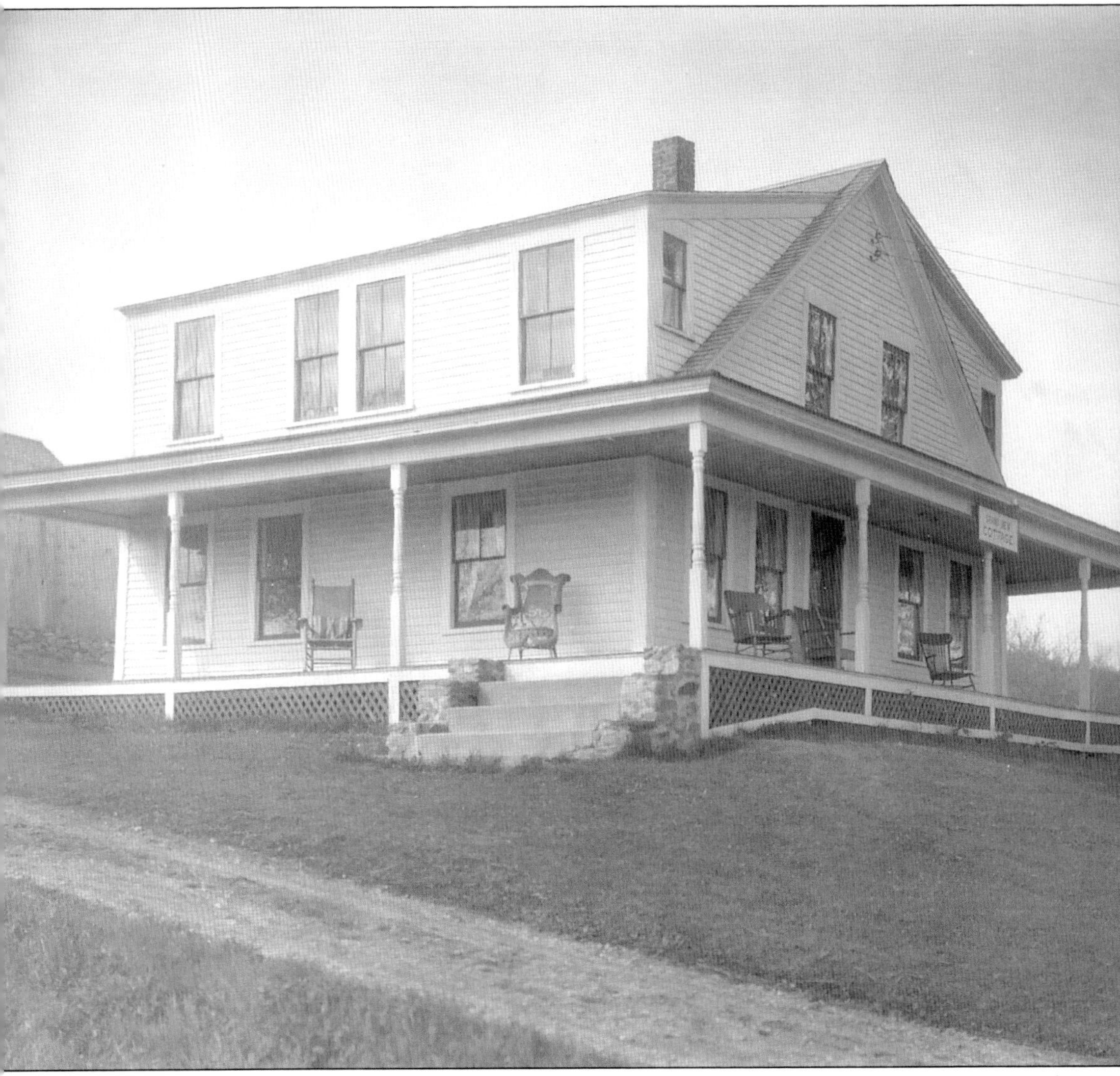

In 1929, Grand View Cottage on South Road was a small lodging house run by Peter Cassidy. Later, the Burlock family owned it. Many northern New Hampshire residents, even today, piece together a living from seasonal woods and agricultural work. From a Berlin logging family, Harvey Burlock continued this tradition by cutting wood part of the year and working on farms during the summer. (Bethlehem Heritage Museum.)

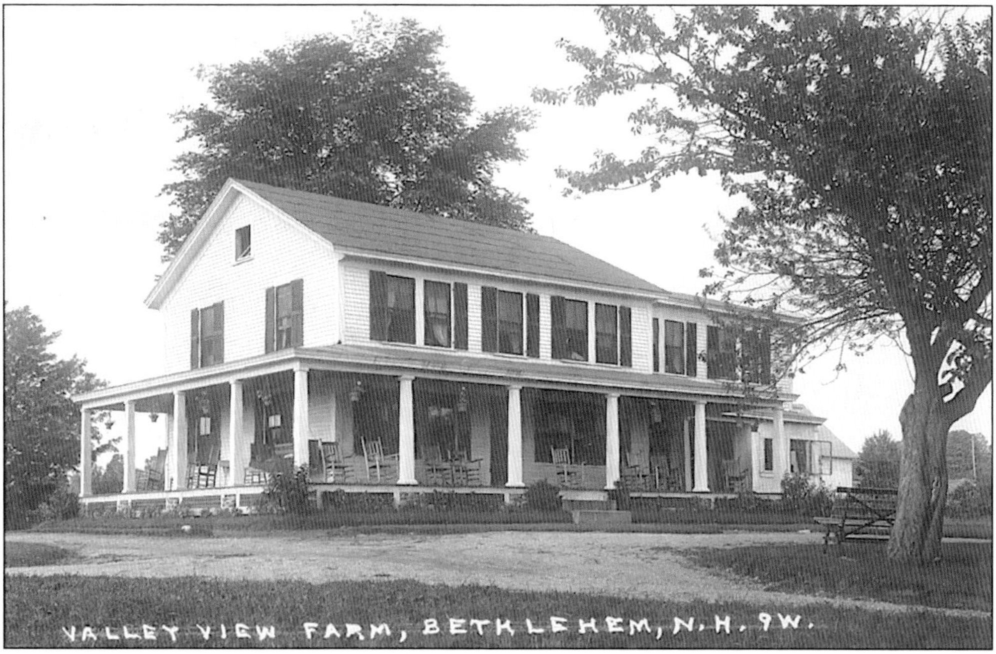

The Valley View property was a farm from 1803 to the mid-1920s, when the farmhouse was converted into an inn holding some 35 guests. Lots of good, farm-fresh food was one of the Valley View's hallmarks; some of the local teenagers chose to work there because of the diet they were offered. The location was private, too, well off Route 302 and nestled in the woods adjoining the Bethlehem Country Club course. A trout pond and a swimming pool were other features. Owners included Fred and Muffin Stevenson and John McCauley. (Paul Hudson.)

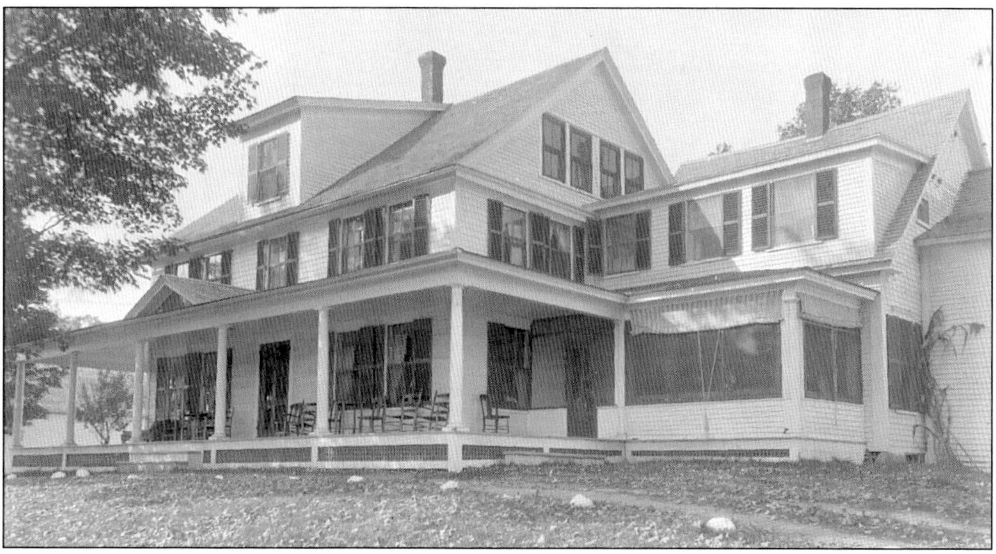

The Wallace family owned Wallace Farm from 1824 to 1935. Like many farm families, they began to rent rooms to guests when the White Mountains and Bethlehem became popular. In the 1930s, it cost $17.50 per week to stay at Wallace Lodge. Guests would enjoy the fresh milk, eggs, poultry, and vegetables produced on the farm. Later owners, the Davidsons, expanded the farm to include four motel units and five cabins. (Bethlehem Heritage Museum.)

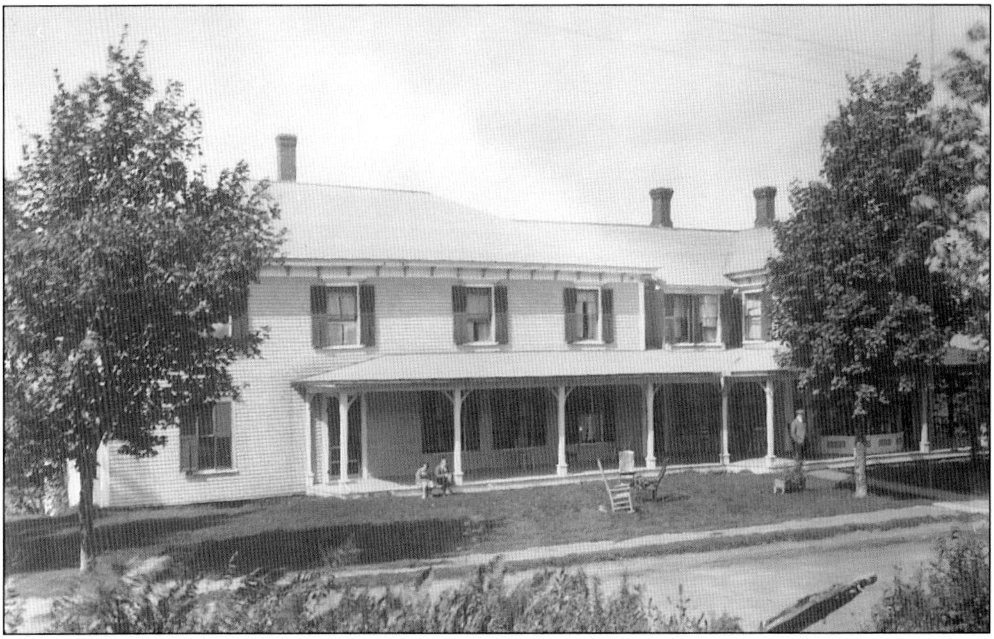

The Idlewild Hotel, which stood on Lewis Hill Road, was also known as the West End Hotel and the Roosevelt. It was one of the early Jewish hotels; as of 1929, proprietor K. Forman advertised observance of the Jewish dietary laws. The Idlewild burned in 1958. (Bethlehem Heritage Museum.)

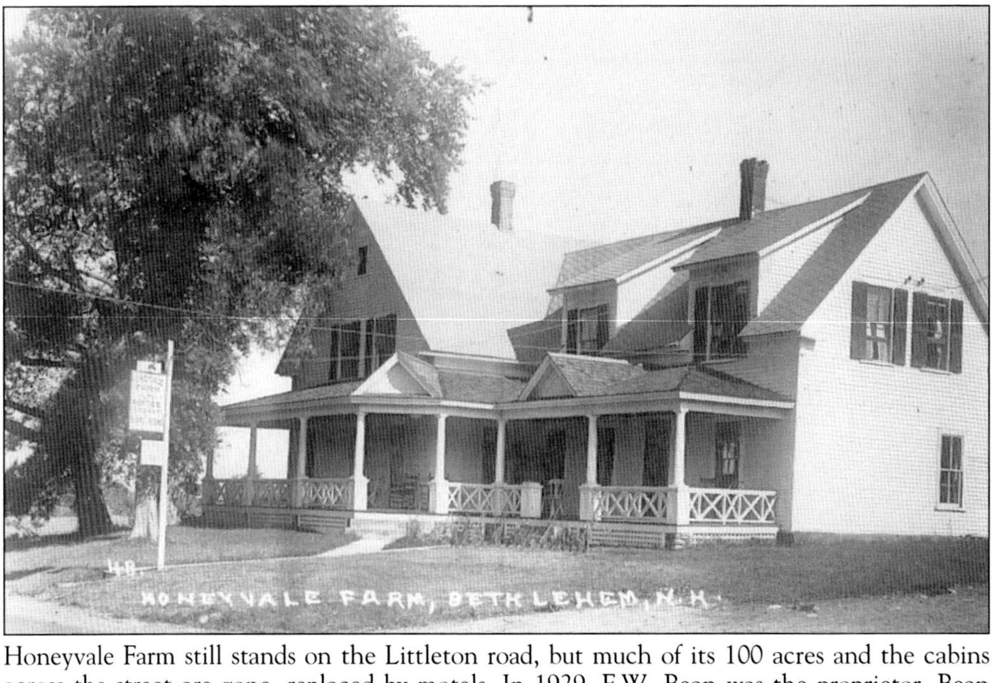

Honeyvale Farm still stands on the Littleton road, but much of its 100 acres and the cabins across the street are gone, replaced by motels. In 1929, F.W. Bean was the proprietor. Bean featured Honeyvale's home cooking and automobile storage in his directory advertisement. (Paul Hudson.)

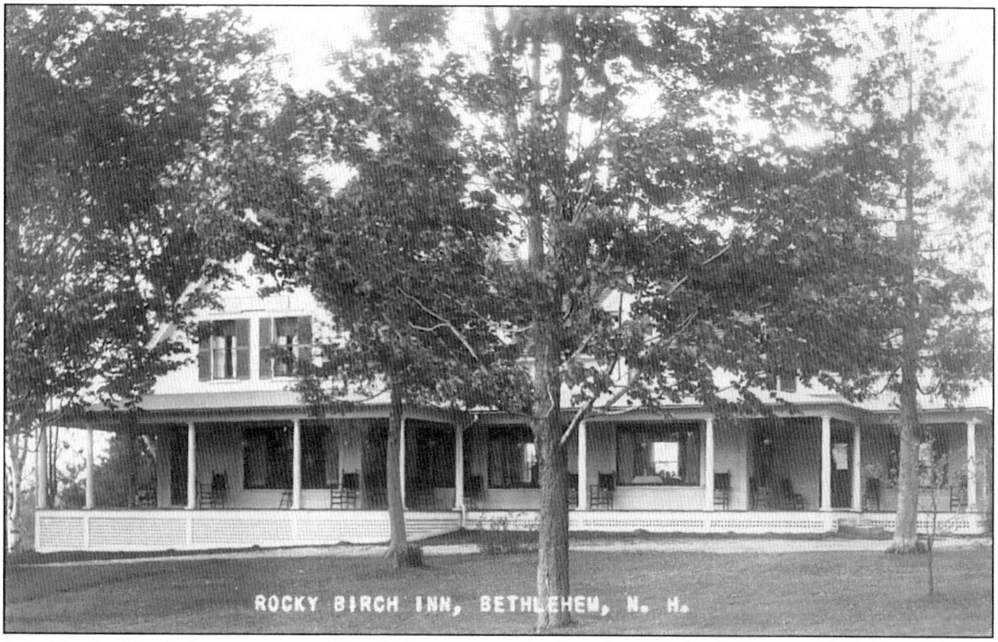

The Rocky Birch Inn accommodated 60 guests and offered steam heat, private baths, and a new garage. Peter Cassidy and Mrs. Harry Day were two of the proprietors. The Rocky Birch burned in 1980, and the Snowy Mountain Campground now occupies the site. (Paul Hudson.)

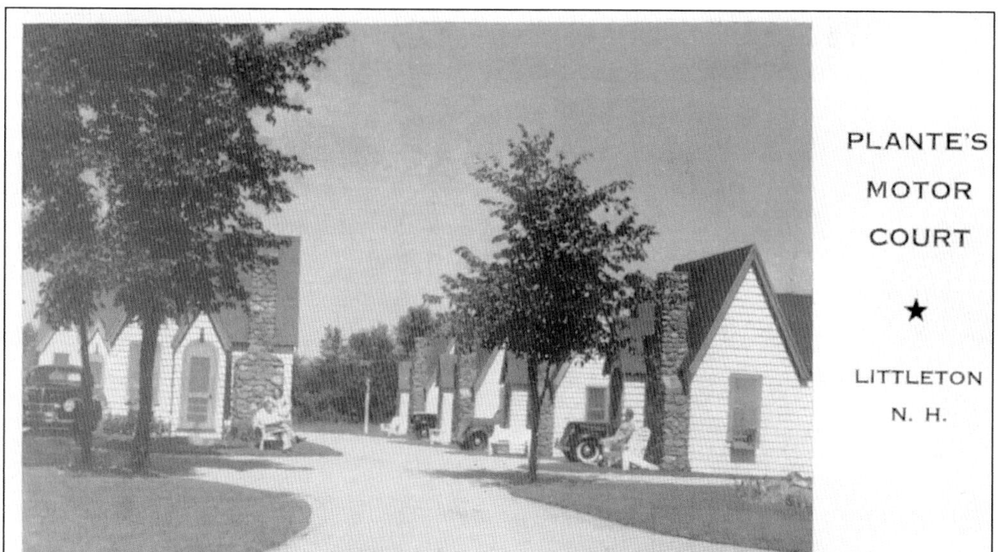

Changing travel patterns and tastes resulted in the development of a stretch of motels and cabins on Route 302 near Honeyvale Farm and the Rocky Birch. Plante's Cabins are now called Hearthside Village, and they are still quaint and playhouse-like. They are located on the corner of Cherry Valley Road on the former site of the Free Will Baptist church. (Paul Hudson.)

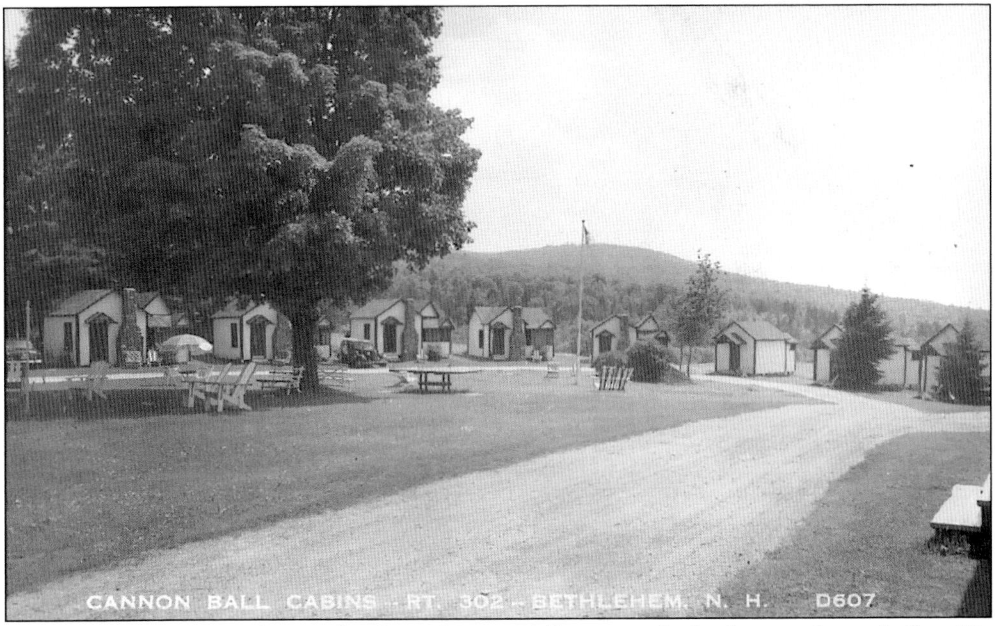

The Cannon Ball complex at the foot of Long Hill consisted of cabins, a dance hall, a 70-foot hardwood bowling alley, a main building, and a residence. Winifred Gearwar operated the business for many years. The cabins were donated to Copper Cannon Camp in Franconia. The main building is now a residence. (Paul Hudson.)

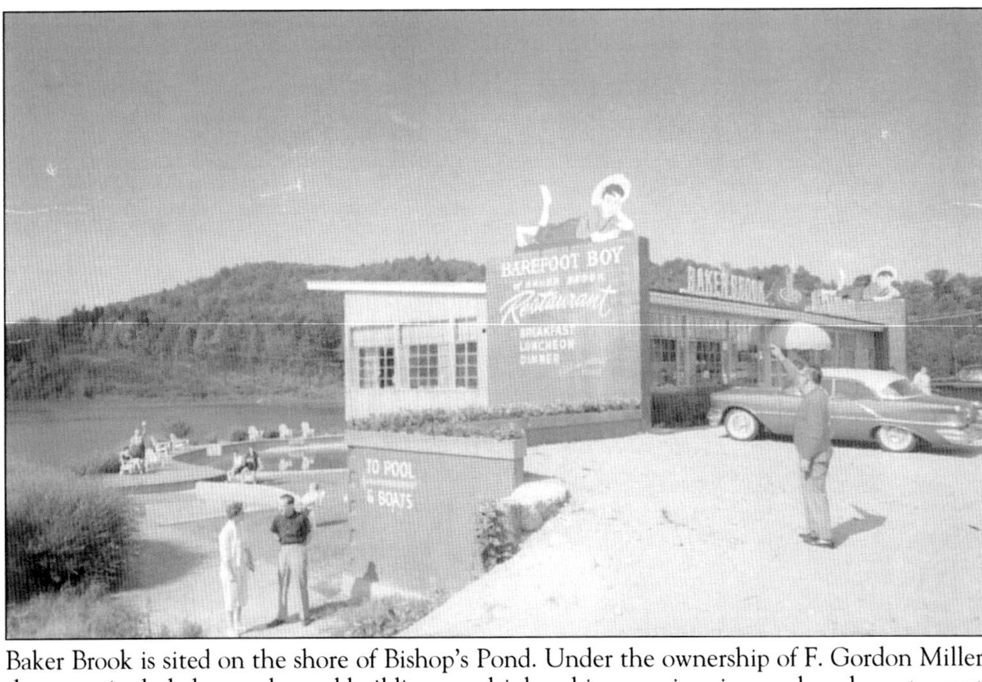

Baker Brook is sited on the shore of Bishop's Pond. Under the ownership of F. Gordon Miller, the resort included several motel buildings, multiple cabins, a swimming pool, and a restaurant. Baker Brook is favored by Hassidic visitors in the summer. The restaurant and pool no longer operate. (Bethlehem Heritage Museum.)

Two

Eclectic Cottages

As Bethlehem developed, people with means built summer homes near the hotels. This convenient arrangement provided privacy and freedom, while allowing participation in the social season. Larger hotels, such as the Maplewood, built and rented their own cottages. Some residents rented their own houses or built rental properties.

The summer home building period lasted from 1873 to the late 1920s. Bethlehem's cottages are marvelously eclectic, representing the wide variety of styles popular in the Victorian and pre–World War I eras. Many draw from more than one style, and they all abound in delightful period detail both inside and out.

Almost all of the buildings depicted in this chapter still exist. Most are in excellent condition and are used as primary homes, inns, or summer homes. Bethlehem is fortunate that so many charming cottages survived the economic and physical circumstances that spelled the demise of the hotels.

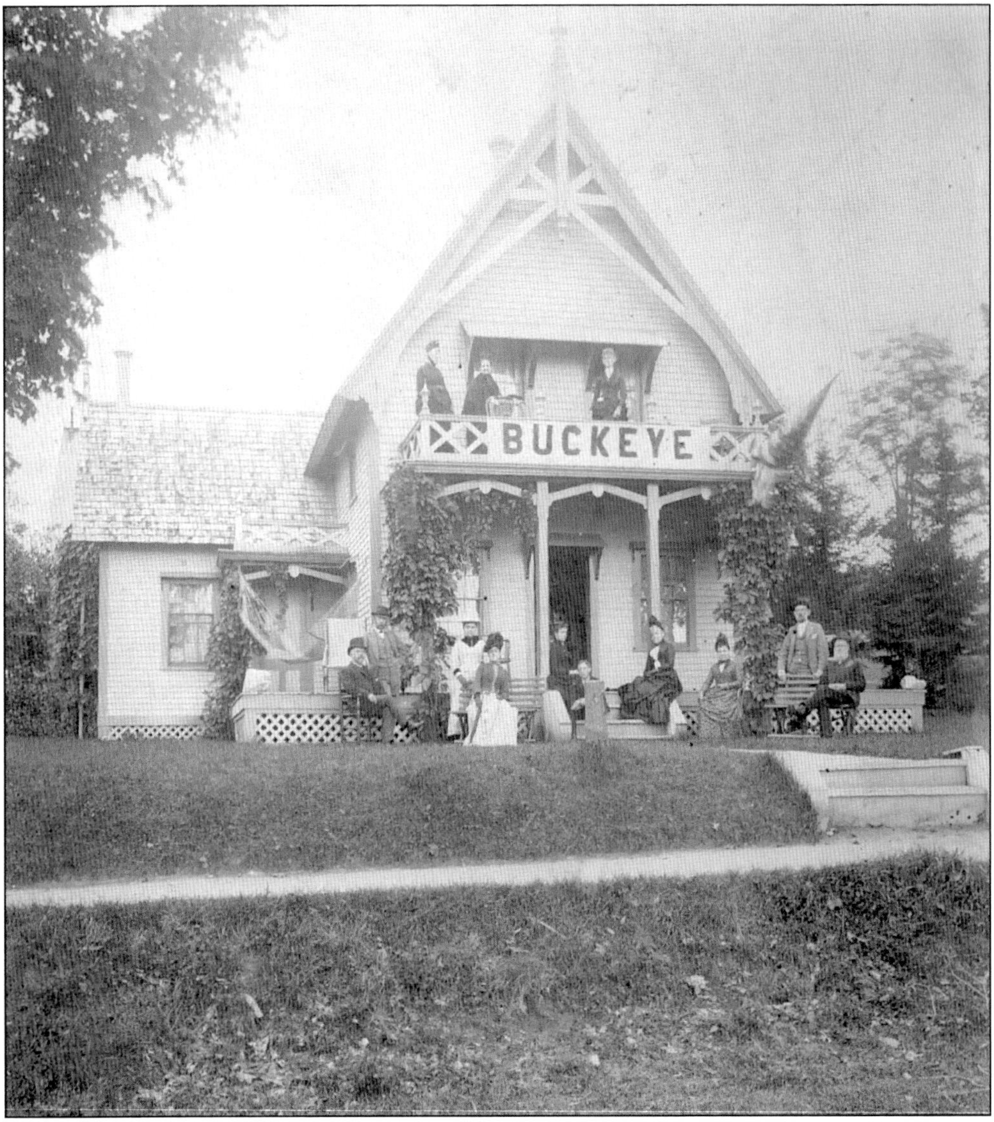

Built in 1873 by Gov. Henry Howard, Buckeye Cottage was the first summer home in Bethlehem. It features Gothic Revival architecture and stands on the corner of Strawberry Hill and Main Street. (Bethlehem Heritage Museum.)

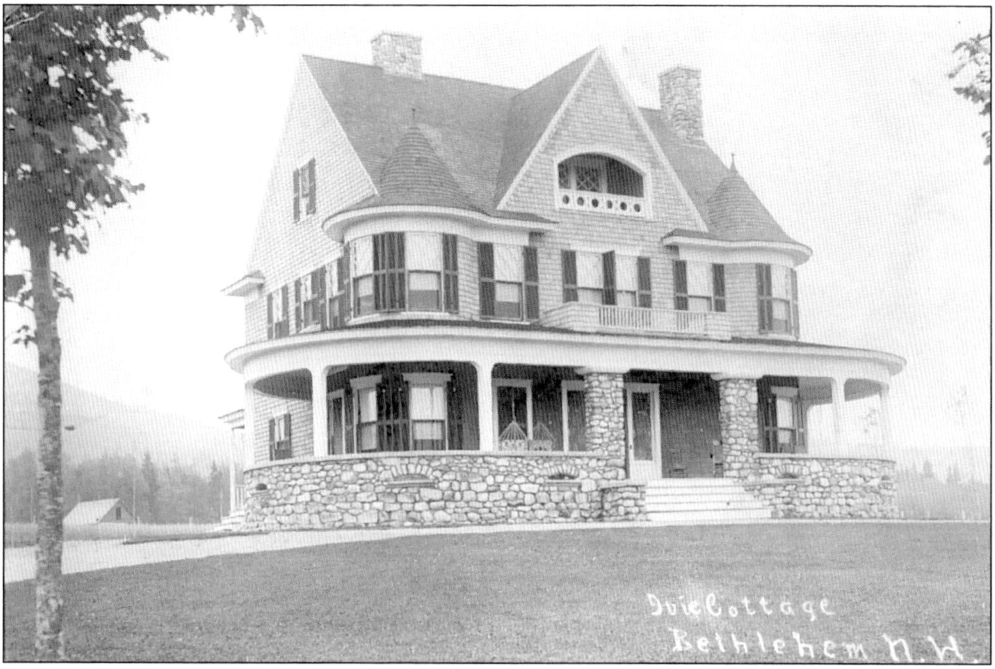

Sylvanus D. Morgan, architect and builder of the Mount Washington Hotel, built the English Tudor–style Ivie Cottage in 1908. Alvin E. Ivie, the owner, was married to Henrietta Creighton, an heiress to the Woolworth fortune. The cottage boasts maple, oak, mahogany, and ash woodwork, curved interior walls, stained-glass windows, and Italian tile fireplaces. Two wings were added to the cottage in 1913. Famous guests include inventor Thomas Edison. Also, actors Barbara Hutton and Cary Grant are rumored to have stayed there. Currently, Ivie Cottage is a bed and breakfast called the Mulburn Inn. (Bethlehem Heritage Museum.)

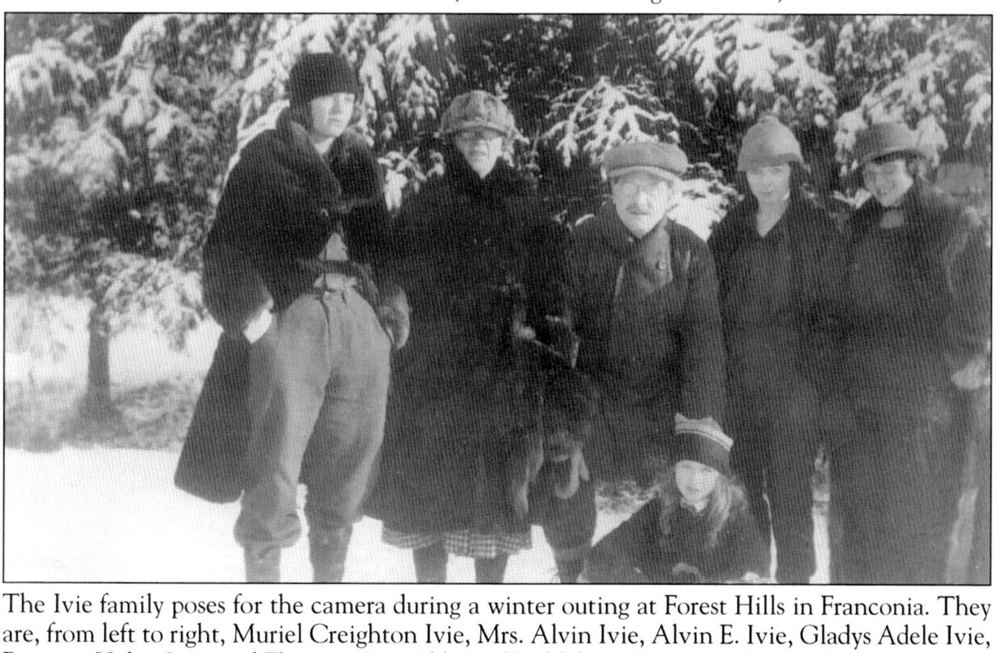

The Ivie family poses for the camera during a winter outing at Forest Hills in Franconia. They are, from left to right, Muriel Creighton Ivie, Mrs. Alvin Ivie, Alvin E. Ivie, Gladys Adele Ivie, Beatrice Helen Ivie, and Florence Ivie Abbott. (Bethlehem Heritage Museum.)

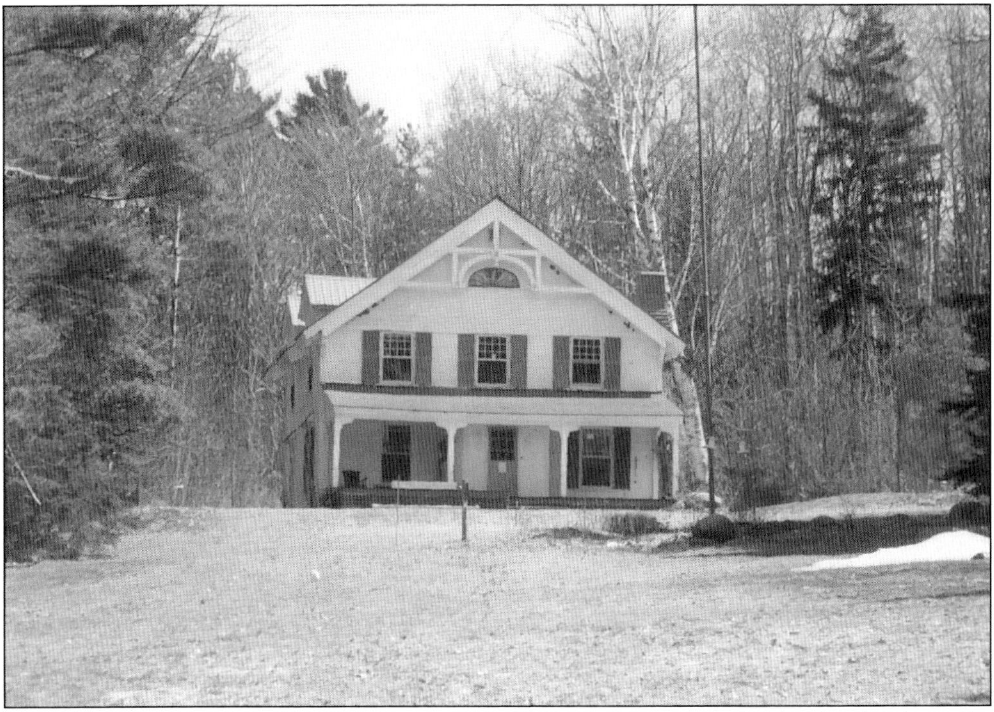

Parva Domus was the second cottage built in Bethlehem, in 1880. Elizabeth Cleveland was the owner. It is located on Lewis Hill Road, across from Lemen Cottage. (Elizabeth Ward.)

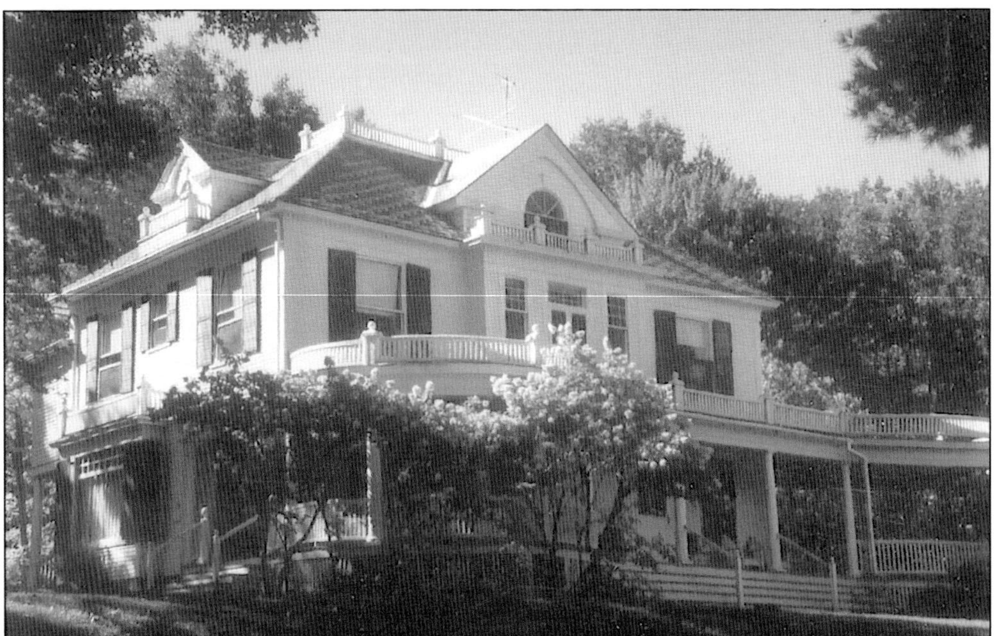

Famous architect Stanford White designed this lovely cottage for the sister of J.P. Morgan. Later owners included the Poors of Standard and Poors. (Kathleen J. Parrish.)

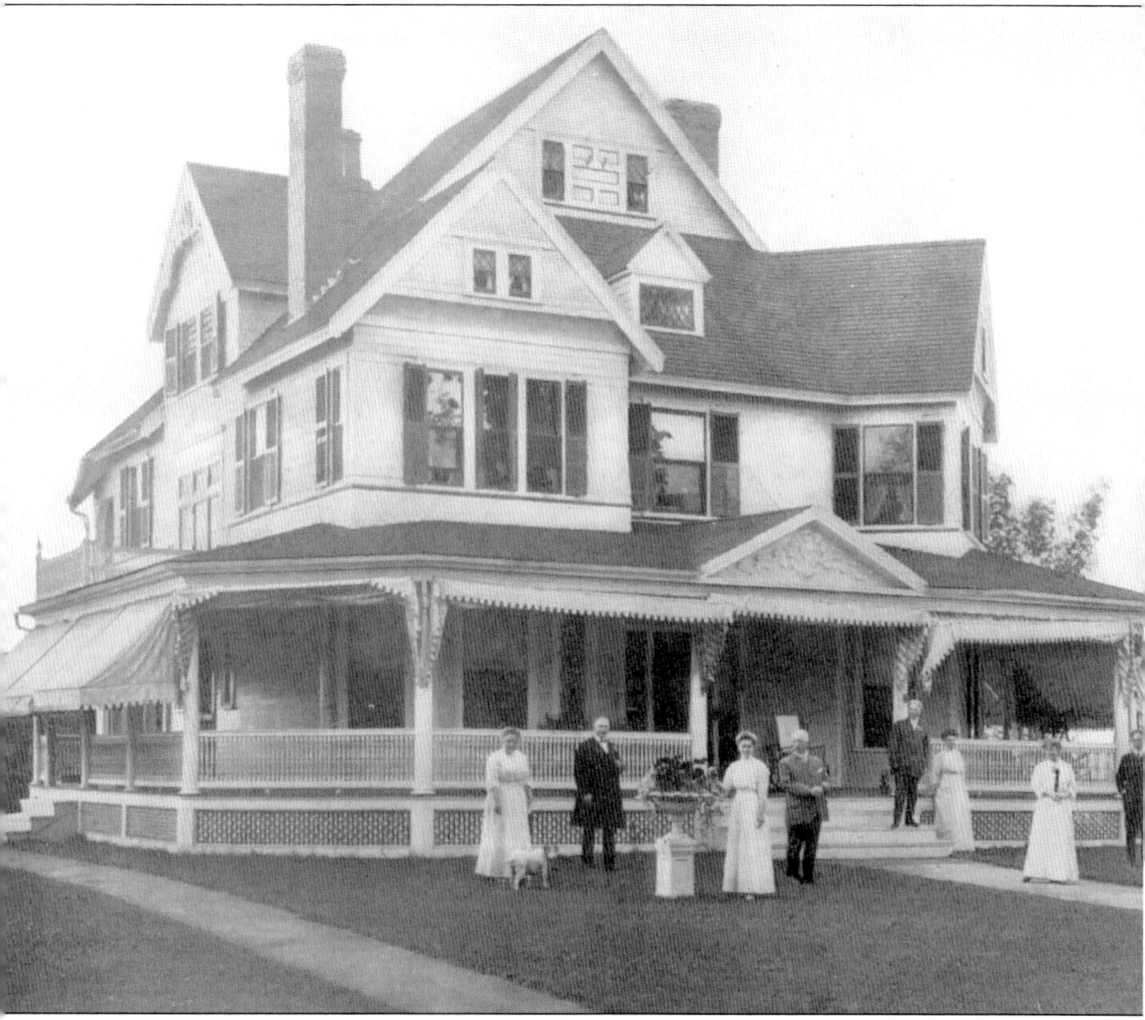

Sylvanus D. Morgan built the Red Gables for Mrs. W.O. Kelner in 1893. After serving as a summer cottage for several owners, Red Gables became the Howard House Annex. During that period, every room was converted into a bedroom. After painstaking renovation, the house is now a bed and breakfast owned by Ben and Sally Gumm. It features oak interior woodwork, Victorian exterior trim and shingle work, and decorative molding. (Bethlehem Library.)

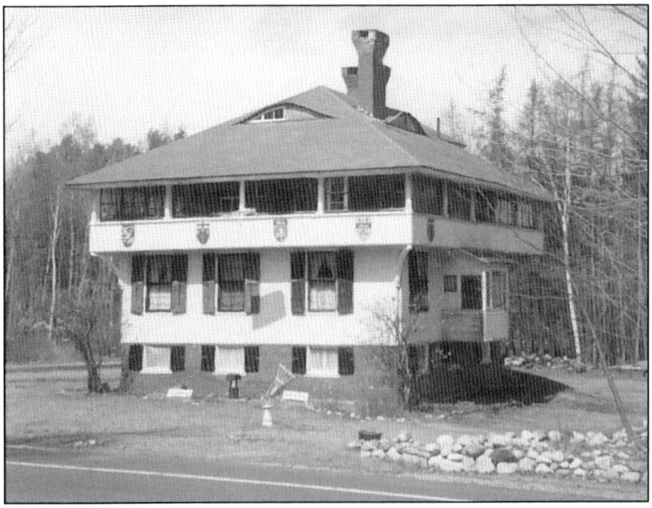

The Lodge, reminiscent of a fort in its architecture, stands near the Maplewood cottages. Norman Franzeim, director of the Maplewood Caddy Camp from 1915 to 1949, owned it for many years. In 1958, he donated a part of the cottage's land for the Caddy Shrine, which is still maintained by the Caddy Association. (Elizabeth Ward.)

MAPLEWOOD IN THE WH

LINCOLN COTTAGE (12)

One of our best cottages, is 400 feet east from the hotel. It faces south, has piazzas on three sides and overlooks Maplewood Park and Gardens. It is surrounded by ample grounds and has a good walk to the hotel.

On the ground floor are two large bedrooms, dining-room, kitchen and two bath-rooms, also an extra toilet for servants. There is a large heater in the cellar which supplies steam for the entire house

There are on piazza floor, a large living room with windows on three sides, a fire-place and closet; three other large rooms two connecting with bath-room; back of these, one room suitable for servant.

There are three large chambers above, also bath-room, with plenty of storage room and closets.

This cottage can be arranged for housekeeping.

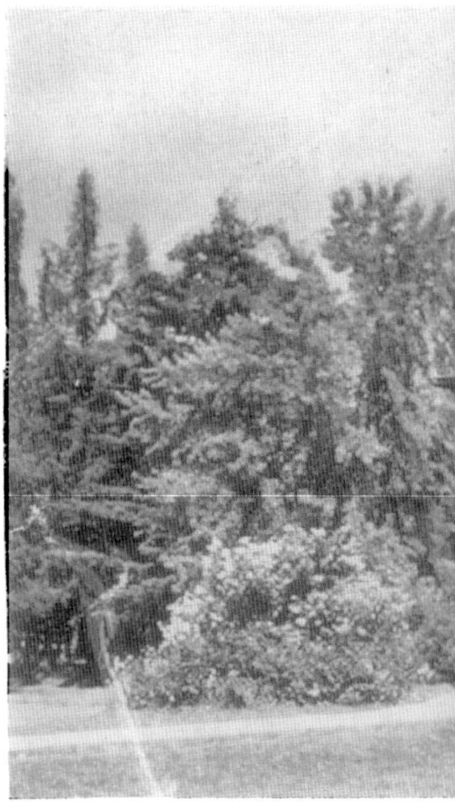

(Diagram of rooms on re

Lincoln Cottage was one of 15 cottages owned by the Maplewood Hotel. (Norm Chapman.)

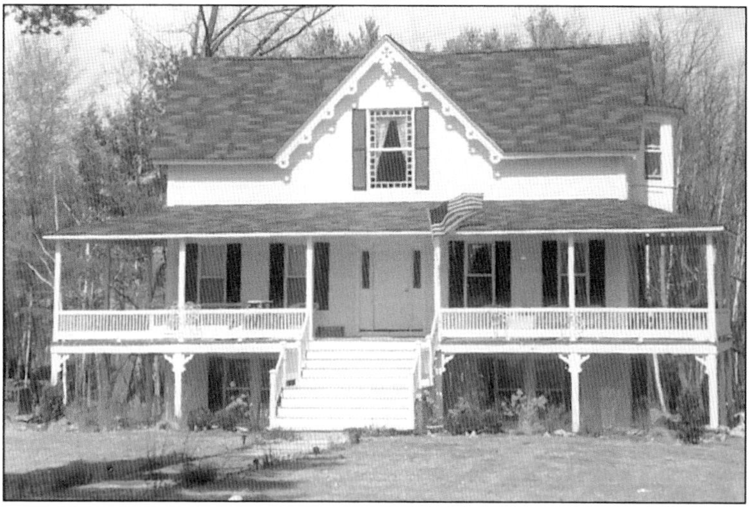

Cottage No. 14 stands west of Lincoln Cottage. Several years ago, it stood surrounded by new growth and looked like it was past saving. Fortunately it was purchased and renovated. (Elizabeth Ward.)

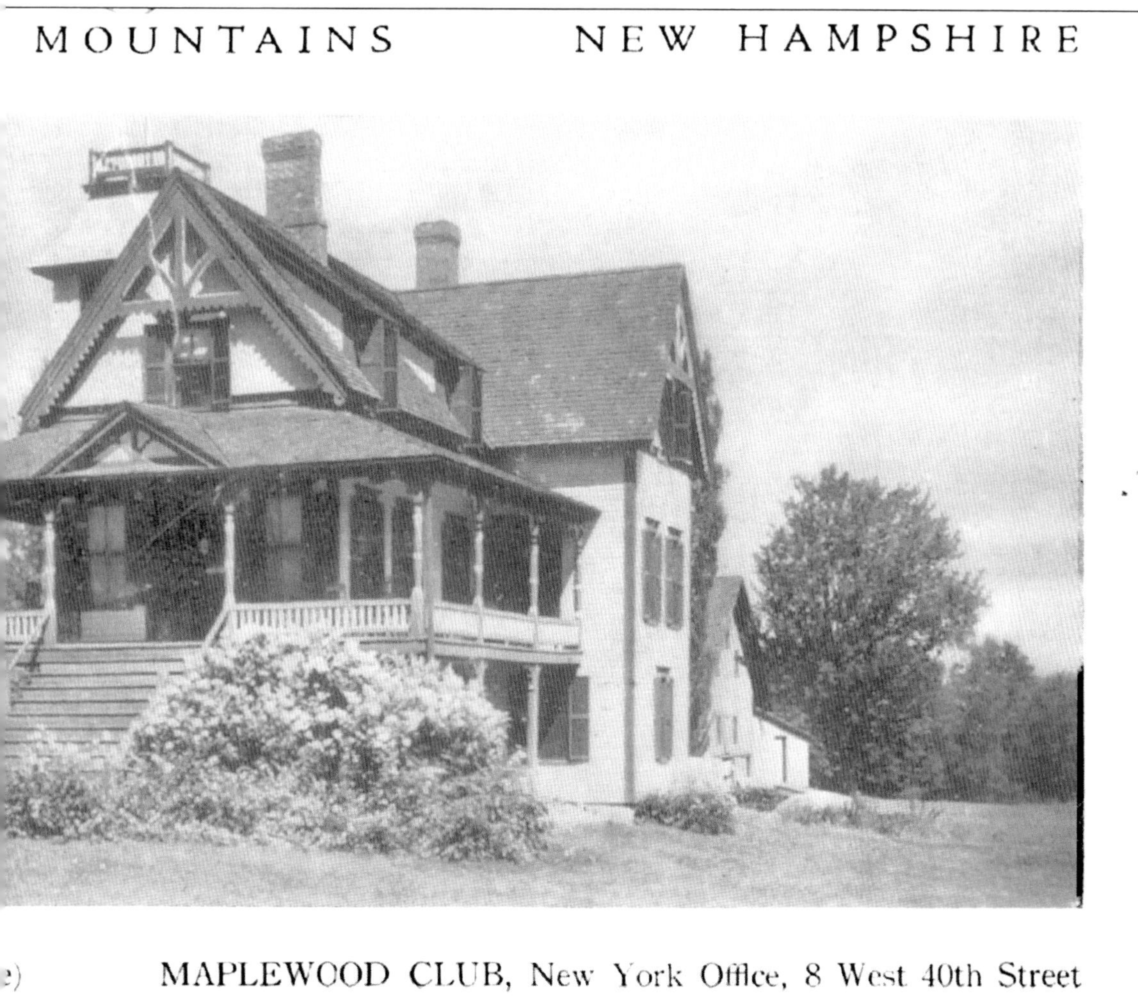

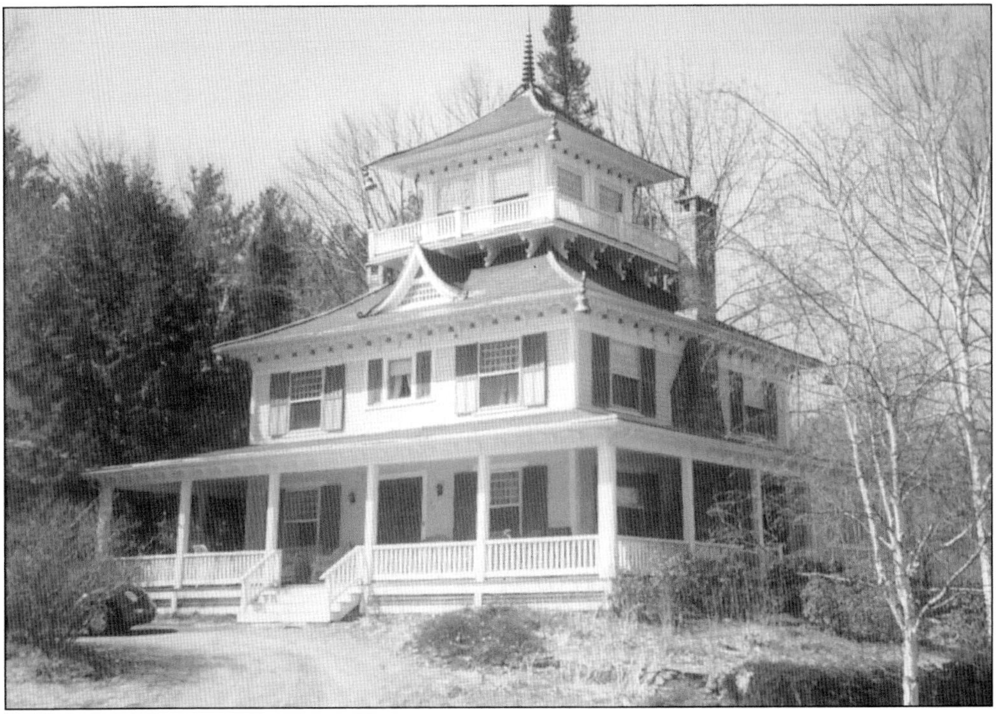

With its tiered construction, curved roof, and bells and dragons, Bell Cottage is reminiscent of an Oriental pagoda. Built by a Methodist minister in 1892, Bell Cottage was the third summer home in Bethlehem. Other unusual features include the cupola and the 32-over-one windows. (Elizabeth Ward.)

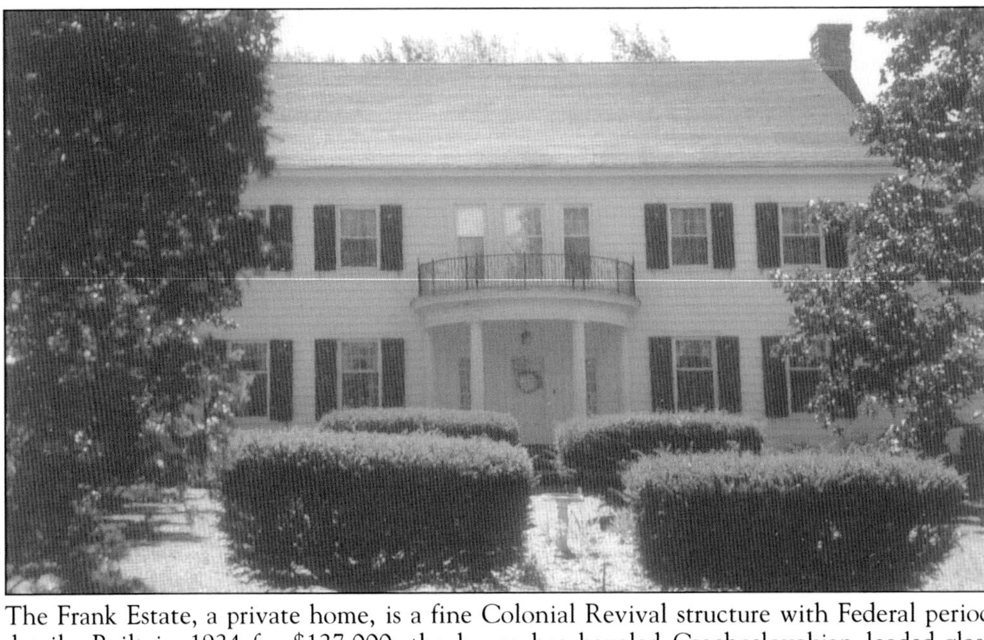

The Frank Estate, a private home, is a fine Colonial Revival structure with Federal period details. Built in 1924 for $127,000, the house has beveled Czechoslovakian leaded-glass windows in the sun room, large gracious rooms, and an operating servant bell system. (Kathleen J. Parrish.)

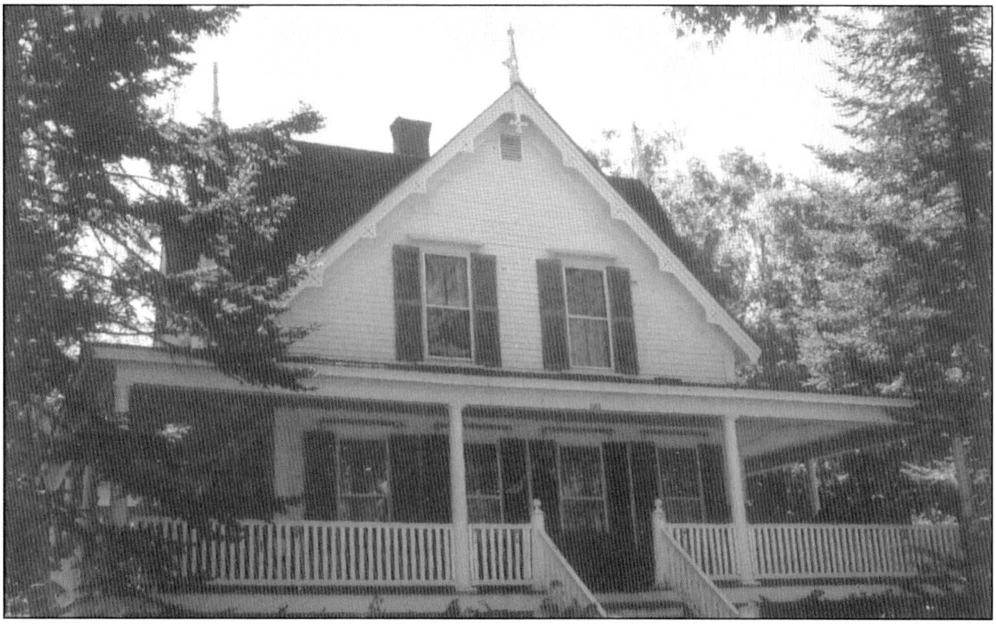

Poplar Cottage is another example of Gothic Revival architecture. Built in 1876 by Isaac Cruft, who built the Maplewood Hotel, it served as his summer cottage. Later, the Ivie family bought it, and some of the land was used for the Ivie Memorial Chapel. Today, the barn is used as an antique store by Chris Curran and Gerry Fanning. They are only the fourth owners in more than 125 years. (Kathleen J. Parrish.)

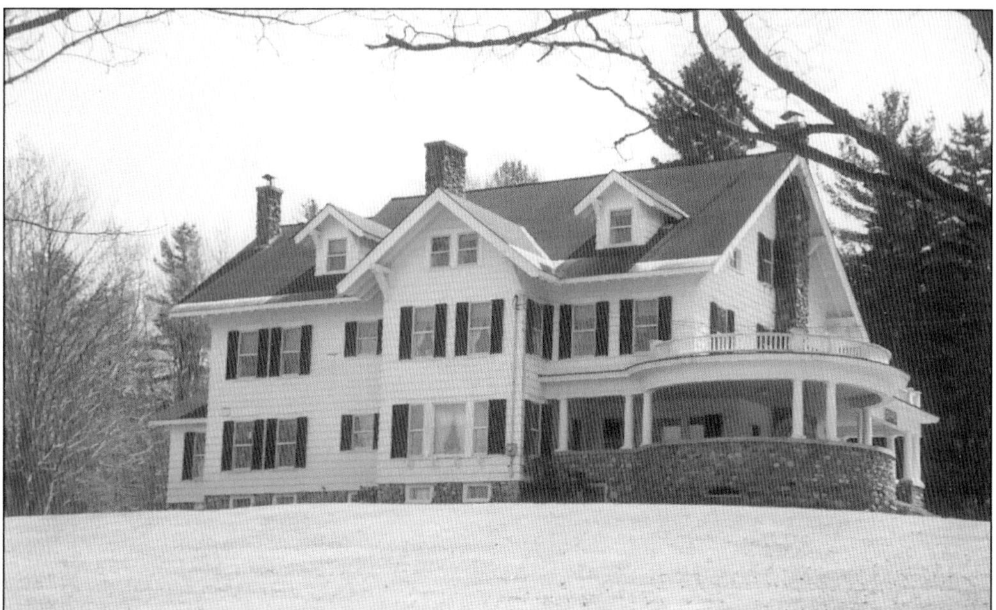

The Grande Victorian, as it is currently known, is a beautiful example of Colonial Revival architecture. Sylvanus D. Morgan designed and built the cottage in 1905. Note the roof brackets, curved porch, dormers, and fieldstone masonry. The ghost of a small boy is said to run up and down the stairs and to peer out the windows on occasion. The house is now a bed and breakfast owned by Steve and Fran Marszalkowski. (Elizabeth Ward.)

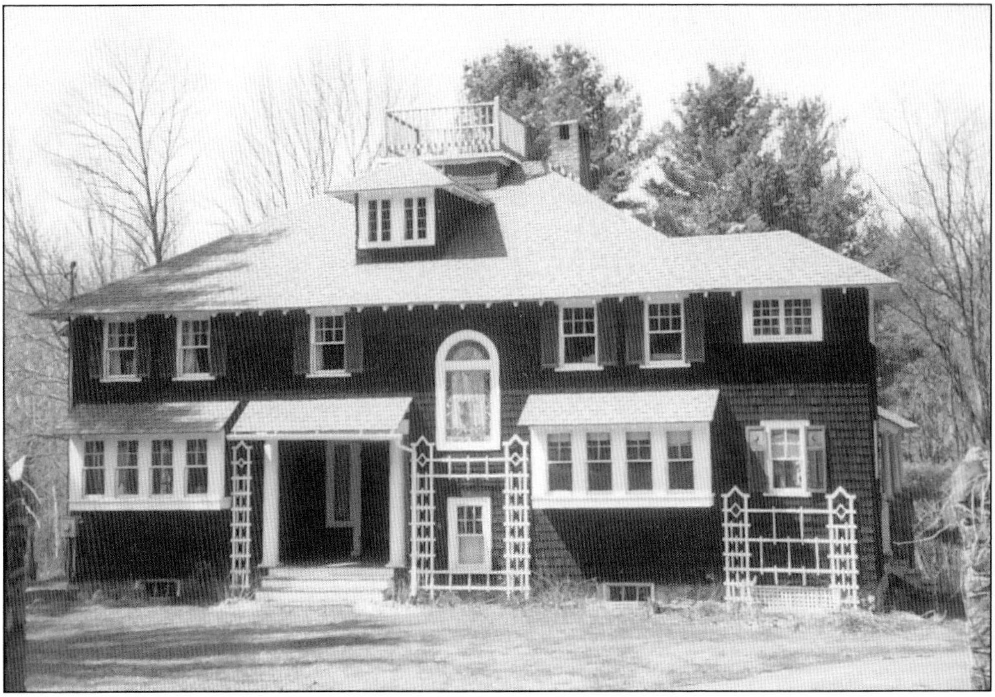

Lemen Cottage is a wonderful example of a Colonial Revival house with Craftsman influence. It is one of two cottages that Waldo Whitcomb built in 1916 or 1917 for Mr. Lemen on Lewis Hill Road. (Elizabeth Ward.)

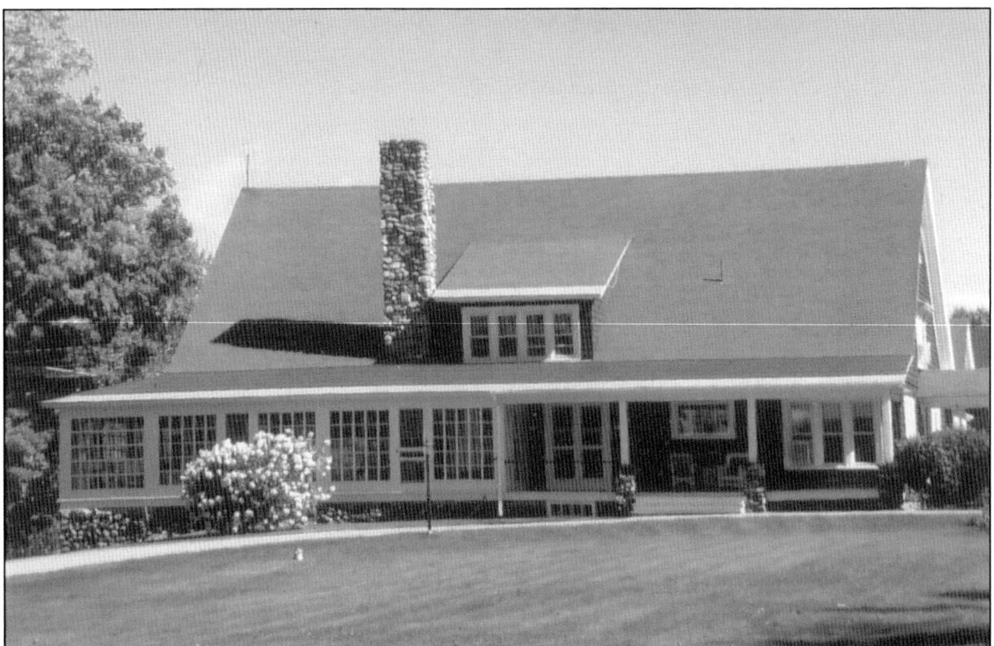

The cottage known as Three Acres is located on Congress Street on the site of the Bethlehem House, which burned *c.* 1908. The cottage was used as a rental property for years. George Noyes and his family owned it from 1949 to 1998. (Kathleen J. Parrish.)

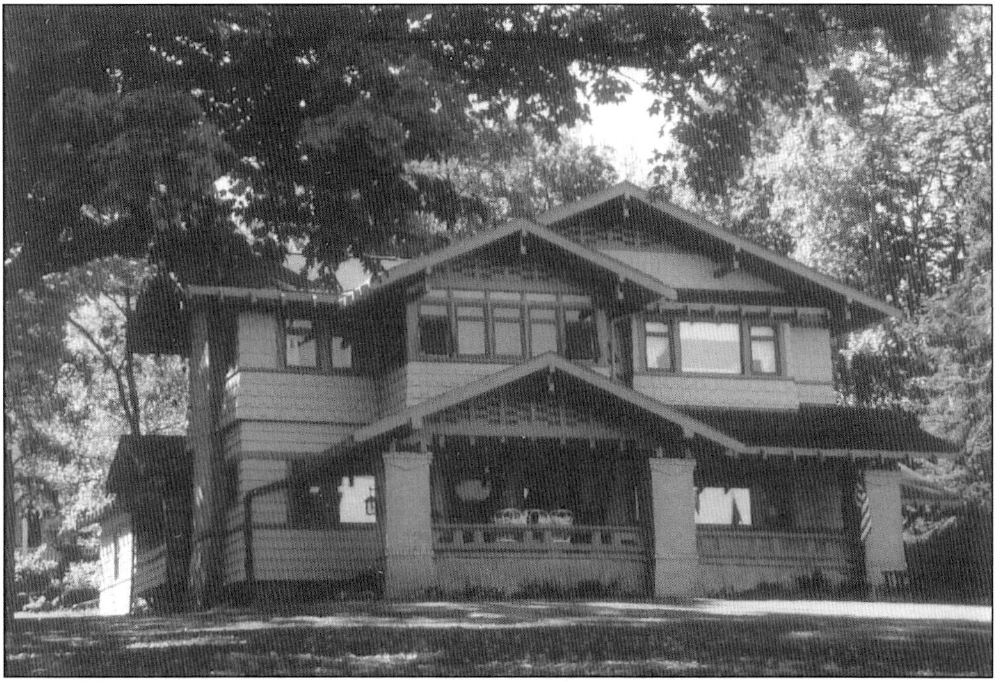

After a visit to see architect Frank Lloyd Wright's work in Chicago, Sylvanus D. Morgan designed and built a Prairie-style cottage on the grounds of the Upland Terrace. The house was a gift to Karl and Florence Ivie Abbott for their 1918 wedding. (Kathleen J. Parrish.)

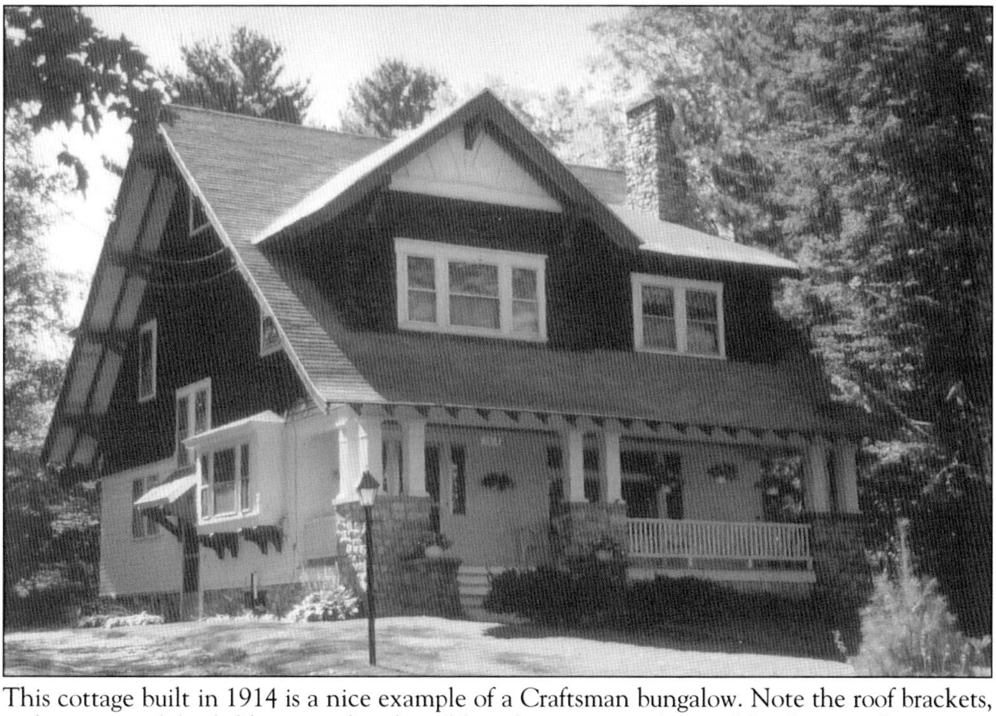

This cottage built in 1914 is a nice example of a Craftsman bungalow. Note the roof brackets, wide eaves, and the fieldstone pedestals and foundation, a use of natural local materials common in Arts and Crafts architecture. (Kathleen J. Parrish.)

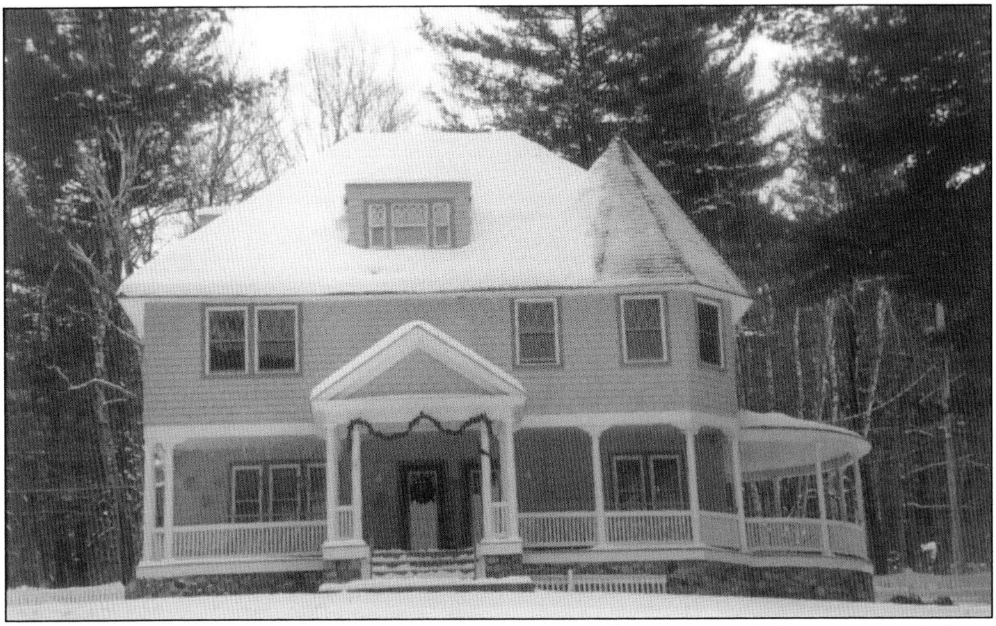

W.M. Sayer built four cottages along Main Street as rental properties. Cubans, many of whom were high-level government officials, rented them during the 1920s. Later, two of the buildings were divided into apartments, including the one pictured here. Now owned by the nonprofit housing organization AHEAD, they have been newly renovated. (Elizabeth Ward.)

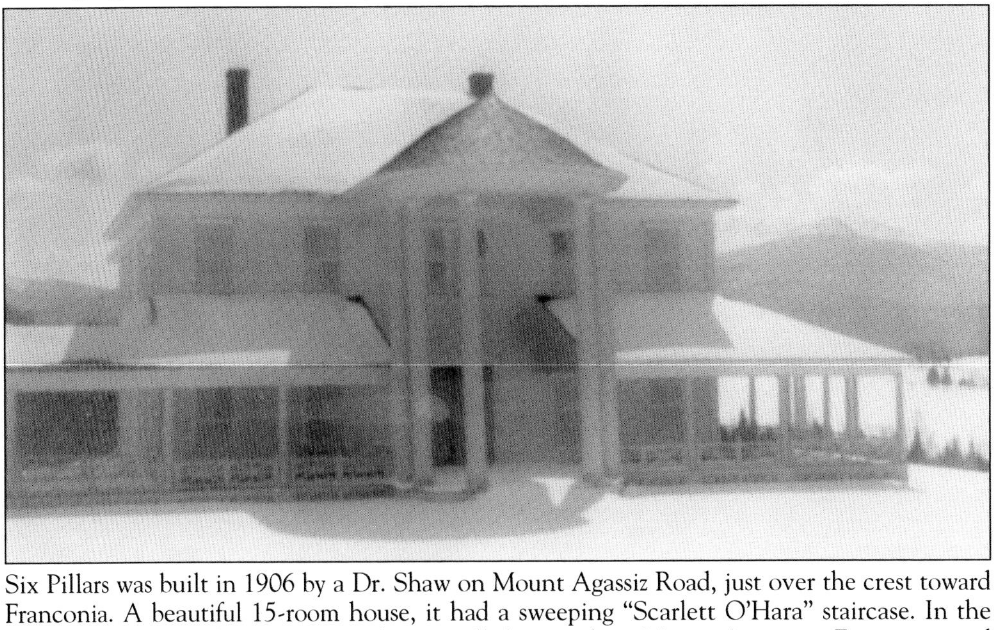

Six Pillars was built in 1906 by a Dr. Shaw on Mount Agassiz Road, just over the crest toward Franconia. A beautiful 15-room house, it had a sweeping "Scarlett O'Hara" staircase. In the early 1900s, the landscape was mostly open all the way from Mount Agassiz to Franconia, and Six Pillars and other houses in the vicinity had an unobstructed view of Franconia Notch. One resident remembers a former owner who was so afraid of germs that she always dressed in white and sent her chauffeur to do the shopping. This woman would ask the local children to dress up and parade in front of her porch to be inspected. She rewarded each with a dollar. (Courtesy of Dartmouth College Library.)

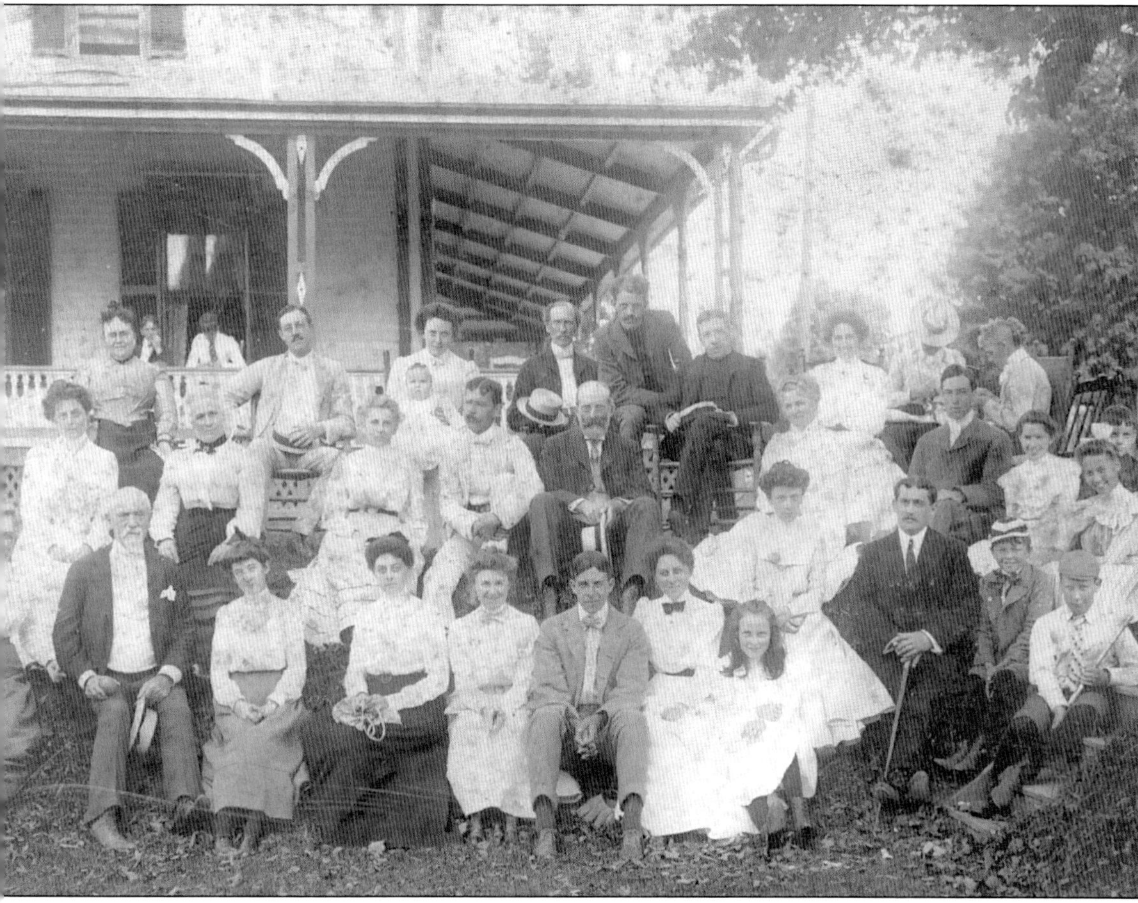

The Cowie and Campbell families from Rahway, New Jersey, spent many summers in Bethlehem. People identified in the back row (at left) in this 1901 photograph are Margaret Clarkson Campbell, George Howard Cowie, Caroline Campbell Cowie with baby George Howard Cowie Jr., and Orville D. Campbell. (Bethlehem Heritage Museum.)

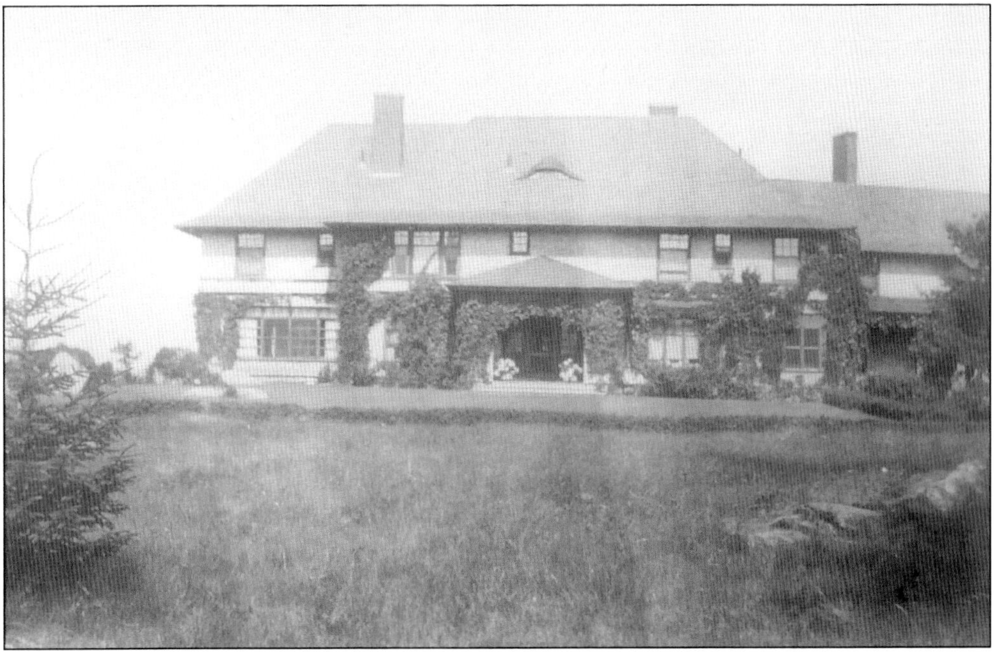

Located off Prospect Street on grounds measuring 200 acres, the cottage called Stonecrest is one of the largest in Bethlehem. It was built *c.* 1902–1905 by the Macbeth family, who were related to the Glessners of the Rocks Estate. This photograph shows the house before the round stone porches were added to the left wing. At that time the house was called Glamis. (Bethlehem Heritage Museum.)

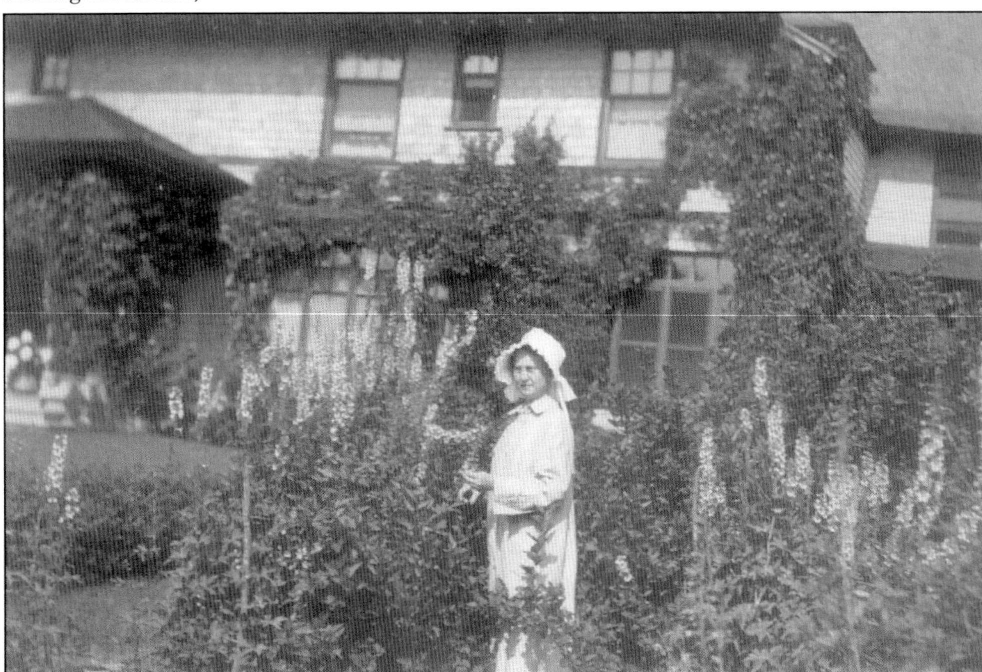

Mrs. Macbeth had several elaborate gardens, including a cutting garden near the stone carriage house. (Bethlehem Heritage Museum.)

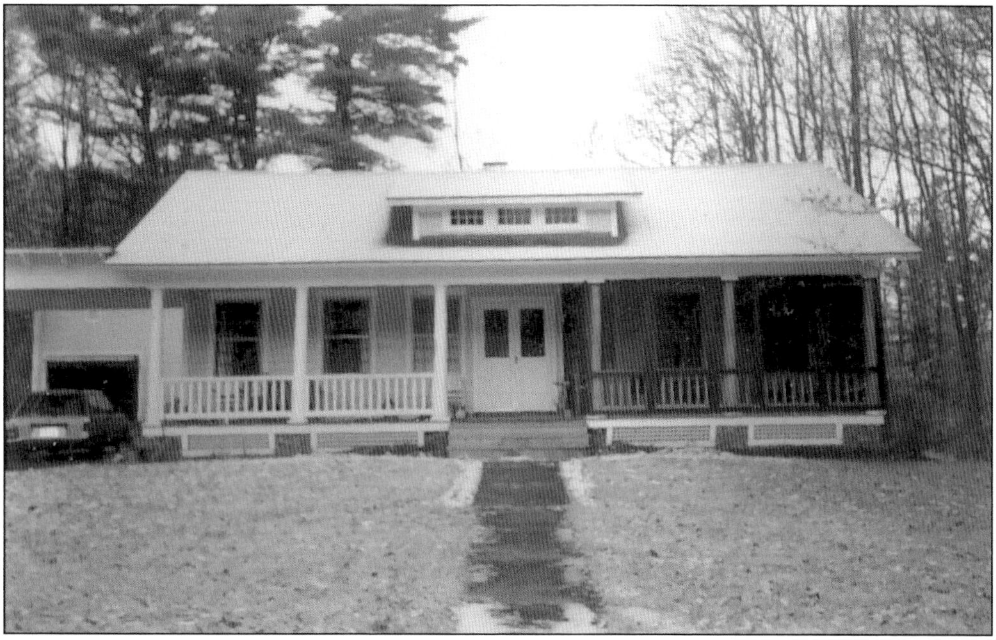

Dr. William Jeffries built the Kentucky, an Aladdin kit house, on Maple Street. In the early part of the 20th century, Sears Roebuck and Aladdin sold many houses through catalogs. The various components of a house—precut, bundled, and labeled—arrived by train, and local carpenters put them together. (Elizabeth Ward.)

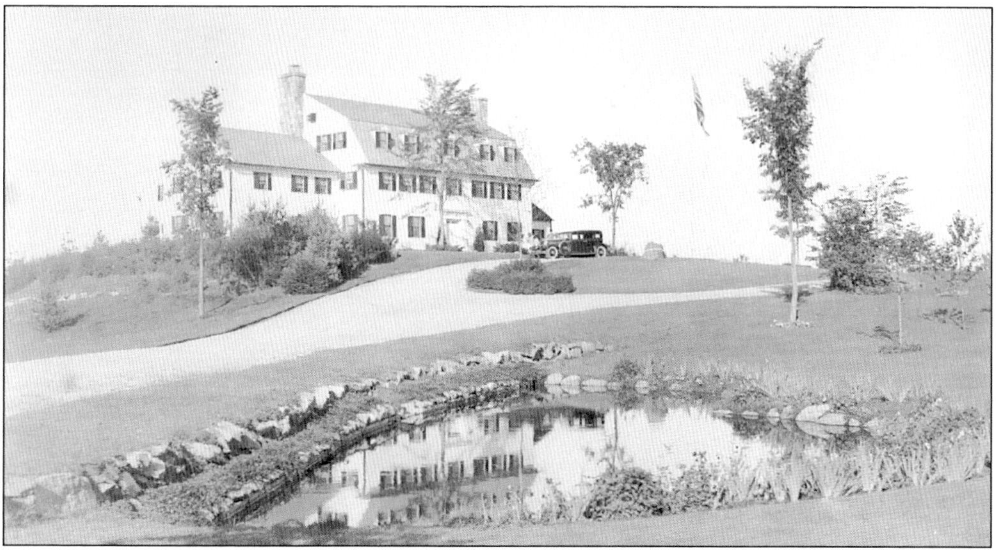

Adair was built in 1927 by Washington, D.C. lawyer Frank Hogan as a wedding gift for his daughter Dorothy Hogan Guider. Designed by a Mr. Peck and built by Bernard Harvey, the house cost $150,000. Due to family connections, the Guiders hosted many distinguished guests over the years. Hogan was an attorney for Theodore Roosevelt, Andrew Mellon, Evelyn Walsh McLain, and Edward L. Doheny of Teapot Dome fame. Hogan's cousin James Byrnes was governor of South Carolina, secretary of state, and a Supreme Court justice. Actress Helen Hayes was a good friend of Hogan's daughter. Adair is now a bed and breakfast owned and operated by Bill and Judy Whitman. (Bill and Judy Whitman.)

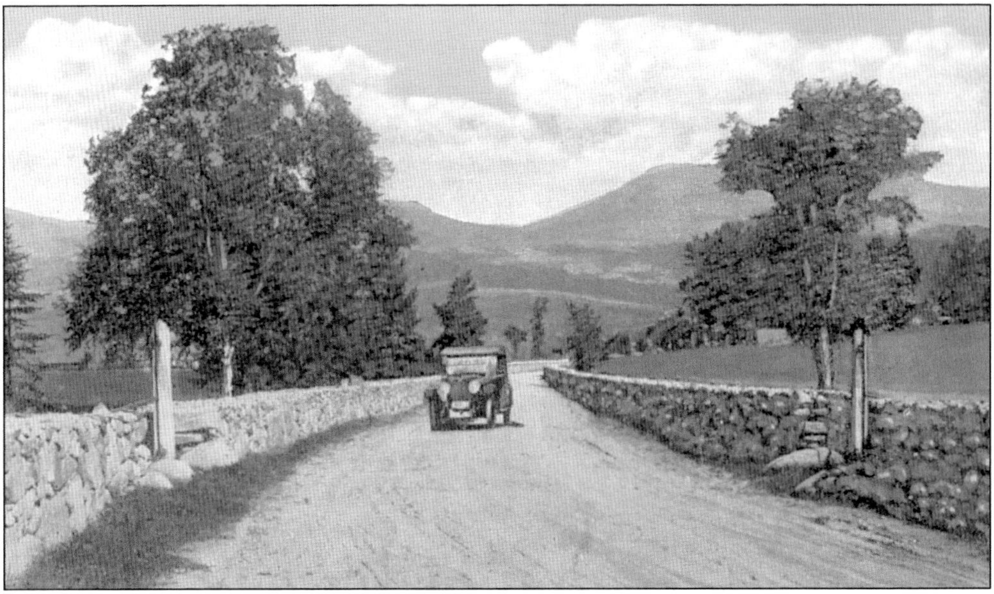

In 1883, John J. Glessner of Chicago and International Harvester purchased farmland from Orrin H. Streeter and created the estate known as the Rocks. Other adjoining parcels were also acquired, bringing the total acreage to 1,300. Using stones from the land, a team of 80 men built roads and miles of beautiful stone walls. Today, the estate is owned by the Society for Protection of New Hampshire Forests, which runs a Christmas tree farm and year-round family and educational programs. An interpretive center featuring the estate's history is currently being planned. (Paul Hudson.)

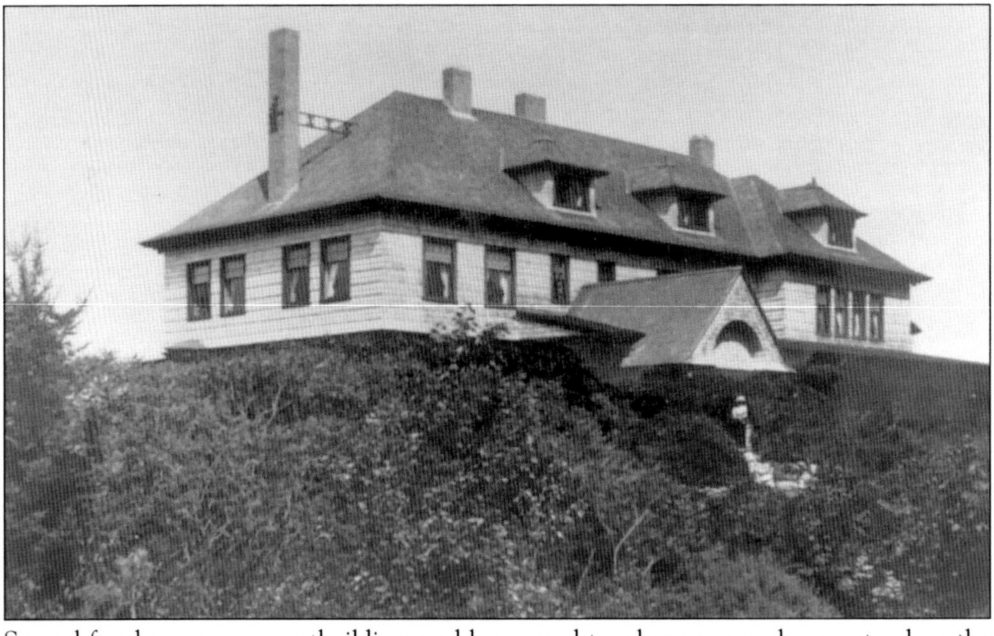

Several farmhouses, many outbuildings and barns, and two large summerhouses stood on the Rocks Estate. George Glessner, John J. Glessner's son, owned this house, called the Ledge. The Glessner family came to the White Mountains for the relief of the son's hay fever, which was quite severe. (Society for Protection of NH Forests.)

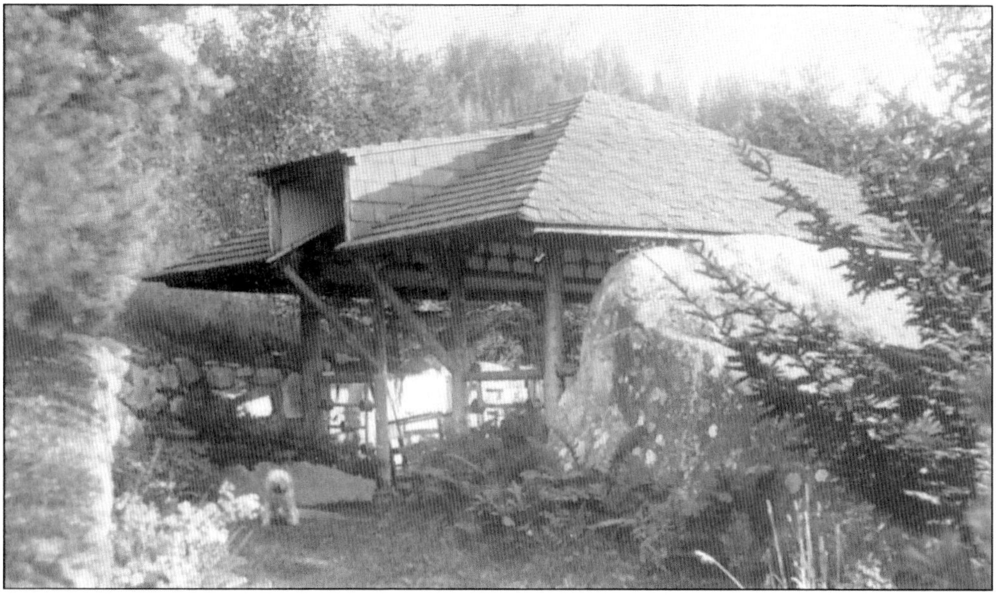

The Big Rock Summerhouse stands along the Mile Path, which circles the property around the back of the main hill. A network of paths winds through the property, past a pool and teahouse, the piggery, the playhouses, the site of the big house, and the springhouses. Mrs. Batchelder, who donated the land, stipulated that some of the paths remain private except during official society tours. The Mile Path is included in that condition. (Society for Protection of NH Forests.)

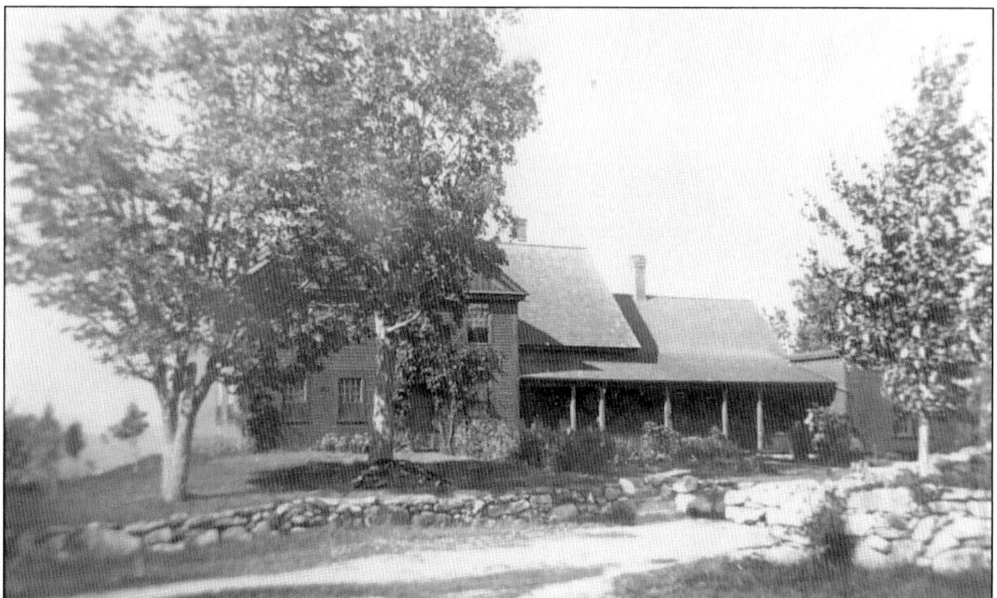

John J. Glessner ran the Rocks as a model farm. He had many employees, some of whom stayed in the farmhouse. The farm had dairy cattle, pigs, sheep, and workhorses. Hay, oats, and corn were grown, and hundreds of cords of wood were cut each year. There was an apple orchard and a chicken barn. Vegetables from the Rocks won many prizes at local fairs. (Society for Protection of NH Forests.)

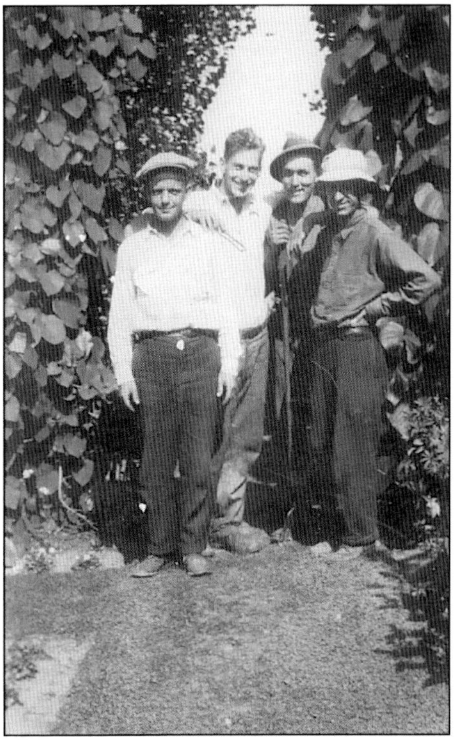

The Rocks flower gardening team poses at the edge of a garden. On the left is Earl Campbell, who spent part of his childhood in Alder Brook, the now vanished logging village on the Whitefield Road. Another gardener, Walter Comeau, was famed for his 8-foot-high sweet peas. The fabulous and extensive gardens were designed by the firm of Frederick Law Olmstead, the famous landscape architect. Cutting flowers were grown in special beds and in a large greenhouse. (Society for Protection of NH Forests.)

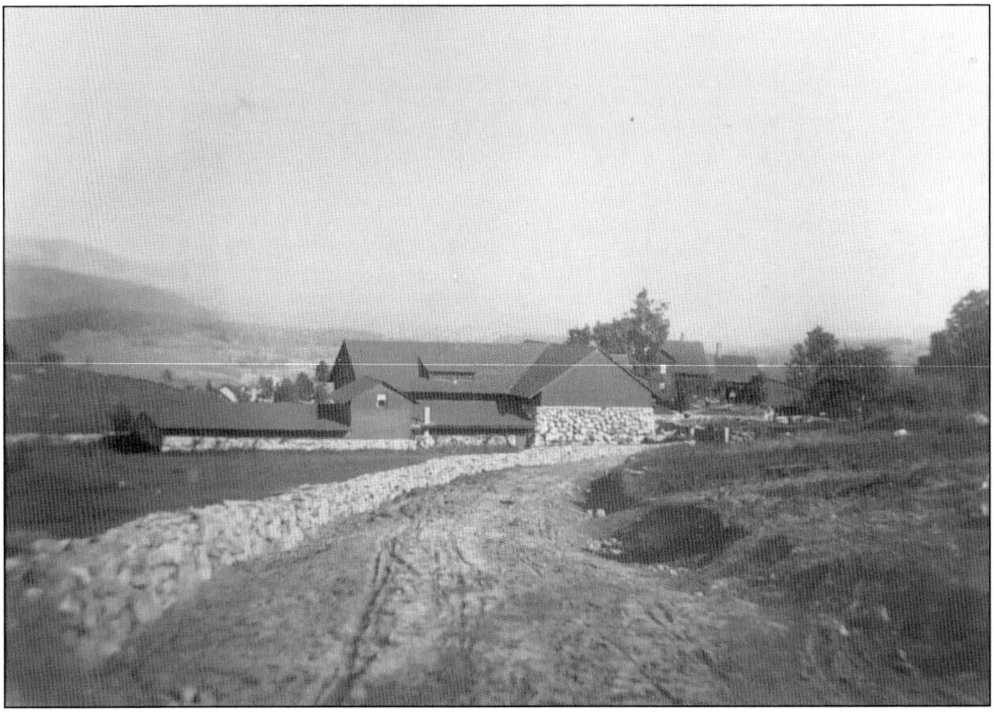

The farm buildings were well built and far more attractive than the usual ones. The carriage barn, with its granite foundation and wood shingle siding, is a good example of the quality design and workmanship that John J. Glessner used. (Society for Protection of NH Forests.)

Three

They Came to Play

The White Mountains region is a beautiful natural environment. With its snow-topped mountains, forested valleys, clear sparkling streams, and crystal cold lakes, the area must have seemed a paradise to people fleeing the heat and discomfort of an urban summer. Late-Victorian interest in the spiritual aspects of nature and the importance of a healthy atmosphere justified the indulgence of an extended stay in the mountains.

However, even the agreeable prospect of eating enormous, delicious meals and rocking on the hotel porch day after day palls after a while. The innkeepers and entrepreneurs of Bethlehem realized early on that they needed to actively entertain their guests and visitors to keep things interesting and yes, to earn additional revenue. Whatever the fad or fashion of the moment was—golf, tennis, bowling, or baseball—the innkeepers strove to meet it. They succeeded admirably. Bethlehem's recreational and social amenities, especially the Gala Day coaching parades, played a large part in creating the town's reputation.

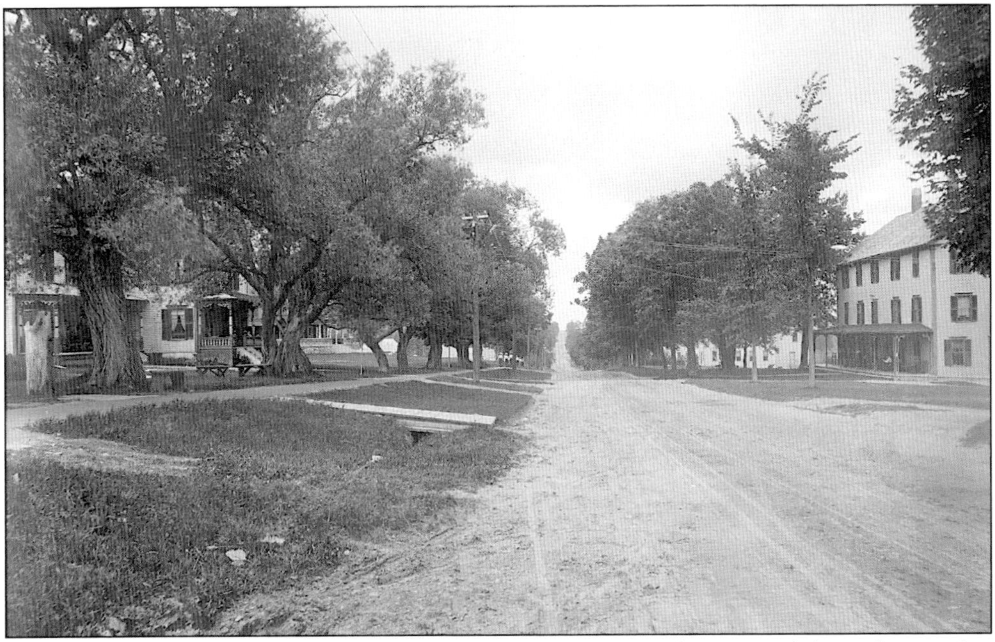

Perhaps the greatest entertainment in Bethlehem was promenading up and down the wooden sidewalks, seeing and being seen. (Bethlehem Heritage Museum.)

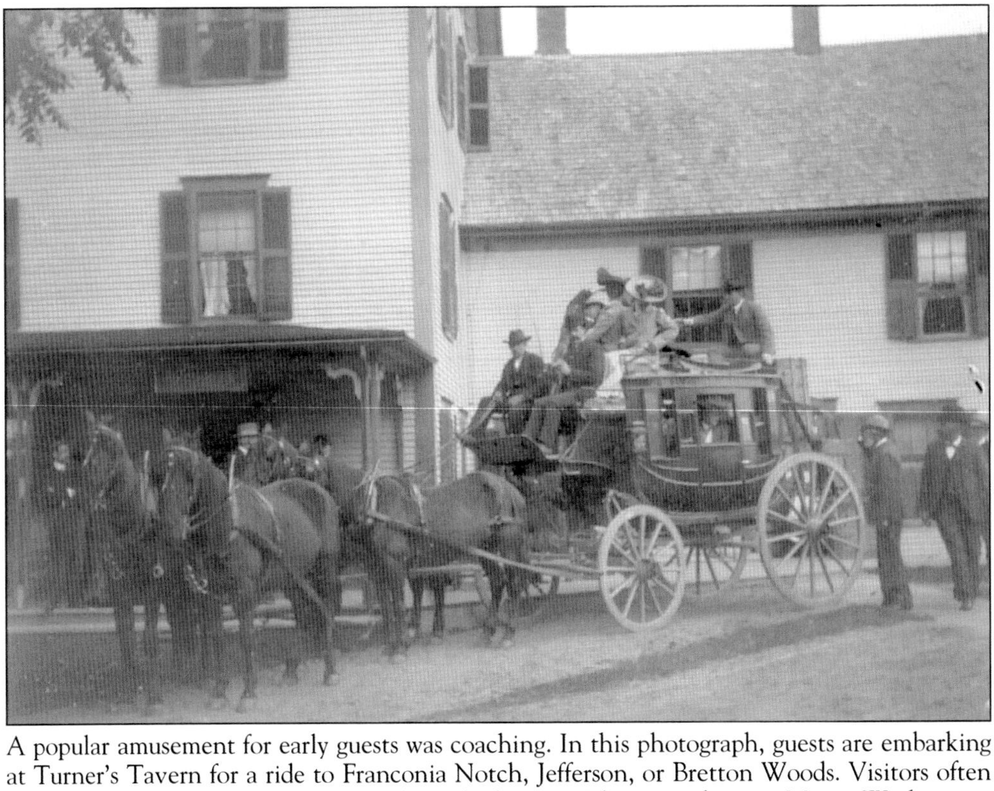

A popular amusement for early guests was coaching. In this photograph, guests are embarking at Turner's Tavern for a ride to Franconia Notch, Jefferson, or Bretton Woods. Visitors often stopped at other grand hotels for a meal or refreshments. The cog railway up Mount Washington was also a popular excursion. (Bethlehem Heritage Museum.)

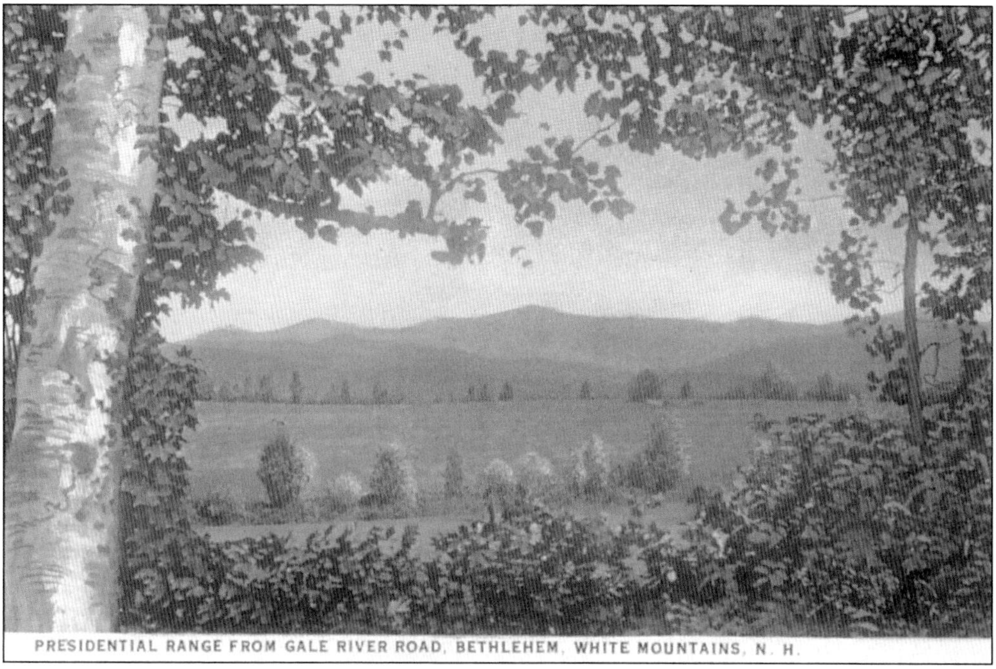

Bethlehem's most famous scenic ride started on tree-shaded Swazey Lane, skirting the bases of Mounts Agassiz and Cleveland and ending in Franconia, near the present Copper Cannon Camp. Fabulous mountain views were visible much of the way. The town closed the road in the 1950s, but the way can still be walked or bicycled. (Paul Hudson.)

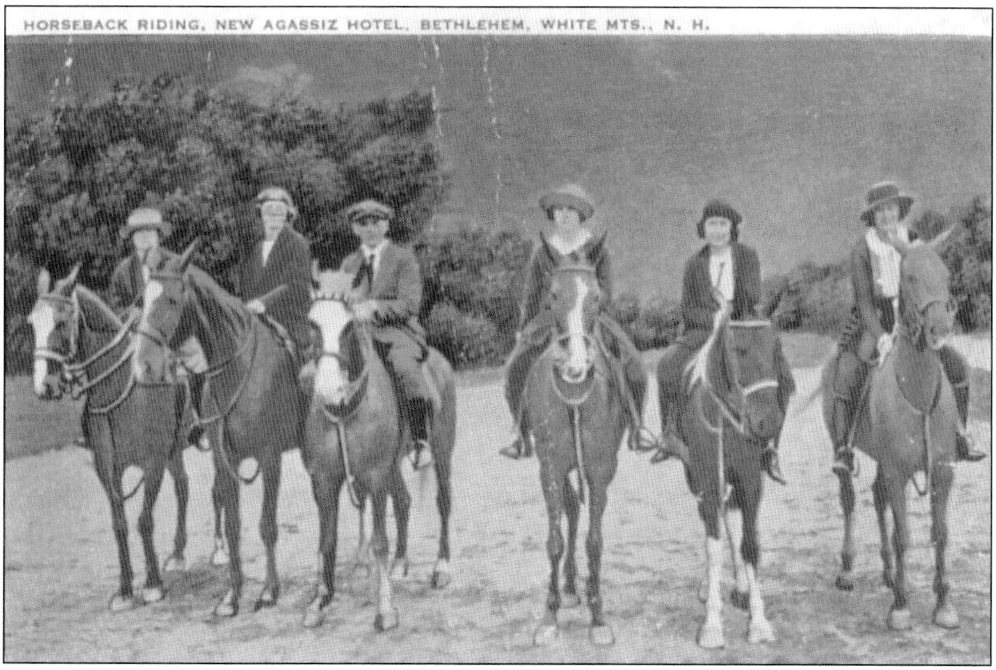

Several hotels kept stables for those guests who wished to ride on Bethlehem's woodland paths. (Paul Hudson.)

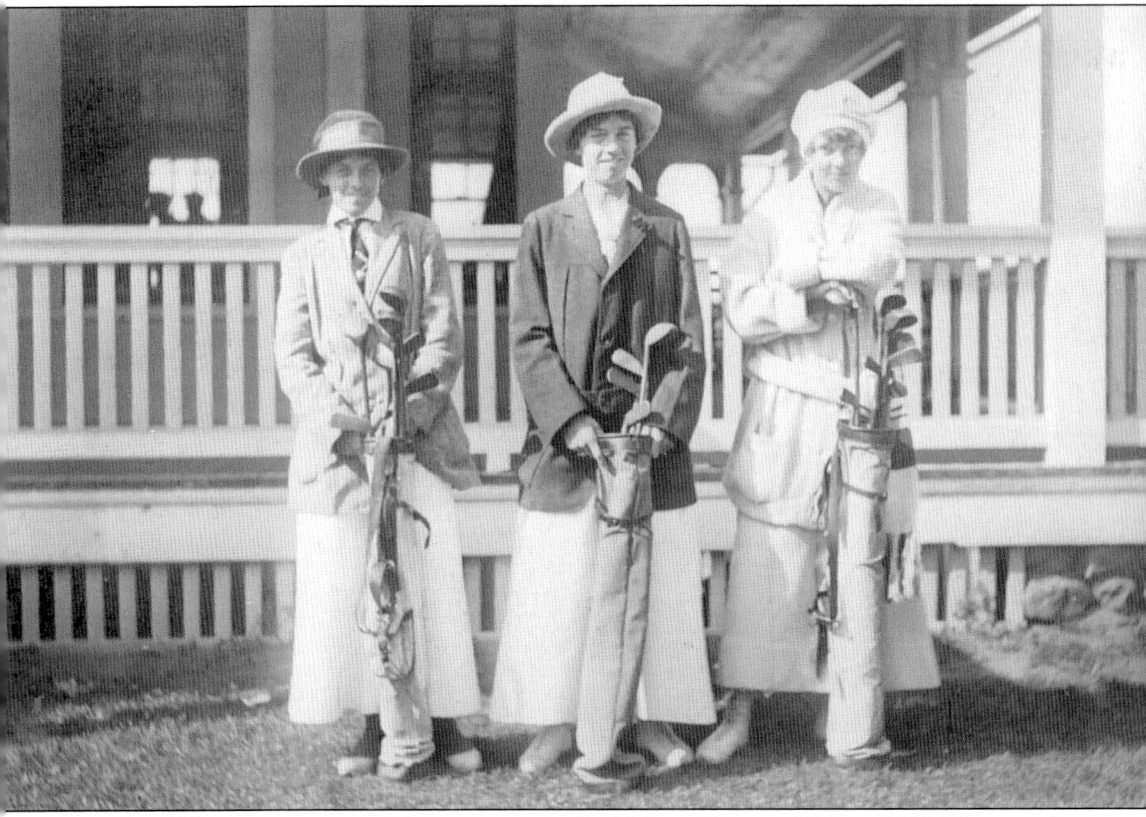

The Abbe sisters pose in golfing attire at the Bethlehem Country Club in 1914. They are, from left to right, Mollie Abbe Estes, Emma Abbe Franziem, and Eleanor Abbe. The sisters golfed as a team and sometimes beat the men. Their father, Fred Abbe, owned the Arlington Hotel. (Bethlehem Heritage Museum.)

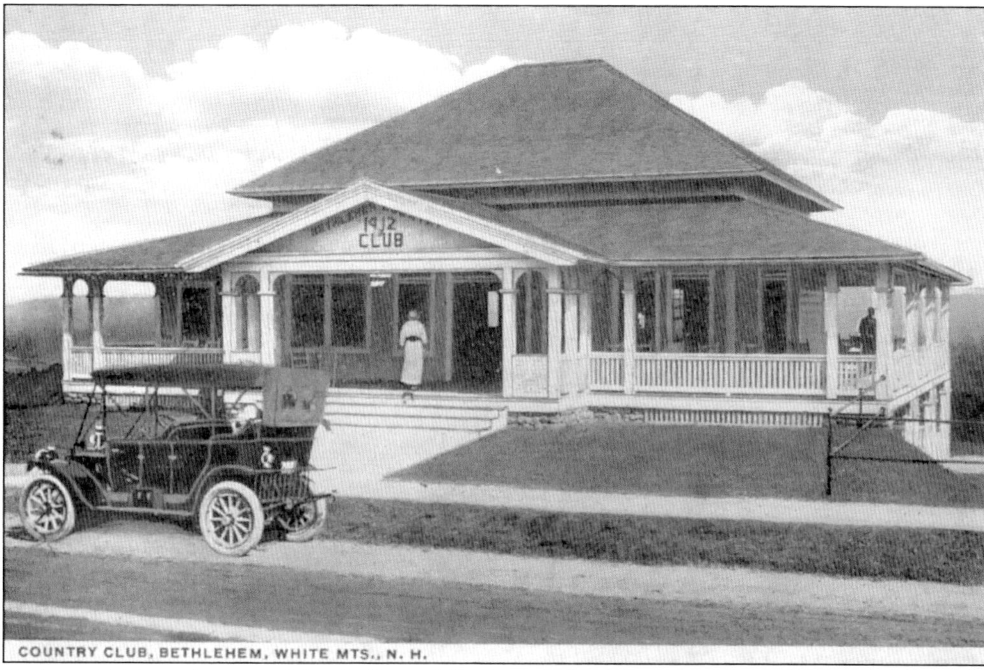

Built in 1912 on the site of the Bellevue Hotel, the Bethlehem Country Club provided locker rooms, reception and assembly rooms, and a refreshment counter for golfers enjoying the nine-hole course designed by Donald Ross. Now an 18-hole course, the country club has operated since 1949 under town ownership. (Paul Hudson.)

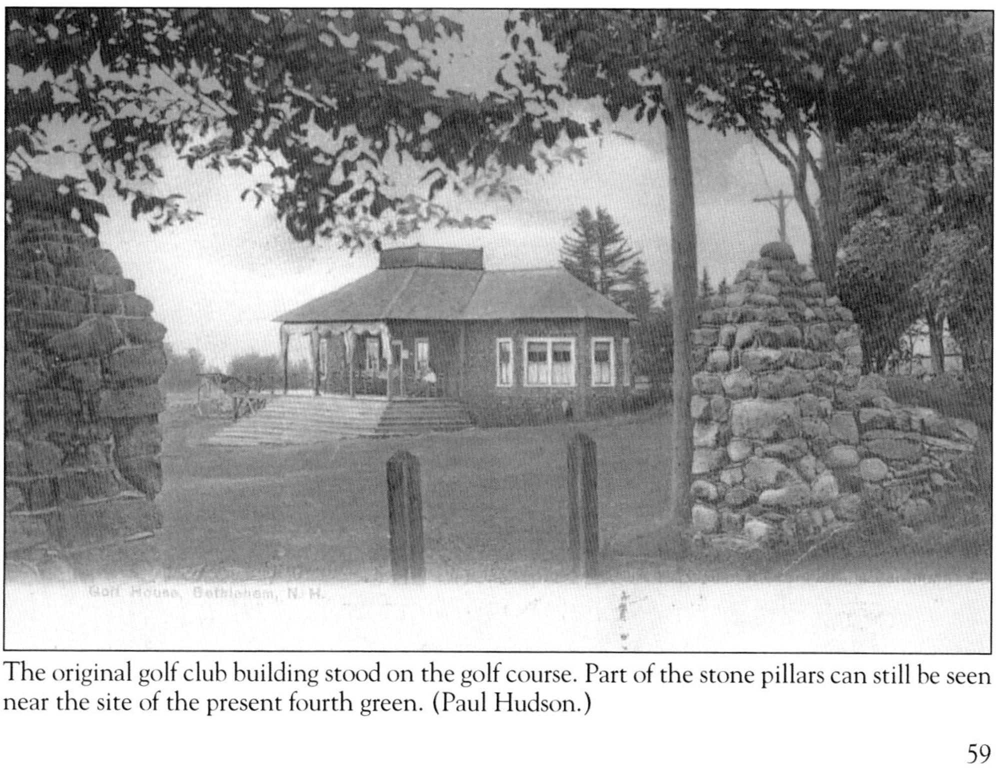

The original golf club building stood on the golf course. Part of the stone pillars can still be seen near the site of the present fourth green. (Paul Hudson.)

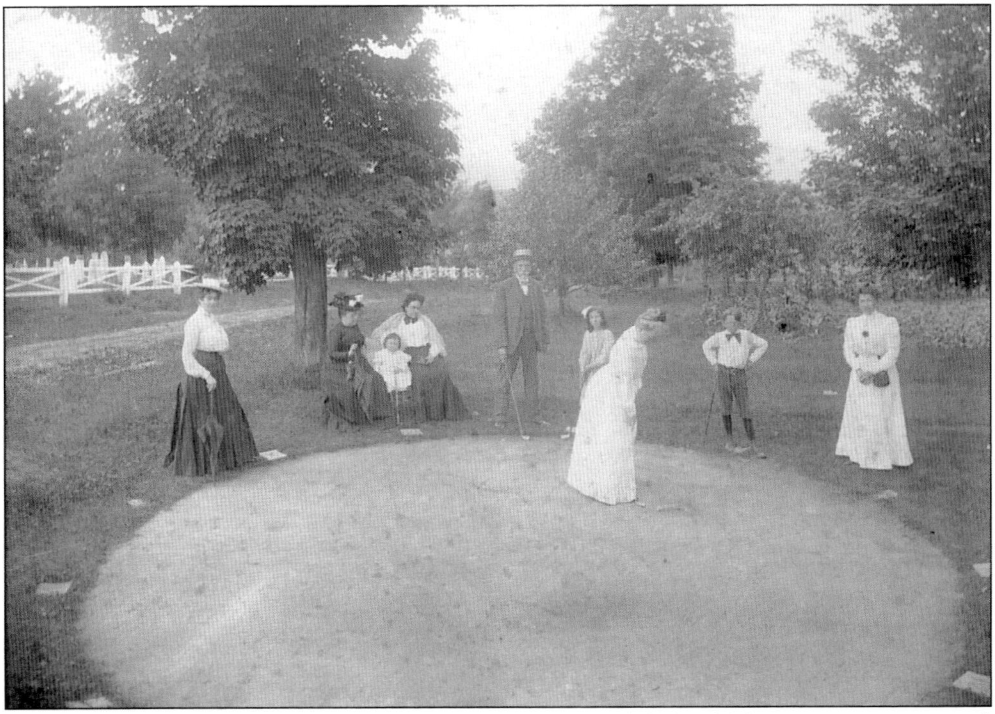

A lady takes her putt on a green at the Bethlehem Country Club. (Bethlehem Heritage Museum.)

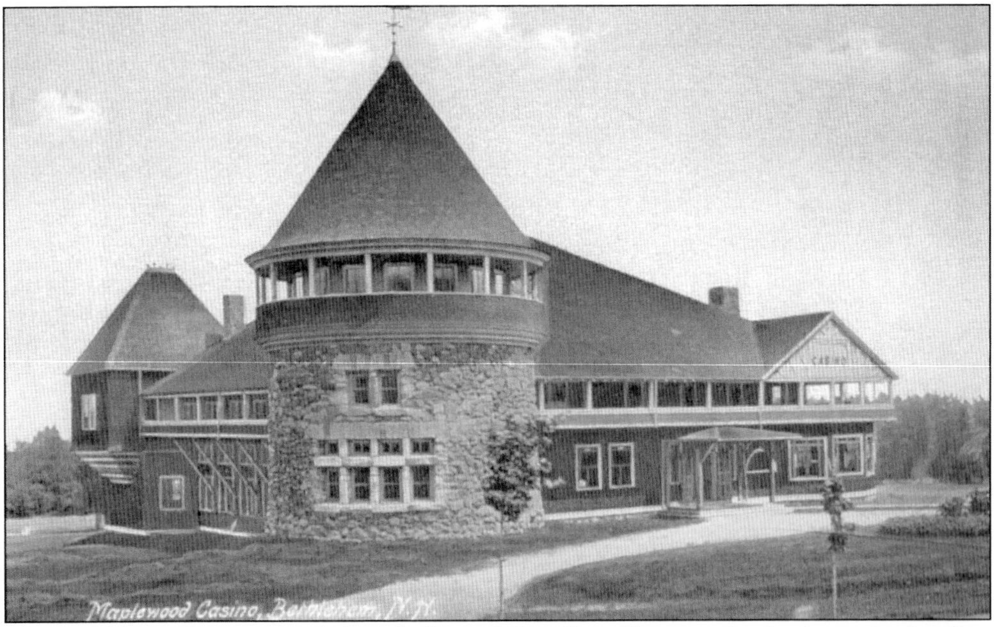

The Bethlehem Casino served the Maplewood Hotel's golf course. It also housed a bowling alley, ballroom, reading rooms, and a theater. Features include beautiful woodwork, fieldstone fireplaces, a stone tower, and a double staircase leading to the ballroom. According to the grandson of a former owner, the casino also hosted gambling operations in the mid-20th century. Another resident speaks of times when roulette tables were quickly turned into dining tables. The golf course now operates as the Maplewood Country Club. (Paul Hudson.)

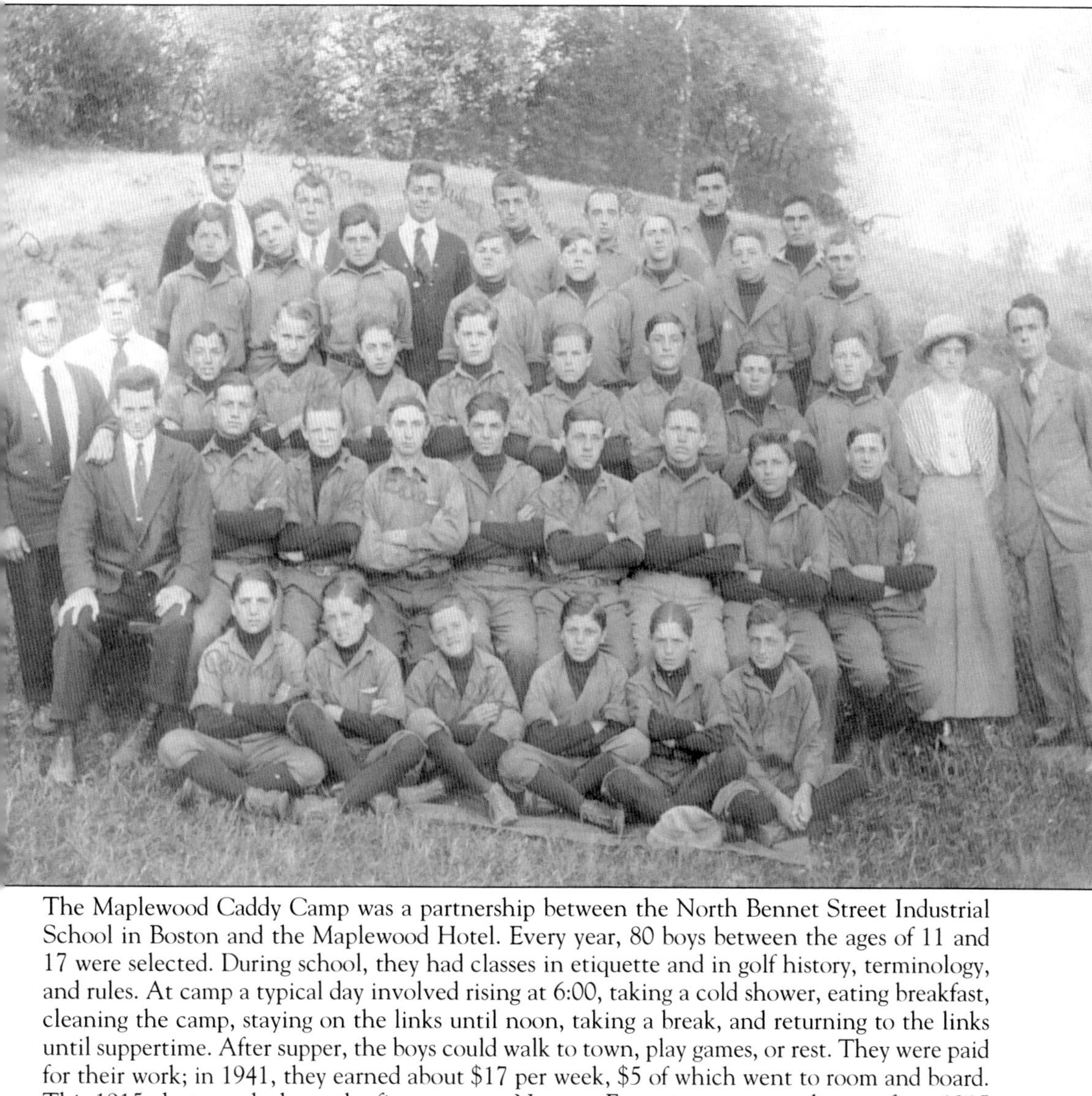

The Maplewood Caddy Camp was a partnership between the North Bennet Street Industrial School in Boston and the Maplewood Hotel. Every year, 80 boys between the ages of 11 and 17 were selected. During school, they had classes in etiquette and in golf history, terminology, and rules. At camp a typical day involved rising at 6:00, taking a cold shower, eating breakfast, cleaning the camp, staying on the links until noon, taking a break, and returning to the links until suppertime. After supper, the boys could walk to town, play games, or rest. They were paid for their work; in 1941, they earned about $17 per week, $5 of which went to room and board. This 1915 photograph shows the first campers. Norman Franzeim was camp director from 1915 to 1949. (Helen Cunningham.)

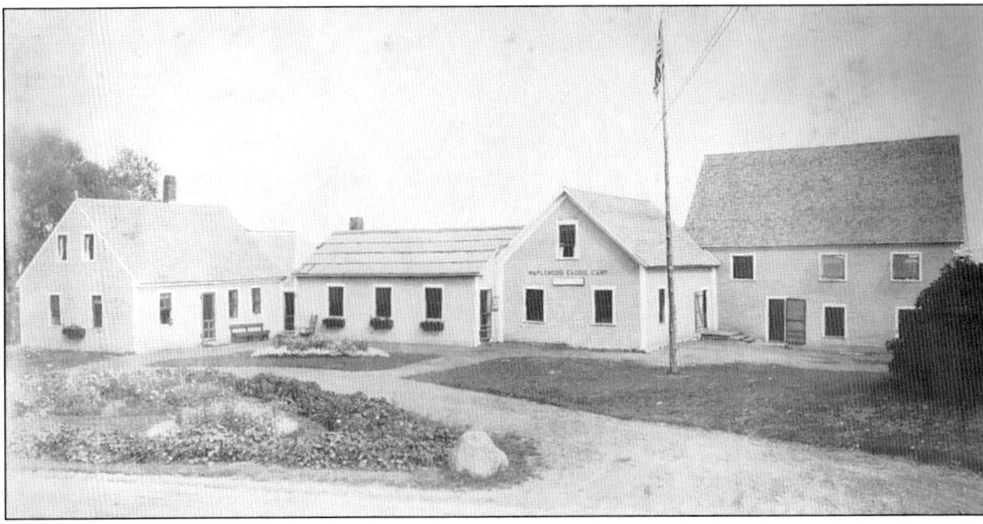

The original Maplewood Caddy Camp buildings stood near the Maplewood Hotel on the present site of the Friendship House. The boys were exposed to successful men who often had a profound influence on them. Some of these men even paid for the boys' college tuition. Many caddies became successful, too, going on to become businessmen, bankers, lawyers, teachers, politicians, and military officers. (Helen Cunningham.)

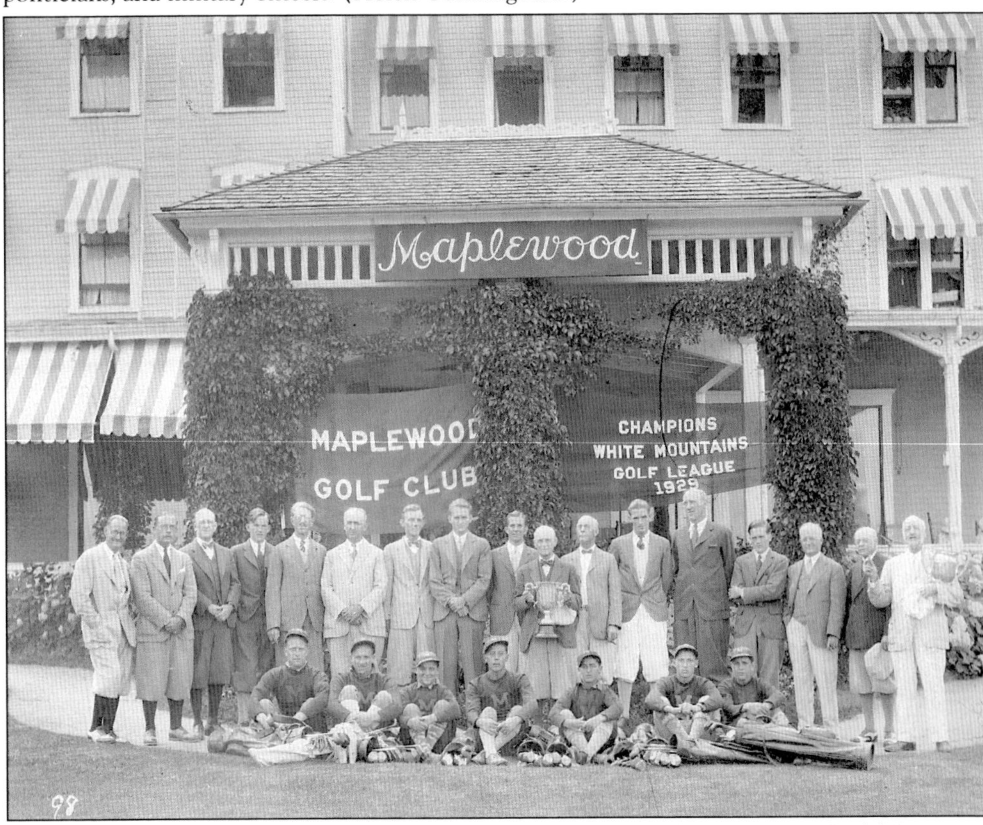

Golf exhibitions, championships, and tournaments were popular events in Bethlehem and throughout the White Mountains. (Helen Cunningham.)

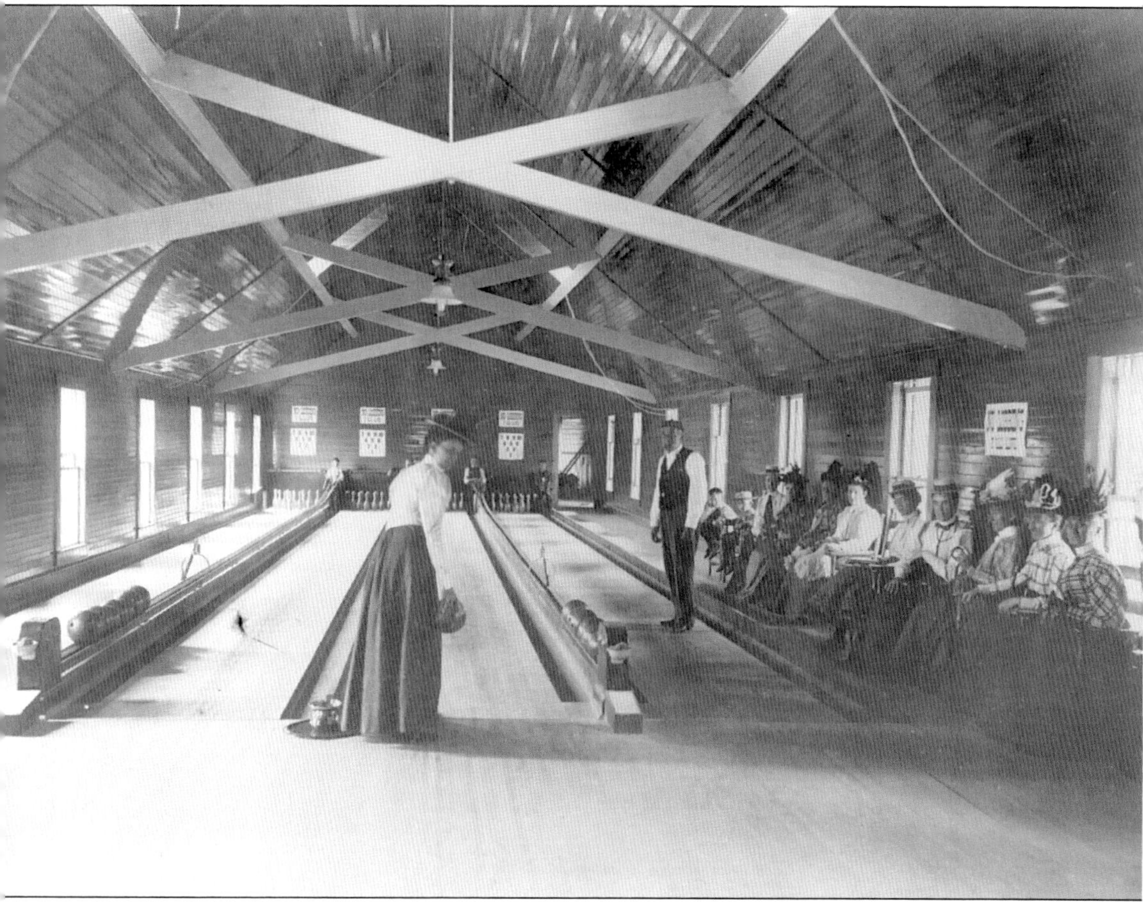

Even genteel Victorian ladies liked to bowl, as this photograph reveals. The Bethlehem Casino, later known as the Bethlehem Bowling Alley, stood next to the Bonardi Block across from the Bethlehem Town Hall. An Irving station now occupies the site. (Dick and Sharon Robie.)

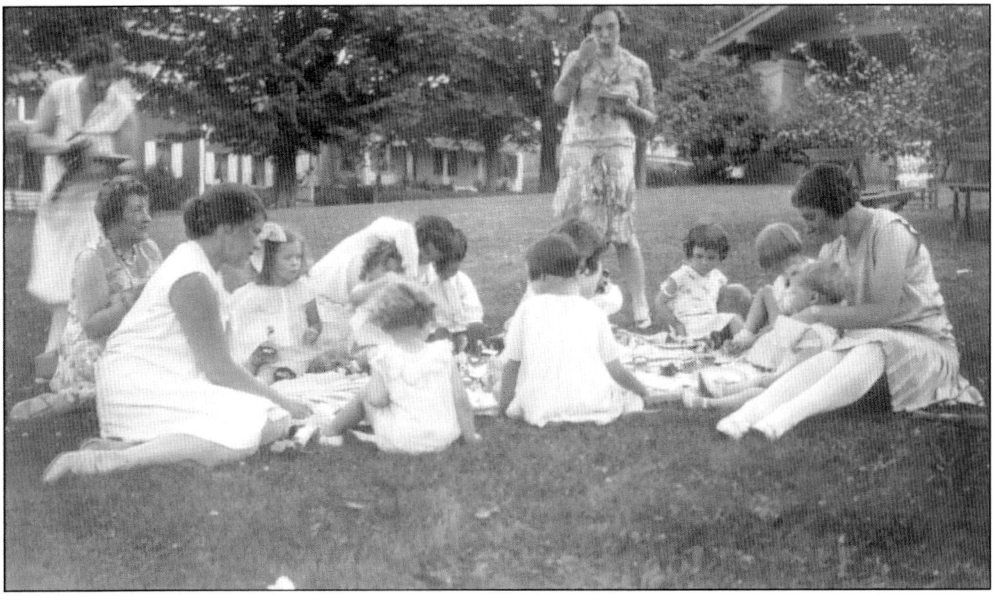

A group of children and their mothers enjoy a picnic on the Upland Terrace lawn. (Bethlehem Heritage Museum.)

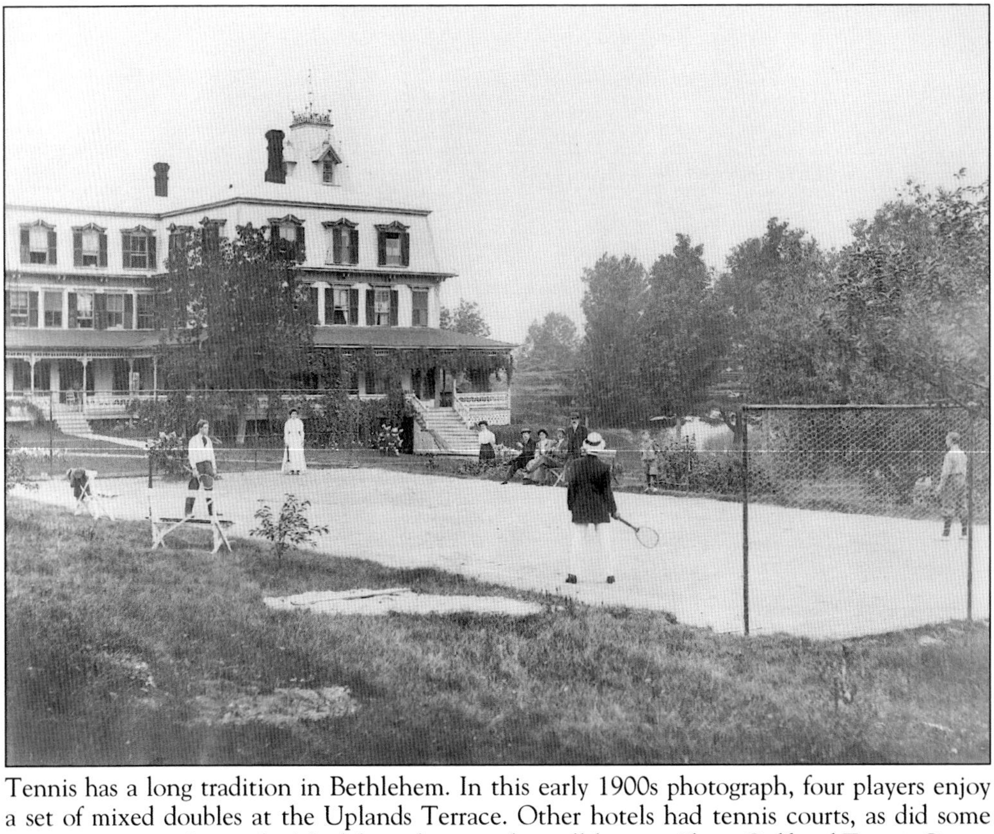

Tennis has a long tradition in Bethlehem. In this early 1900s photograph, four players enjoy a set of mixed doubles at the Uplands Terrace. Other hotels had tennis courts, as did some summer cottages. Later, the Maplehurst became the well-known Chase Golf and Tennis Camp. (Courtesy of Dartmouth College Library.)

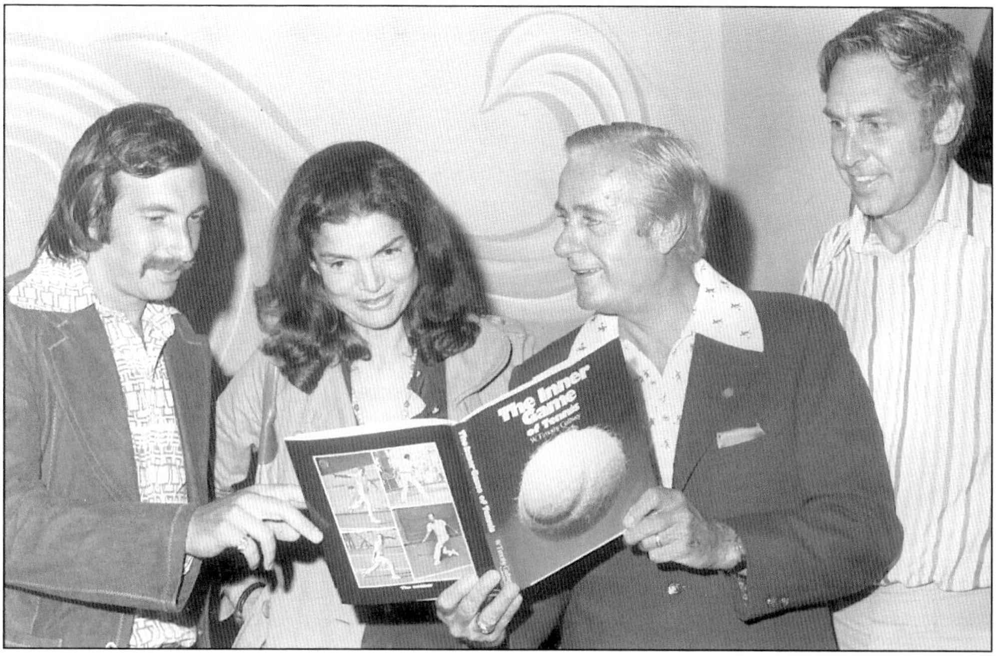

Former First Lady Jacqueline Kennedy Onassis and sportscaster Curt Gowdy discuss the finer points of the game, while Chase Golf and Tennis Camp owner Neil Chase and his tennis pro look on. John F. Kennedy Jr. attended the Chase Golf and Tennis Camp in 1974. Camp staff and townspeople cooperated in helping the Kennedys keep a low profile during their visit. (Bethlehem Heritage Museum.)

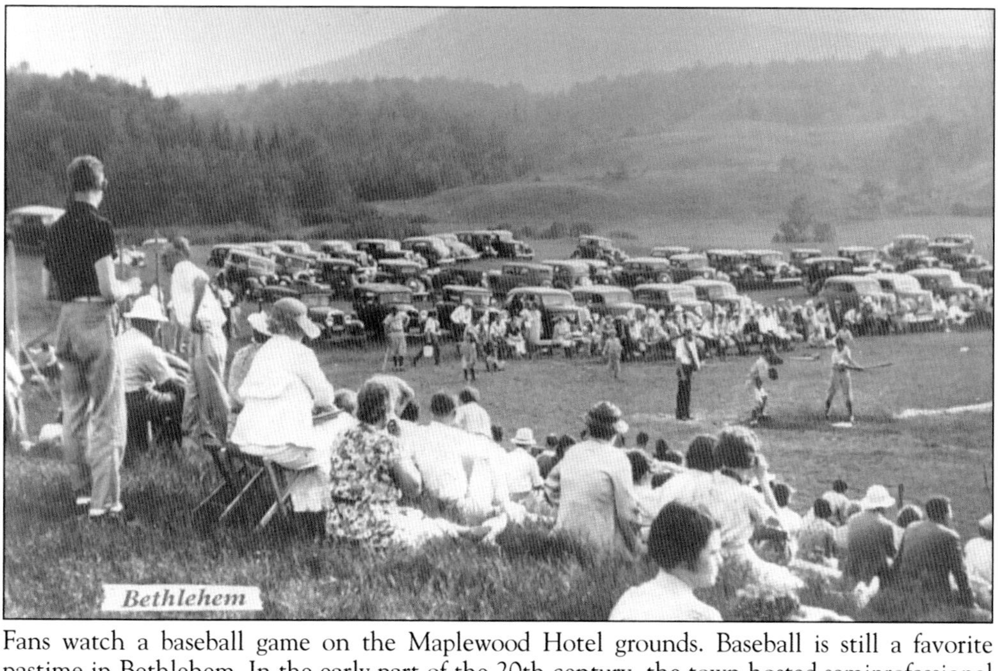

Fans watch a baseball game on the Maplewood Hotel grounds. Baseball is still a favorite pastime in Bethlehem. In the early part of the 20th century, the town hosted semiprofessional teams. Joseph Kennedy, John F. Kennedy's father, played for a team in 1907. (Bethlehem Heritage Museum.)

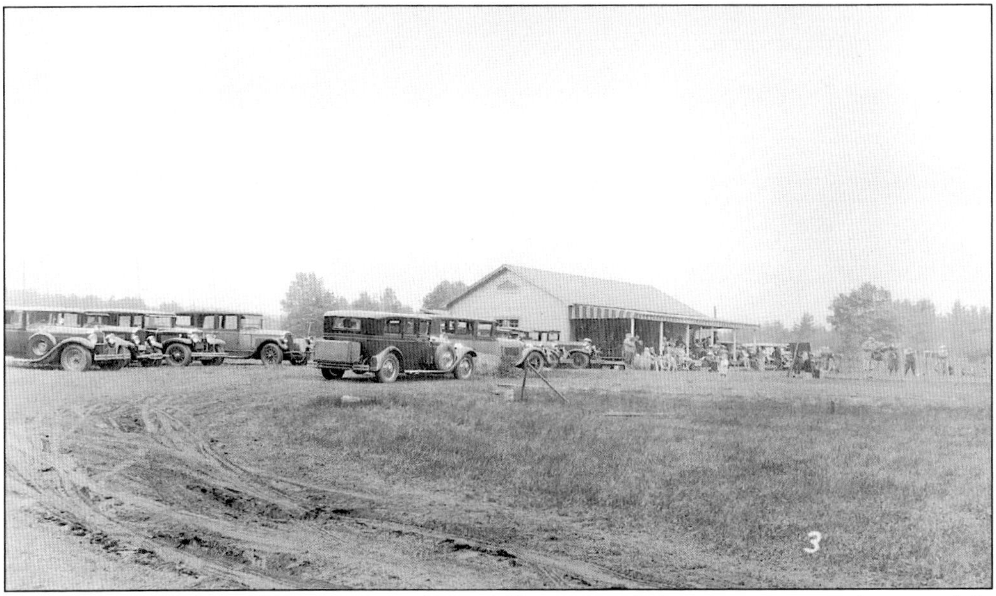

Many Maplewood Hotel guests enjoyed skeet shooting and target practice at the gun club. (Helen Cunningham.)

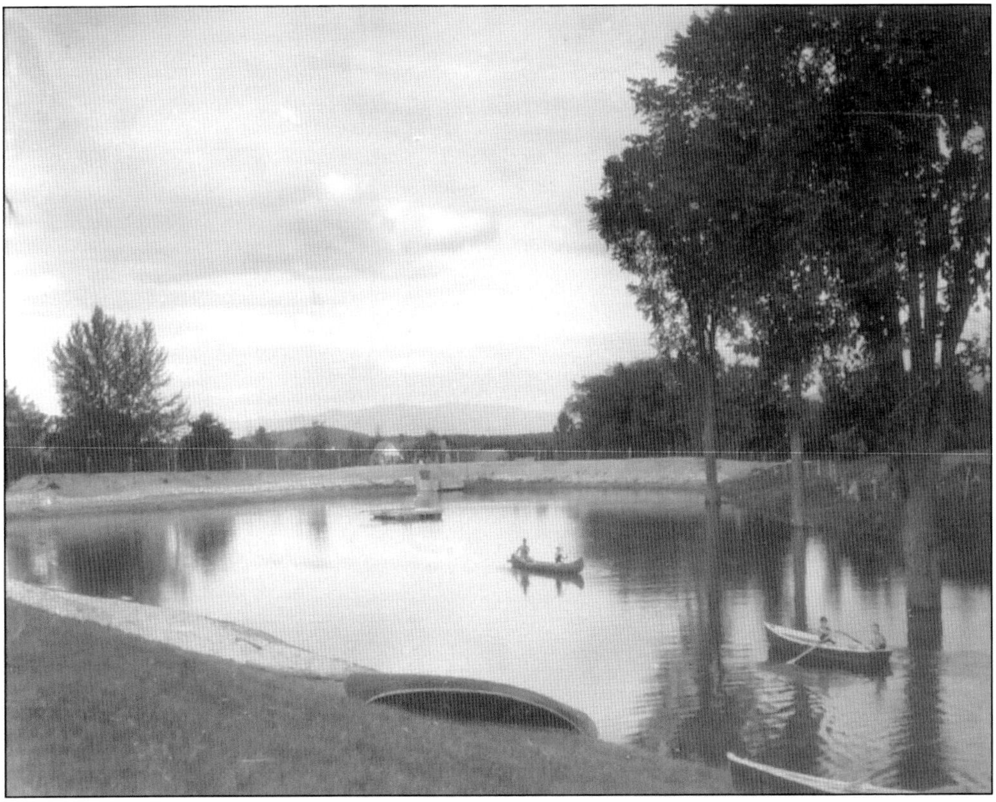

Sunset Lake was right in town behind the present post office. It was fed by a brook that ran under Main Street. After a 1938 disaster in which the dam holding back the lake let go and the water drained away, the town built a public pool. (Bethlehem Heritage Museum.)

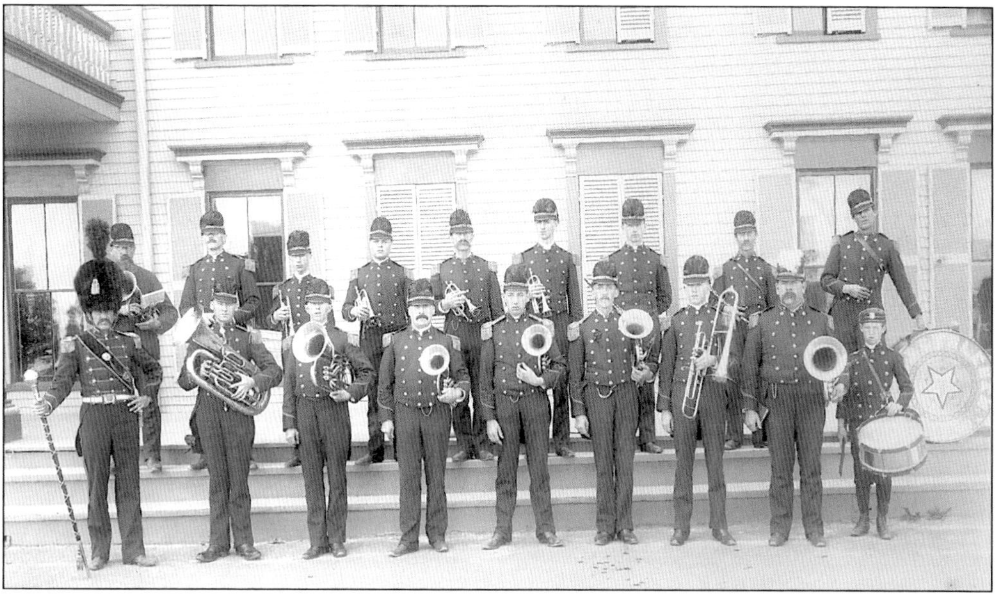

Music was an essential component of Bethlehem's summer life. The Bethlehem Brass Band, which formed in 1888, gave evening concerts at a bandstand in Sinclair Park. Band members are, from left to right, as follows: (front row) two unidentified men; George Buck, postmaster; unidentified; Will Turner; two unidentified men; G. Allen Noyes, Columbia House; and Howard Bartlett; (back row) unidentified; Charles Davis, Hillside House; unidentified; Will Corliss; Warren McGregor; three unidentified men; and Walter Blandin. (Sanborn family.)

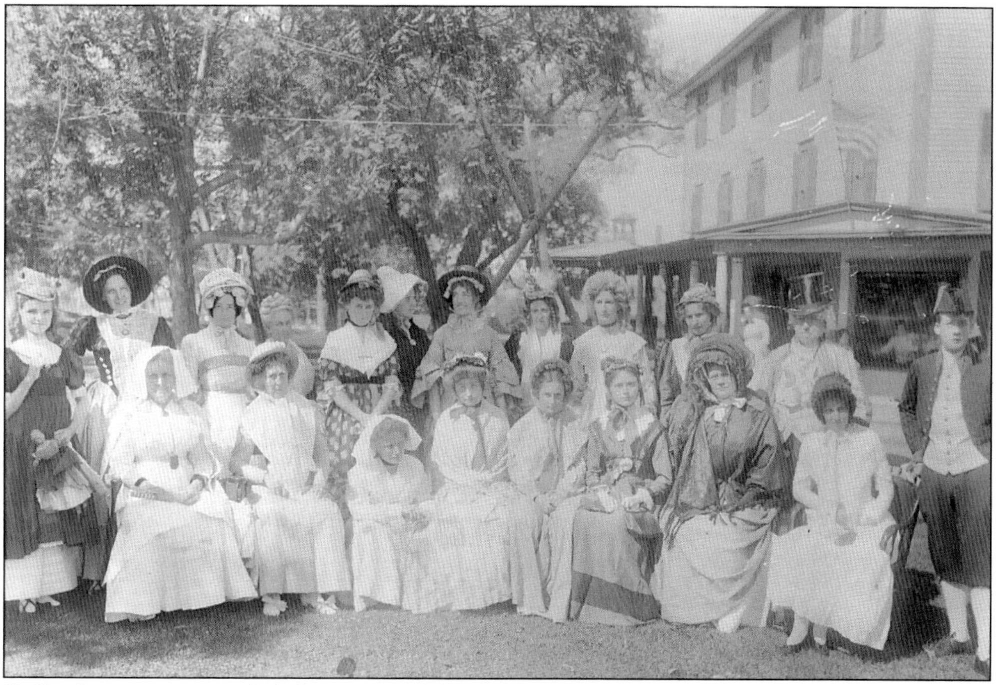

If all other amusement failed, guests could dress up in Mother Goose costumes. Actually, dress-up parties were a favorite Victorian pastime, including costume parties, balls, and picturesque tableaux, often with a moral or romantic theme. (Bethlehem Heritage Museum.)

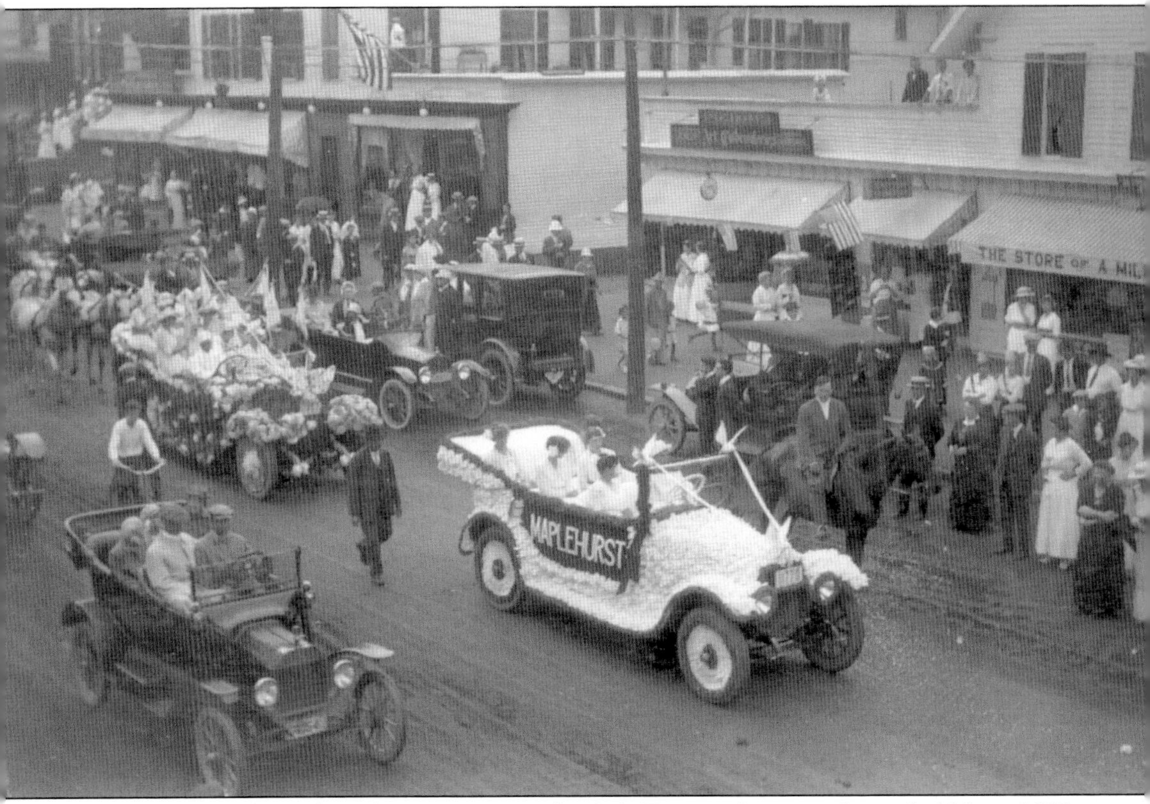

Famed throughout the White Mountains, the Gala Day coaching parade was held from 1887 to 1935 for every year but two—1892 and 1897. When P.T. Barnum attended in 1889, he called it "the second greatest show on Earth." This photograph was probably taken from the second floor of the Sinclair hotel. (Clare Brown, photograph by Morrell Crawford.)

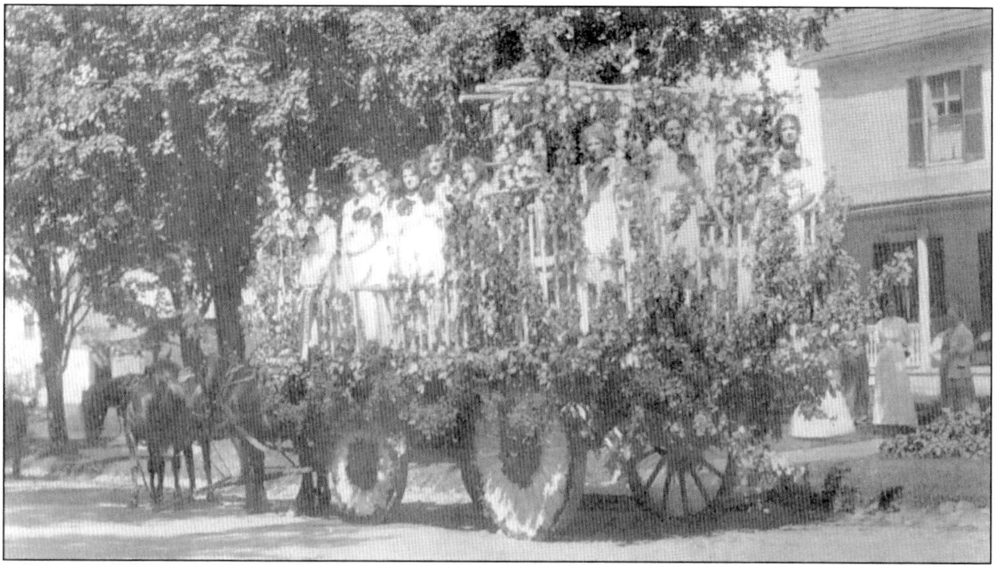

Parade day decorations were quite elaborate, as this 1913 picture of girls on a wagon shows. Each hotel had its own float that was decorated in the hotel's colors, sometimes costing as much as $3,000. The hotels and private homes were also decked out in flags, bunting, and streamers. (Bethlehem Heritage Museum.)

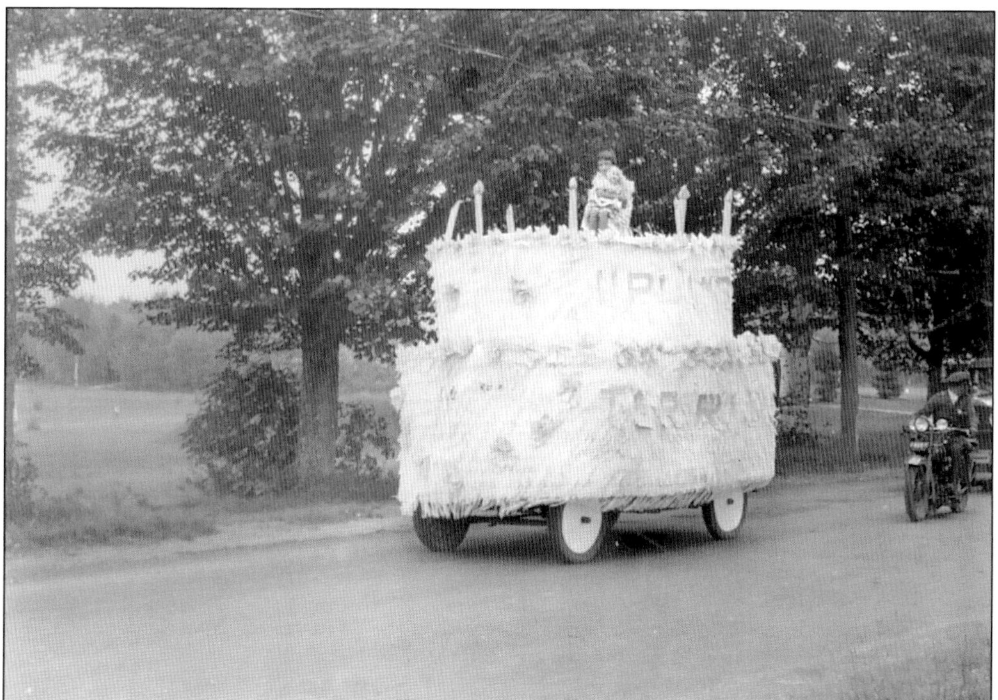

This Upland Terrace float took the cake—it won first prize that year. Oddly, many photographs of it have survived. It must have been a favorite. (Bethlehem Heritage Museum.)

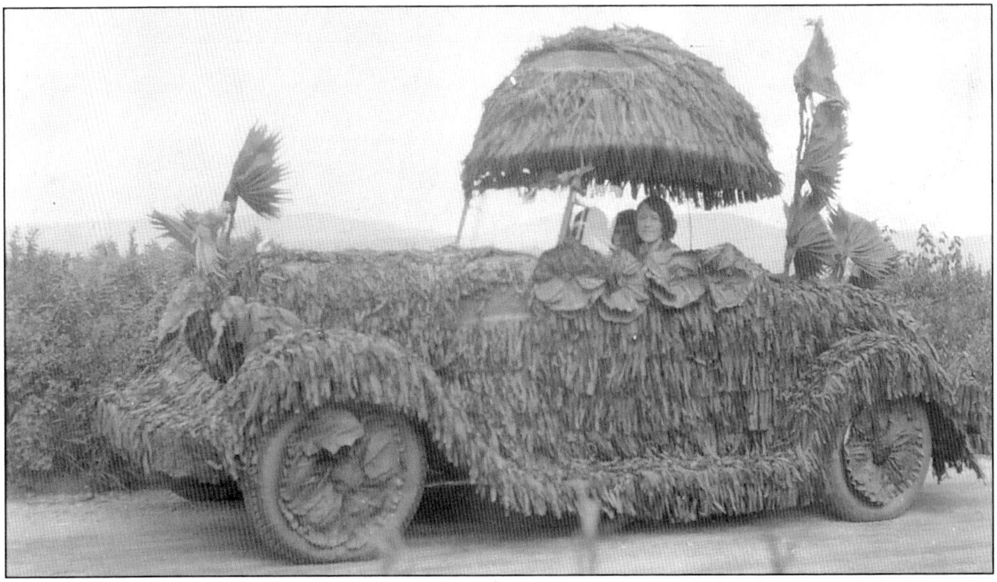

An automobile in a grass skirt was the contribution of Peg Green Parker for a parade held in the early 1920s. (Bethlehem Heritage Museum.)

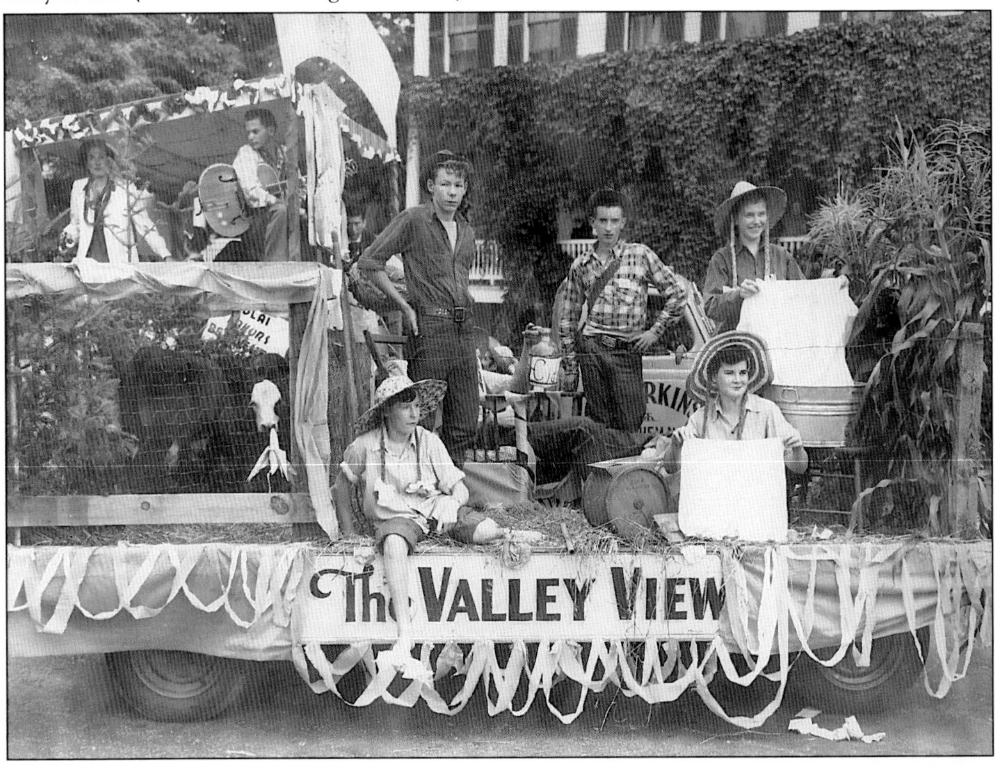

The 1952 Sunfire Festival float entry by the Valley View carried, from left to right, Thelma Gibbs Burlock, Clayton Gibbs, Harvey Burlock, Anita Maguire, Arnold Charland, Bernice Burlock, two calves, a jug of cider (empty), a butter churn, and a tub and washboard. These employees of the Valley View earned a blue ribbon for their efforts. (Harvey and Thelma Burlock.)

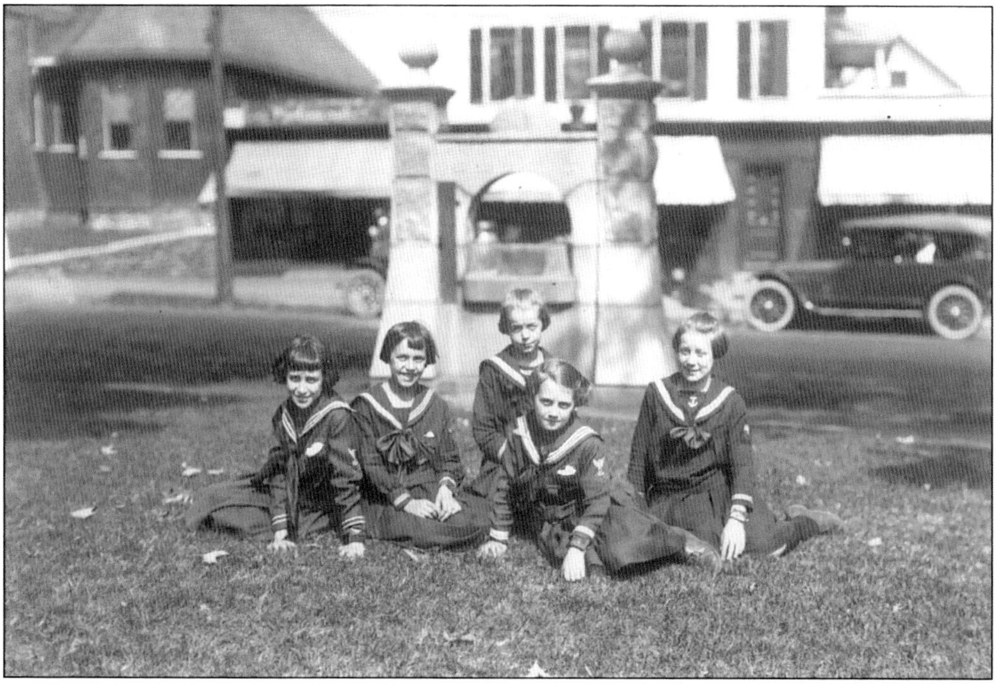

The Dorothy Dix girls pose beside the stone fountain, a landmark on Main Street donated by Gen. George Cruft to commemorate Bethlehem's centennial. The fountain has three bowls—a large one for horses and two small ones at the base for cats and dogs. (Clare Brown, Morrell Crawford photograph.)

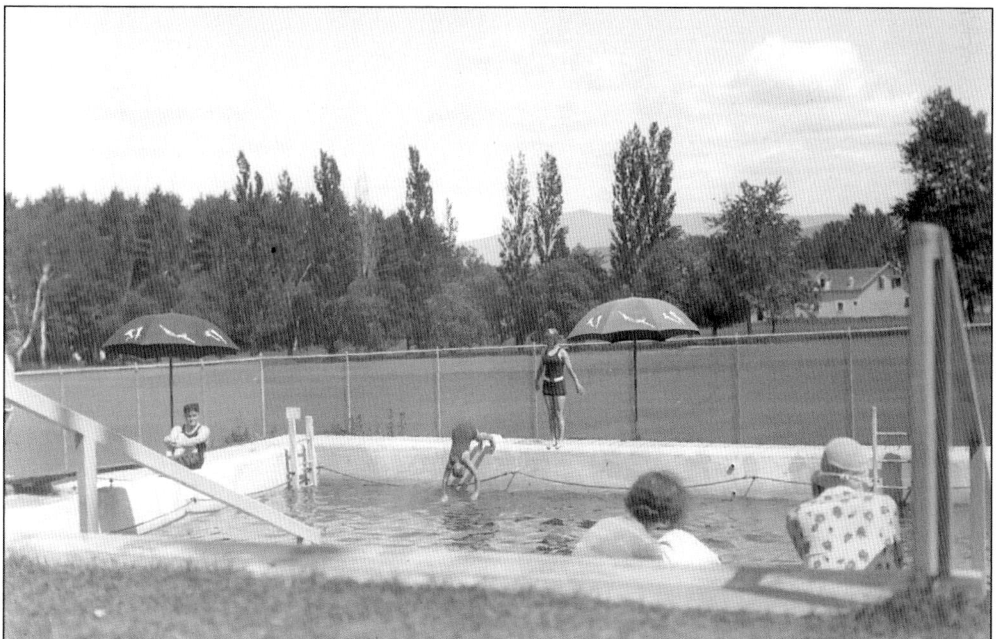

Swimmers in old-fashioned suits frolic at the Maplewood pool in this c. 1920s photograph by Morrell Crawford. Several hotels had their own pools, notably the Sinclair, the Park View, and the Highland. (Clare Brown, Morrell Crawford photograph.)

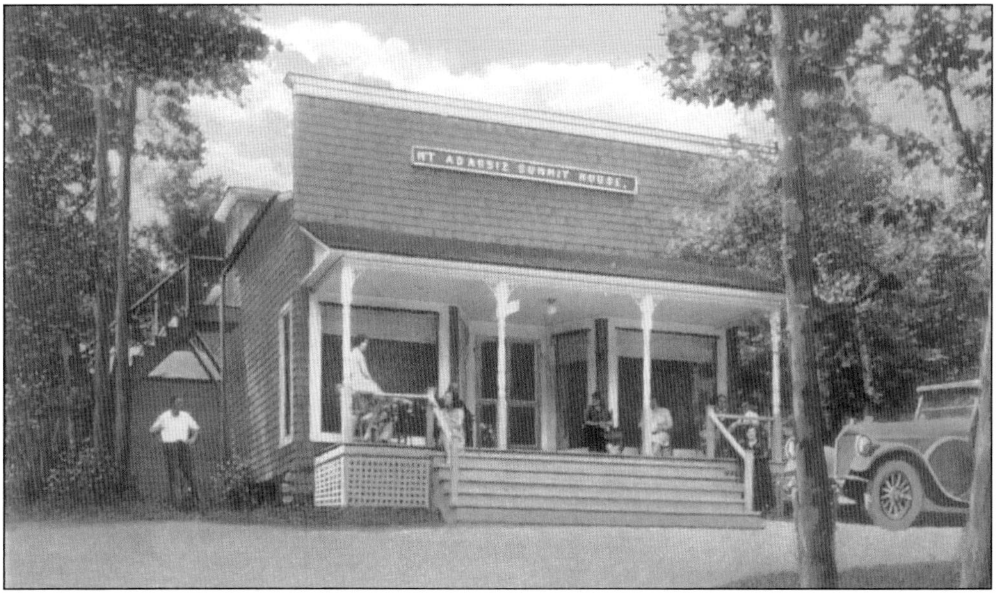

Mount Agassiz is Bethlehem's own little peak, blessed with fabulous views of Franconia Notch and the Presidential Range. Visitors to Bethlehem walked up one of the paths or rode up in a carriage or wagon. Milo J. Corliss built the first road and observation tower. The mountain's name was changed from Peaked Hill in honor of the Harvard professor Louis Agassiz, who studied glacial activity in the area. This postcard shows one of the first summit houses. (Paul Hudson.)

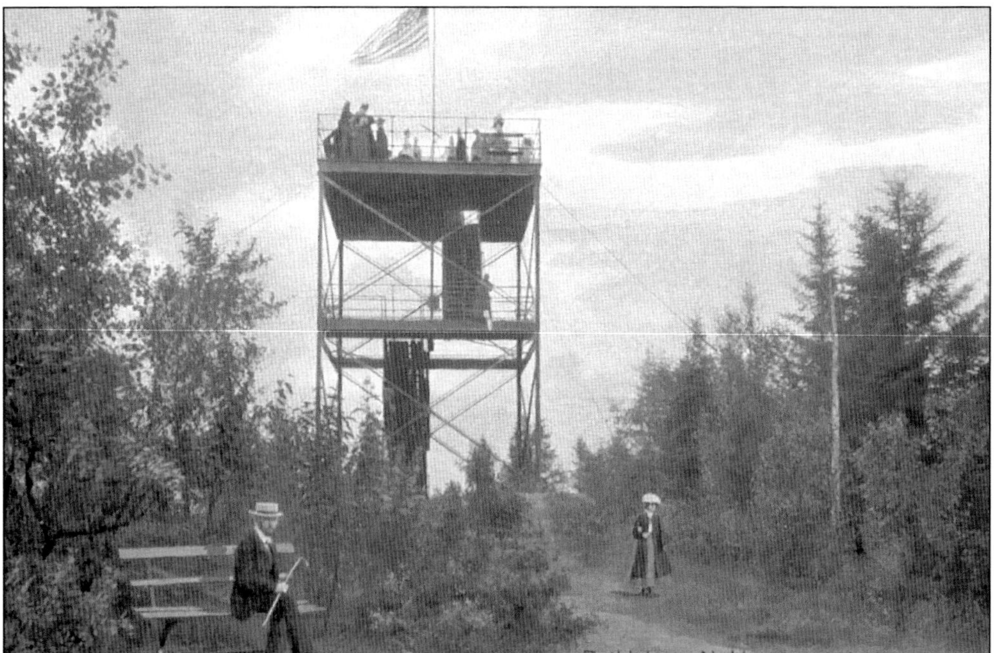

A steel observation tower was built in 1884. According to Hattie Taylor's *Early History*, 317 peaks are visible from the summit, which is 2,500 feet in elevation. The W.S. Phillips family operated the mountain until 1944. (Paul Hudson.)

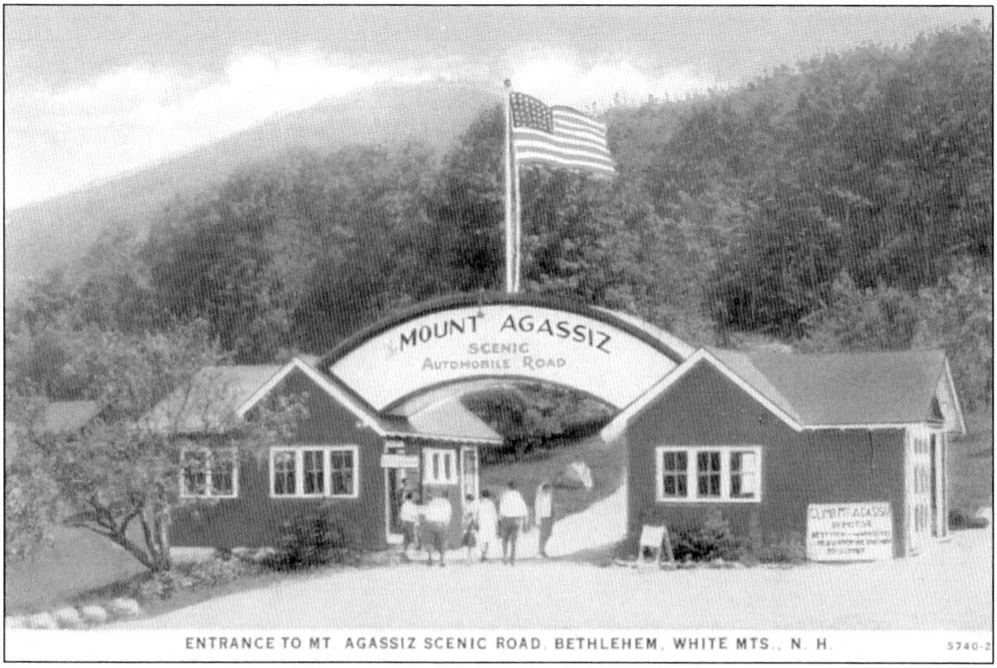

The first automobile ascent of Mount Agassiz was in 1910, and the road was upgraded for automobiles in 1929. The entryway cabins and sign show the evolution of the mountain into a tourist attraction. (David Olson.)

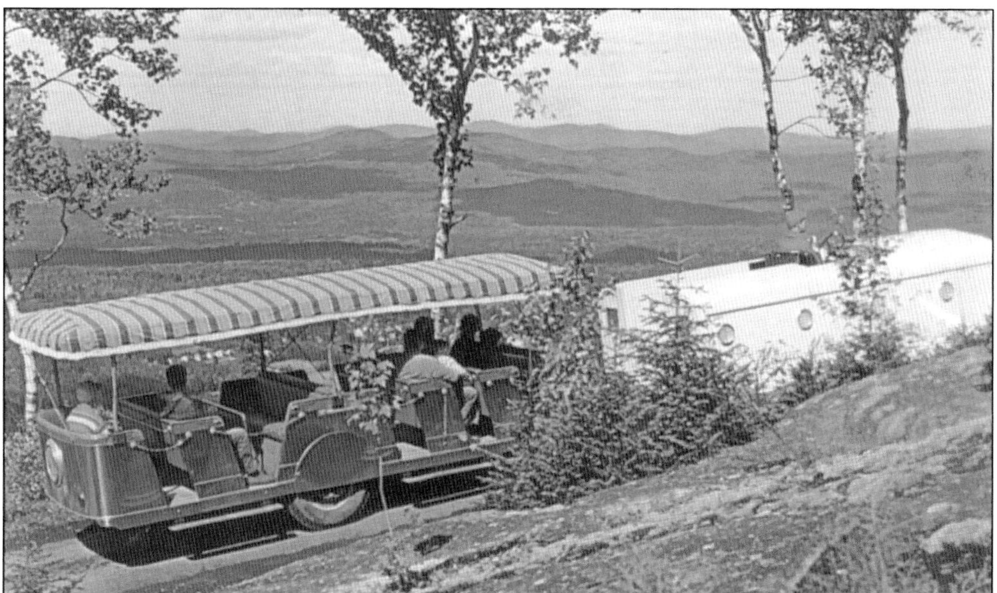

F. Gordon Miller, the last owner to operate Agassiz commercially, ran tourists up the hill in his Magic Mountain Express. (Paul Hudson.)

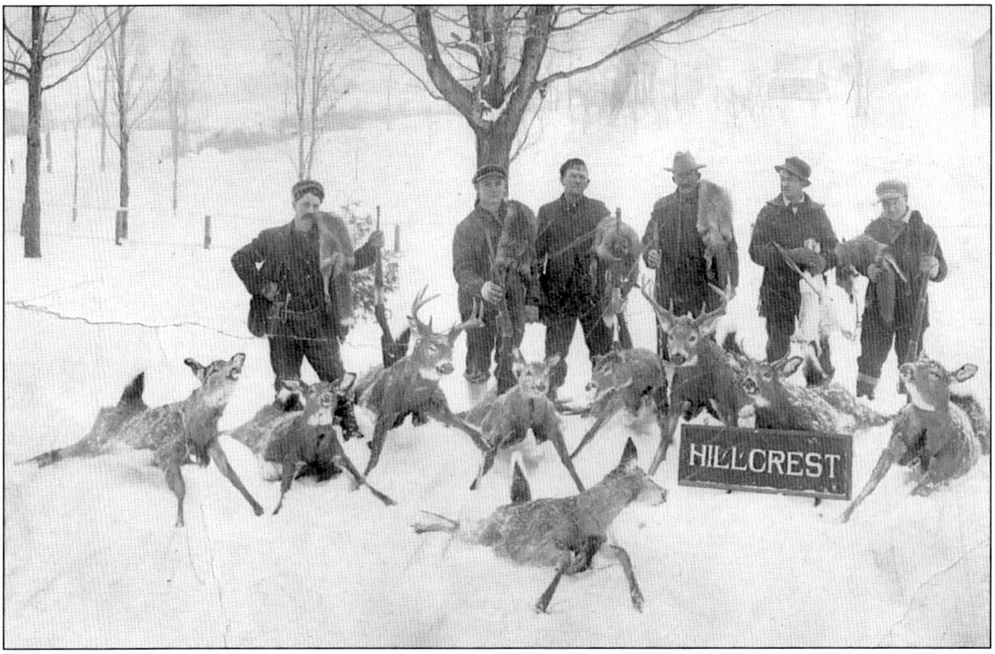

Deer hunting is still a popular northern New Hampshire activity, although nowadays the results might not be displayed in this manner. Fifth from the left is Bryan Ferrin, the owner of the Hillcrest Inn; third from the left is Carl Hoit. (Muriel Brown.)

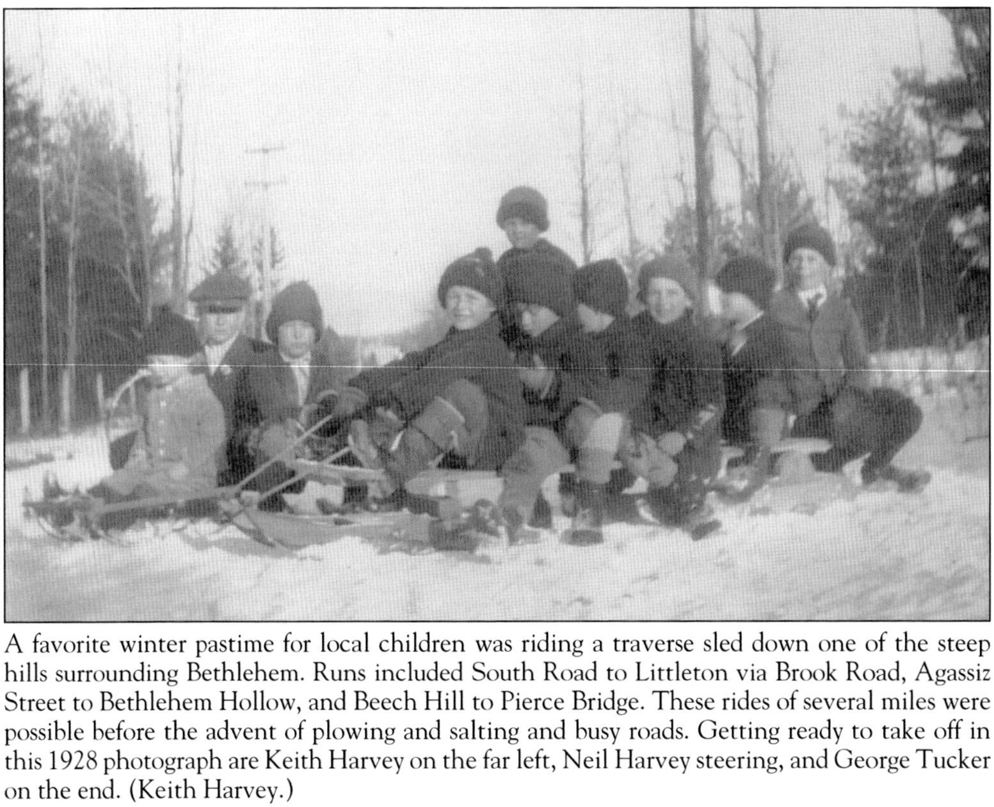

A favorite winter pastime for local children was riding a traverse sled down one of the steep hills surrounding Bethlehem. Runs included South Road to Littleton via Brook Road, Agassiz Street to Bethlehem Hollow, and Beech Hill to Pierce Bridge. These rides of several miles were possible before the advent of plowing and salting and busy roads. Getting ready to take off in this 1928 photograph are Keith Harvey on the far left, Neil Harvey steering, and George Tucker on the end. (Keith Harvey.)

Four

Doing Business

Initially, Bethlehem's economic development was similar to that of many small rural villages. The first settlers cleared land for farms, and soon water-powered mills sprang up to meet local needs. Some of the goods produced were lumber, starch, flour, cider, chairs, and carded wool.

As the hotel trade gained ascendancy, however, most of the economic activity shifted to supporter businesses. George Noyes built his insurance agency around hotel policies. Plumbers, electricians, and carpenters had steady work maintaining hotels and summer homes. Other businesses sold provisions and supplies to the hotels.

The thousands of summer visitors created business opportunities, too. In 1929, Bethlehem had two fine linen shops, seven restaurants, three tearooms, five gift and souvenir stores, and two fruit markets. Five garages serviced visitors' automobiles and provided cars for hire. One way or another, most of Bethlehem's residents depended upon the hotel business for their livelihood.

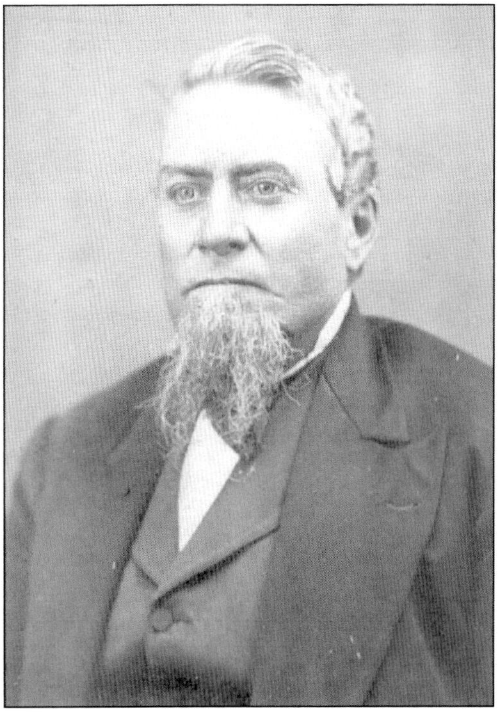

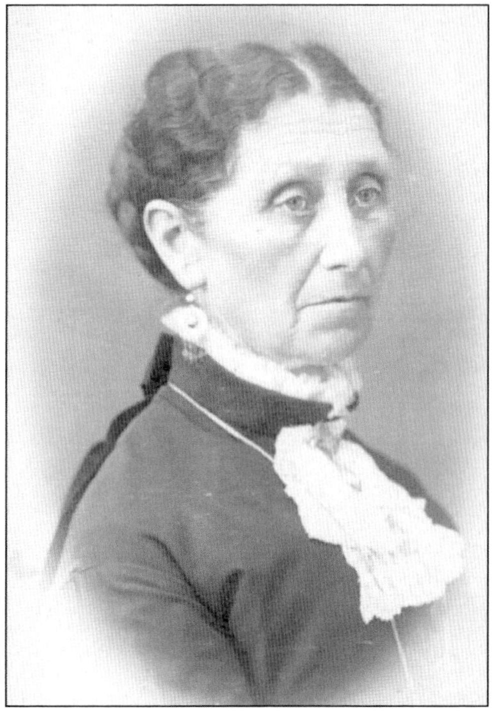

Left: Curtis Coe Clark was a well-known stagecoach owner and driver. Early on, he had a route from Plymouth to Lancaster, but after the advent of northern train routes, he worked the run from the Profile House to the Crawford House. Once the Bethlehem Junction spur was built, he ran the Strawberry Hill Hotel livery in the summer and logged in the winter. Clark was known for his love of good food, tenor voice (he sang in the Profile House stage drivers' quartet), and a fear of bears. (Marilyn Johnson.) *Right:* Abigail Wallace Clark, wife of Curtis Clark, loved to read and cook and was a staunch churchgoer. (Marilyn Johnson.)

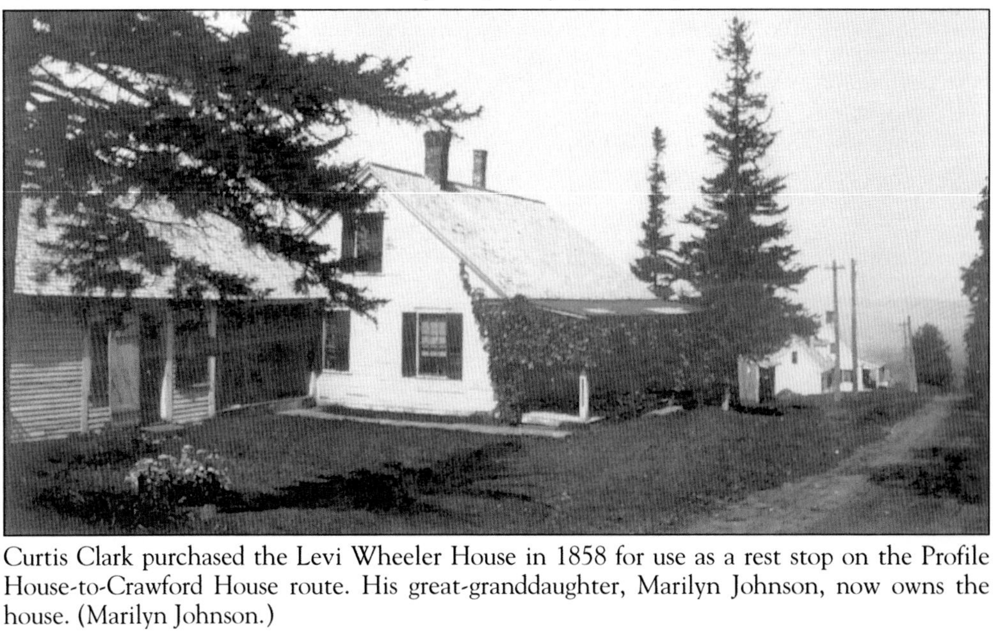

Curtis Clark purchased the Levi Wheeler House in 1858 for use as a rest stop on the Profile House-to-Crawford House route. His great-granddaughter, Marilyn Johnson, now owns the house. (Marilyn Johnson.)

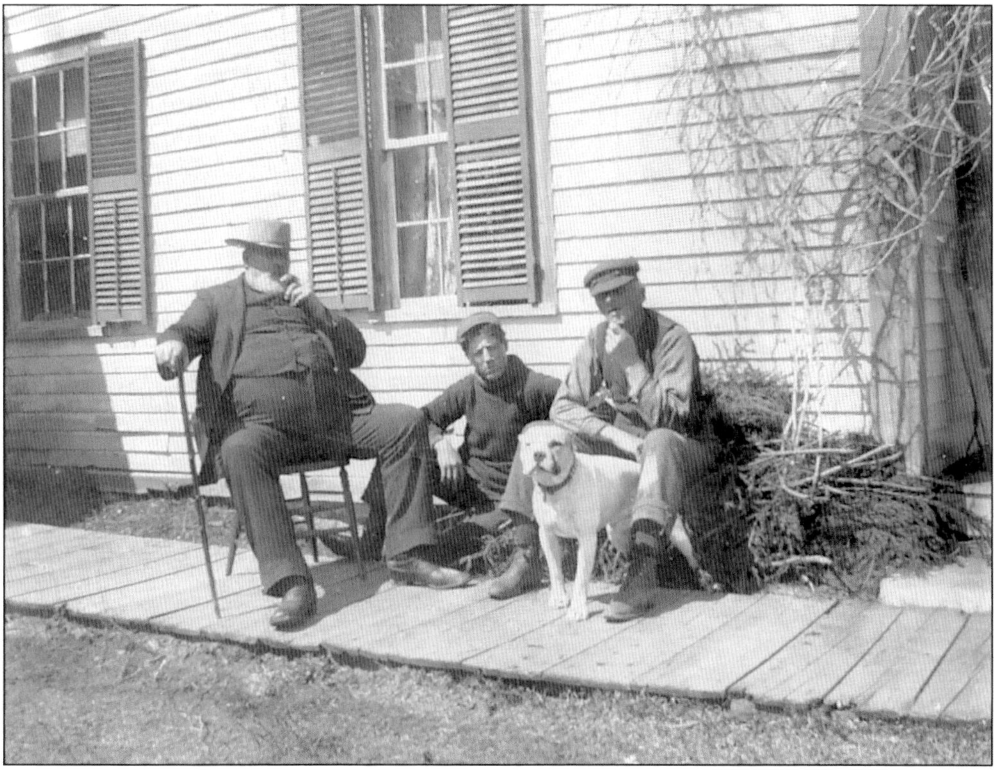

Curtis Clark's brother, Damon Clark, along with Smith Johnson and Clark's son-in-law, Jerry Johnson (all coach drivers), enjoy the sun in front of the Clark house. Some of Damon Clark's routes were Littleton to Plymouth, Haverhill to Lebanon, Littleton to Lyndon, Vermont, and the Crawford House to Jackson. Mail often accompanied passengers on these runs. (Marilyn Johnson.)

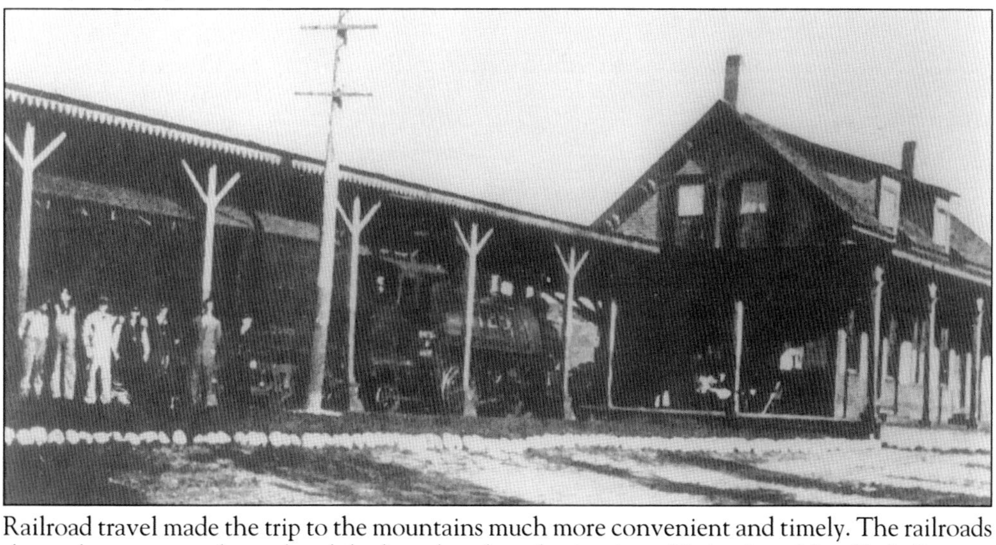

Railroad travel made the trip to the mountains much more convenient and timely. The railroads themselves promoted travel and the large hotels as destinations. Trains from New York, Boston, Portland, Saratoga, Montreal, and Quebec stopped daily at Bethlehem Junction, Pierce Bridge, in the late 1800s. (Courtesy of Dartmouth College Library.)

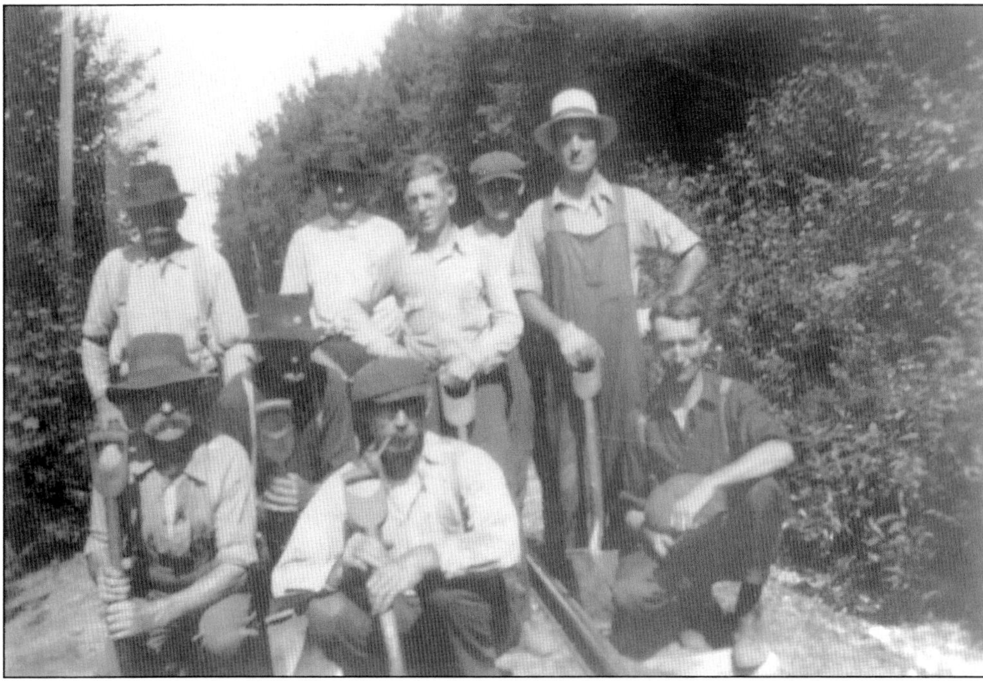

Many local men who lived in Pierce Bridge worked for the railroad. (Muriel Brown.)

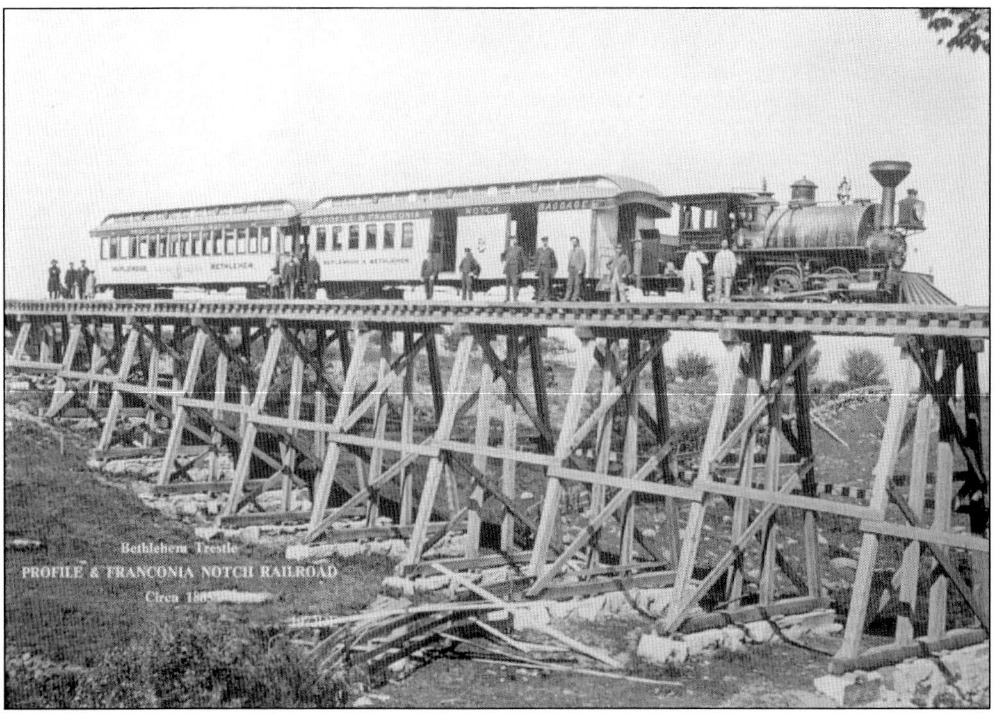

In 1885, a narrow-gauge track was laid up the hill into the village to two new stations—one at the Maplewood Hotel and the other near Park Street. The trestle pictured was located along the end of Elm Street. It was replaced in 1897 by a standard-gauge line and an embankment. Train service into the village ended in 1924. (Bethlehem Heritage Museum.)

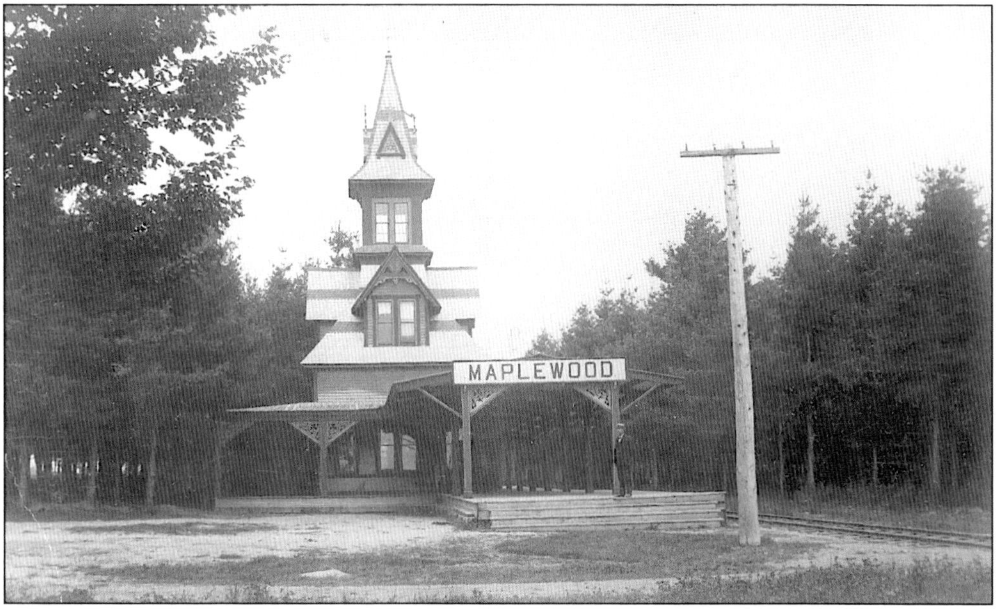

Small but elegant, the Maplewood station was built to serve guests of the Maplewood Hotel and cottages. (David Olson.)

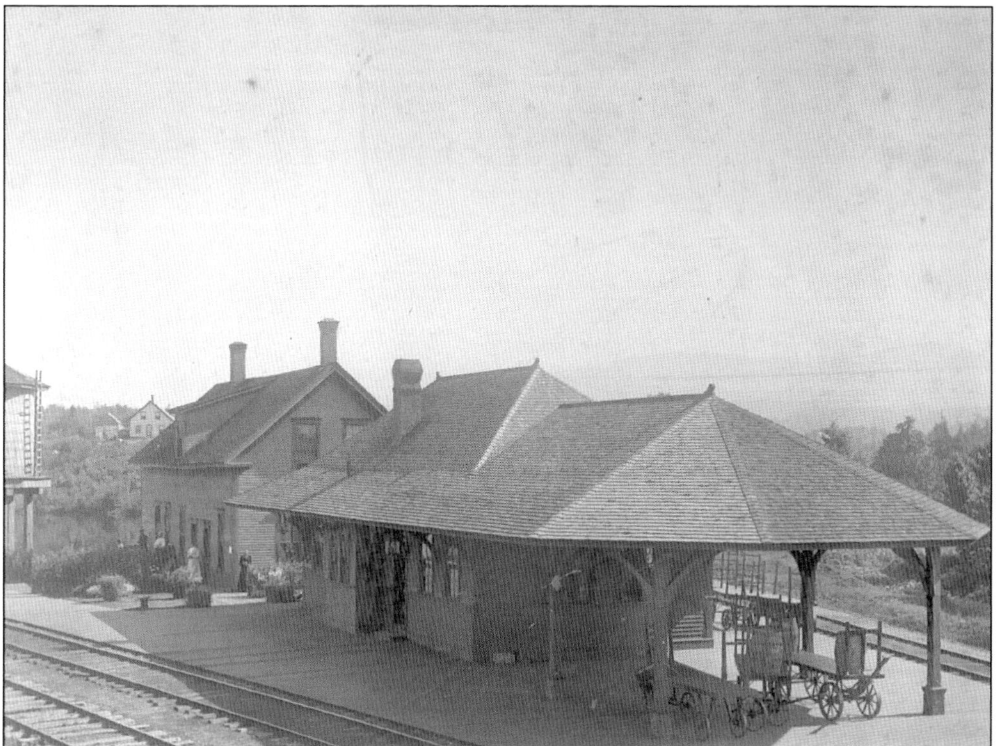

The Wing Road Station once won a prize for its flower beds. Trains went from Wing Road to Littleton and to Whitefield and Lancaster carrying milk, mail, freight, and passengers. Many Bethlehem residents used the train for local transportation. (Bethlehem Heritage Museum.)

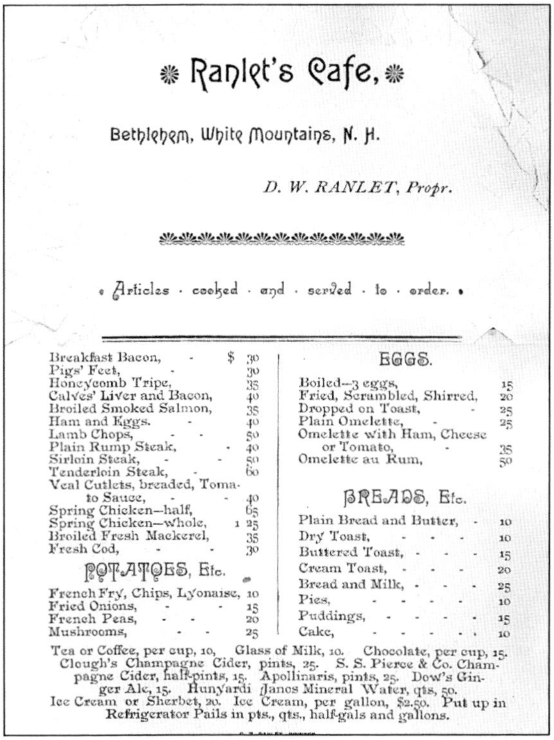

Ranlet's Cafe,

Bethlehem, White Mountains, N. H.

D. W. RANLET, Propr.

• Articles · cooked · and · served · to · order. •

Breakfast Bacon,	$ 30
Pigs' Feet,	30
Honeycomb Tripe,	35
Calves' Liver and Bacon,	40
Broiled Smoked Salmon,	35
Ham and Eggs.	40
Lamb Chops,	50
Plain Rump Steak,	40
Sirloin Steak,	50
Tenderloin Steak,	60
Veal Cutlets, breaded, Tomato Sauce,	40
Spring Chicken—half,	65
Spring Chicken—whole,	1 25
Broiled Fresh Mackerel,	35
Fresh Cod,	30

POTATOES, Etc.

French Fry, Chips, Lyonaise,	10
Fried Onions,	15
French Peas,	20
Mushrooms,	25

EGGS.

Boiled—3 eggs,	15
Fried, Scrambled, Shirred,	20
Dropped on Toast,	25
Plain Omelette,	25
Omelette with Ham, Cheese or Tomato,	35
Omelette au Rum,	50

BREADS, Etc.

Plain Bread and Butter,	10
Dry Toast,	10
Buttered Toast,	15
Cream Toast,	20
Bread and Milk,	25
Pies,	10
Puddings,	15
Cake,	10

Tea or Coffee, per cup, 10, Glass of Milk, 10. Chocolate, per cup, 15. Clough's Champagne Cider, pints, 25. S. S. Pierce & Co. Champagne Cider, half-pints, 15. Apollinaris, pints, 25. Dow's Ginger Ale, 15. Hunyardi Janos Mineral Water, qts, 50.
Ice Cream or Sherbet, 20. Ice Cream, per gallon, $2.50. Put up in Refrigerator Pails in pts., qts., half-gals and gallons.

Breakfast tastes have changed somewhat since this menu was offered in the 1880s. Ranlet's Café was located on Main Street near the corner of Park Street, beside the Ranlet Hotel. In 1895 or 1896, the café building was moved east on Main Street to a position at one end of the Bonardi Block, which was then called the Lewis Block, as Fred Lewis owned it. Ranlet's Café is now the site of the Bethlehem Visitor Center and Museum. (Paul Hudson.)

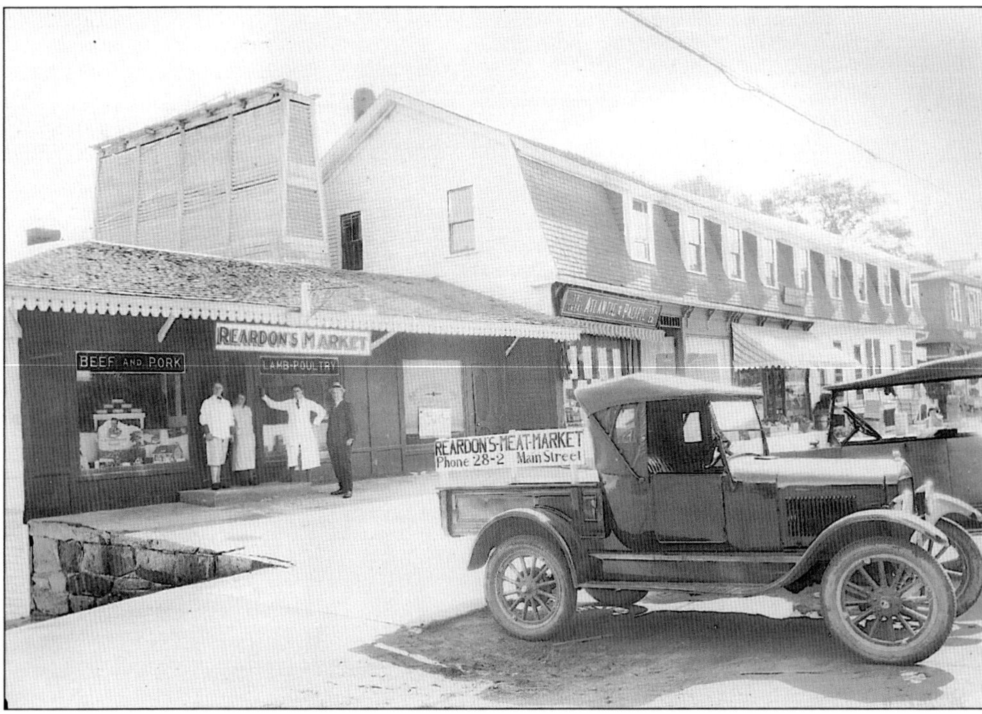

During the 1920s, Reardon's Market was housed in the former Ranlet's Café. William and Leona Reardon offered groceries and a convenient delivery service. They also had a store in Littleton, at 43 Main Street. (Bethlehem Heritage Museum.)

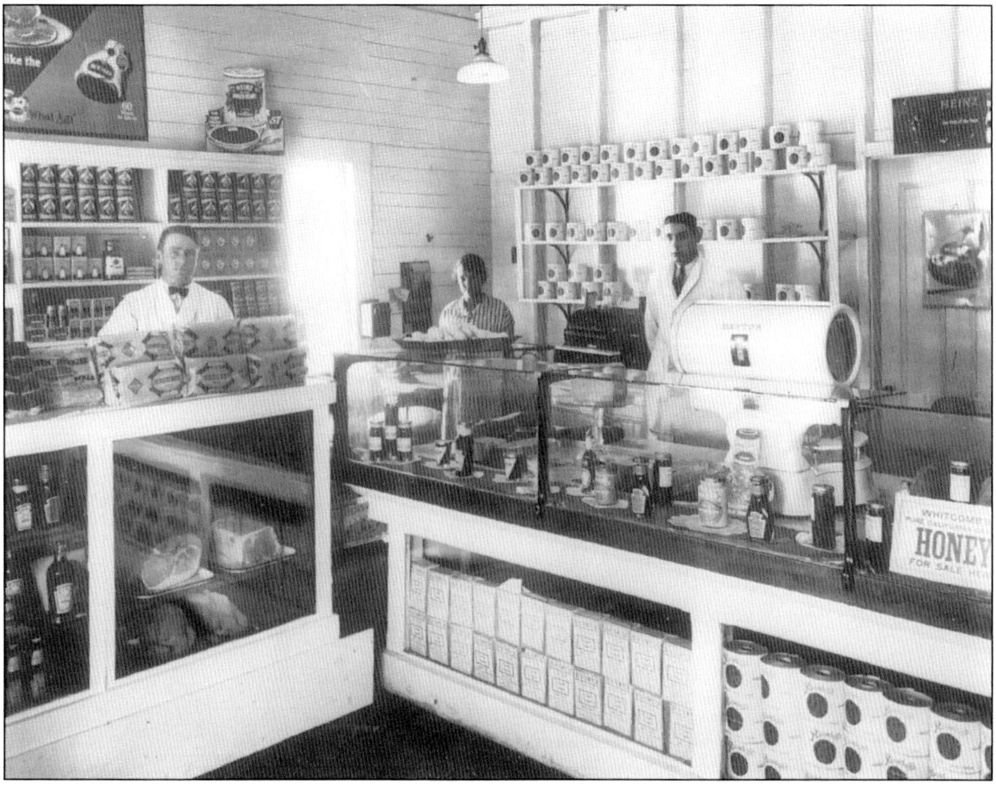

In this photograph, William and Leona Reardon stand behind the counter of their store. (Courtesy of Dartmouth College Library.)

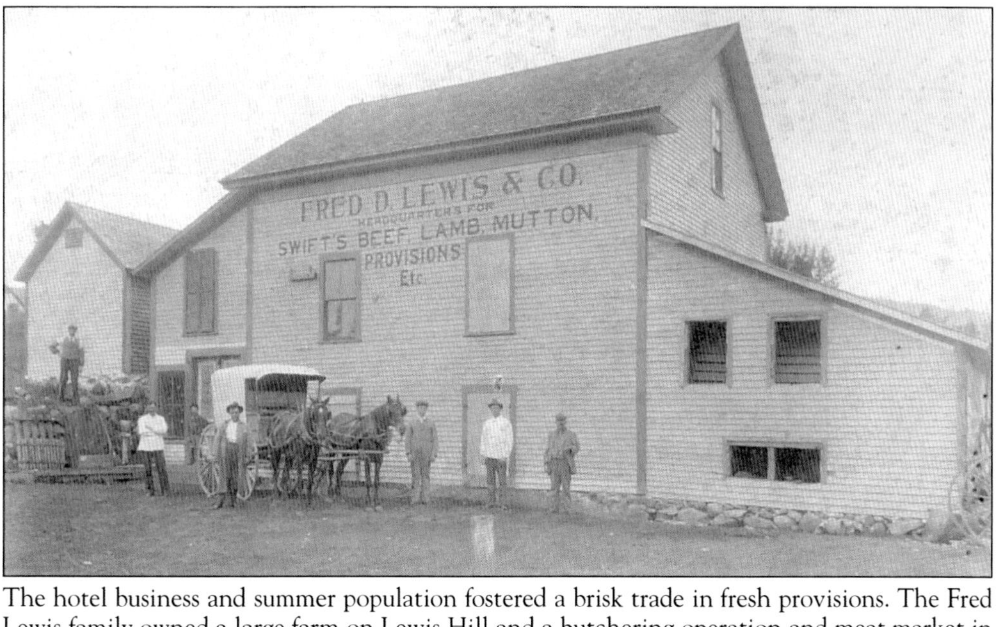

The hotel business and summer population fostered a brisk trade in fresh provisions. The Fred Lewis family owned a large farm on Lewis Hill and a butchering operation and meat market in town. One summer resident remembers the Lewis wagon making deliveries. In later years, the Lewises took in boarders at the farm. (Bethlehem Heritage Museum.)

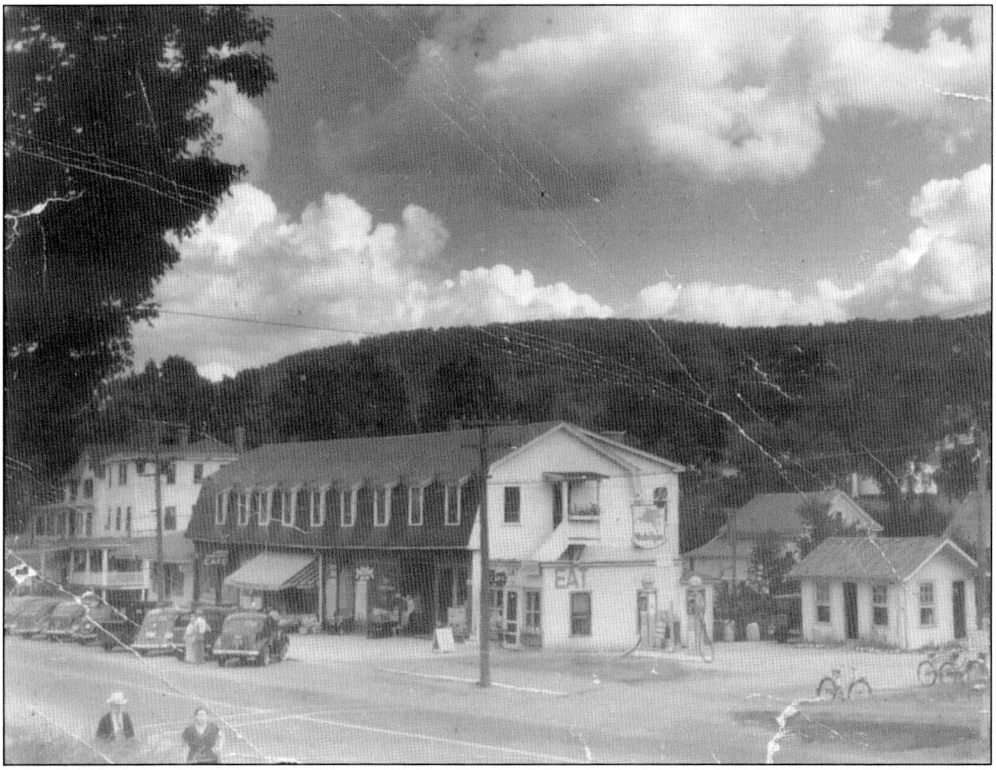

The main part of the Bonardi Block was originally part of the Maplewood Hotel complex, Maplewood Hall. Fred Lewis moved it to Main Street across from the Bethlehem Town Hall. Lewis's Meat Market, C.S. Boston's Candy Store, and the town clerk's office were among the businesses housed here. After Louis Bonardi bought the building in the mid-1920s and opened his grocery business here, it became the Bonardi Block. The Bonardi Block was torn down in the 1970s. (Patsy Bonardi.)

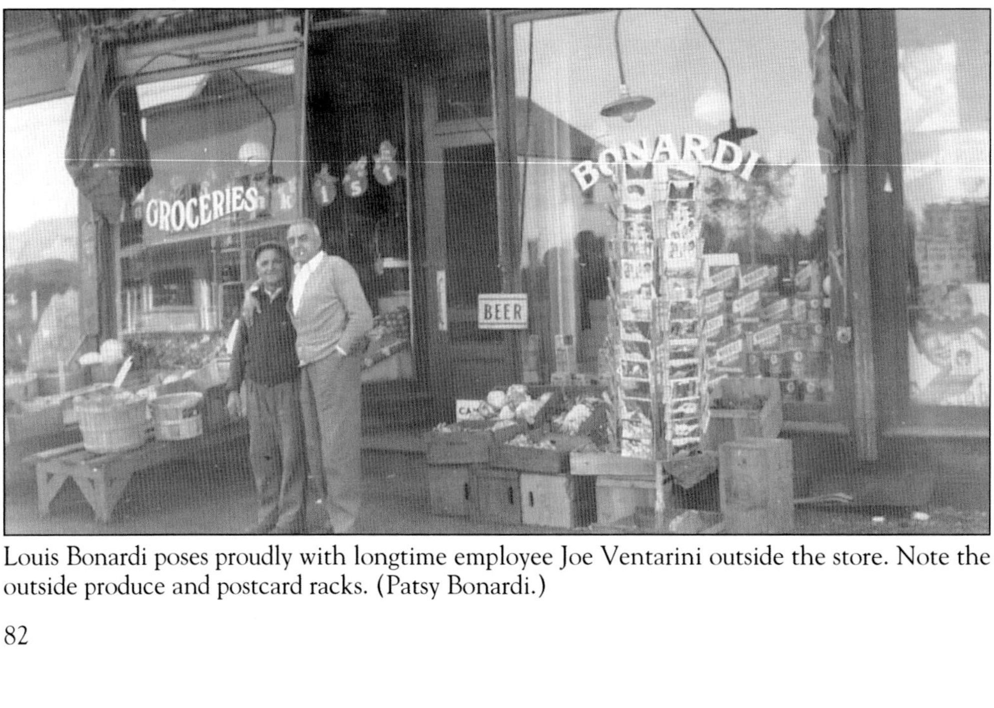

Louis Bonardi poses proudly with longtime employee Joe Ventarini outside the store. Note the outside produce and postcard racks. (Patsy Bonardi.)

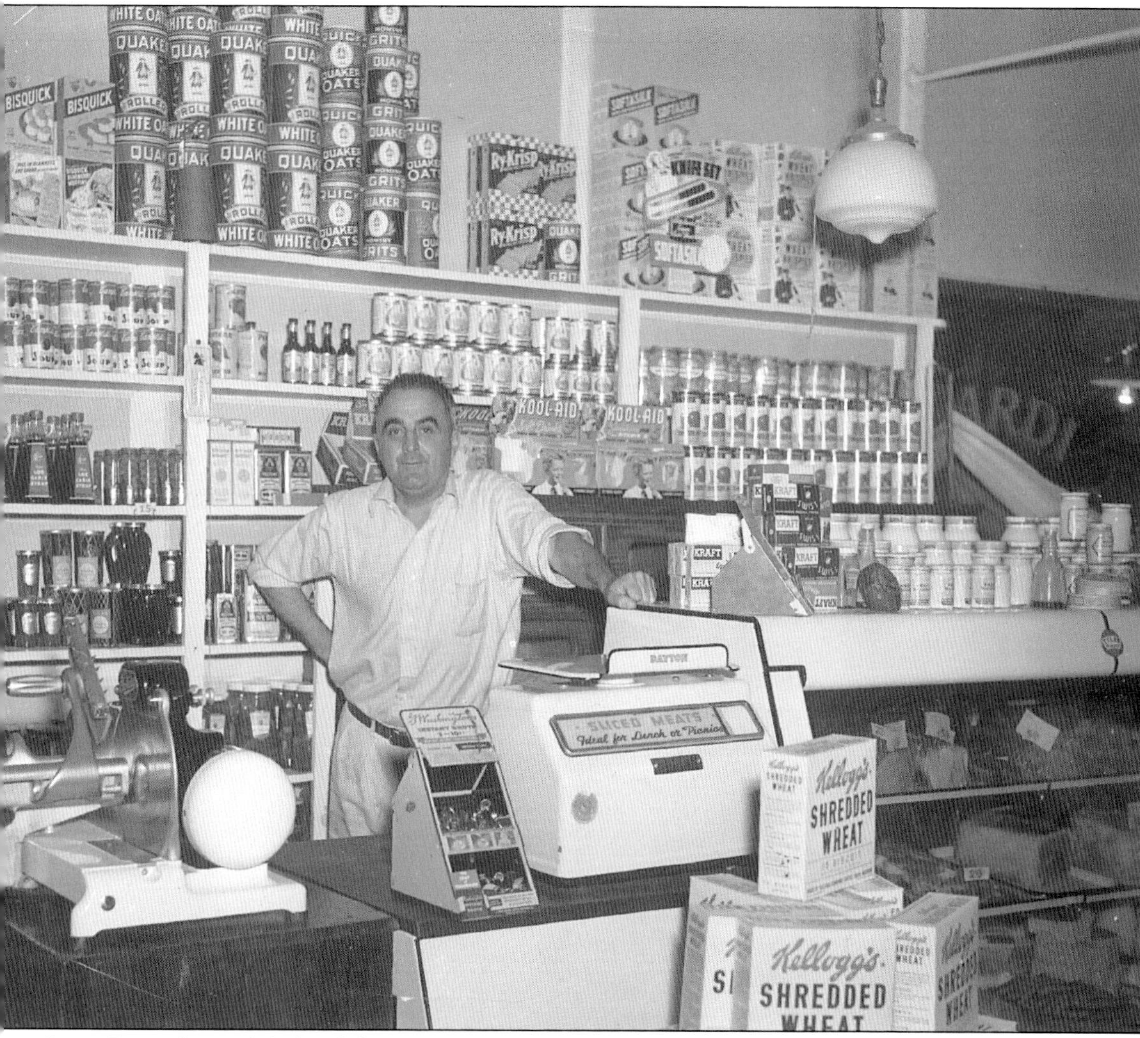

Louis Bonardi stands behind the counter in the Bonardi Market. (Patsy Bonardi.)

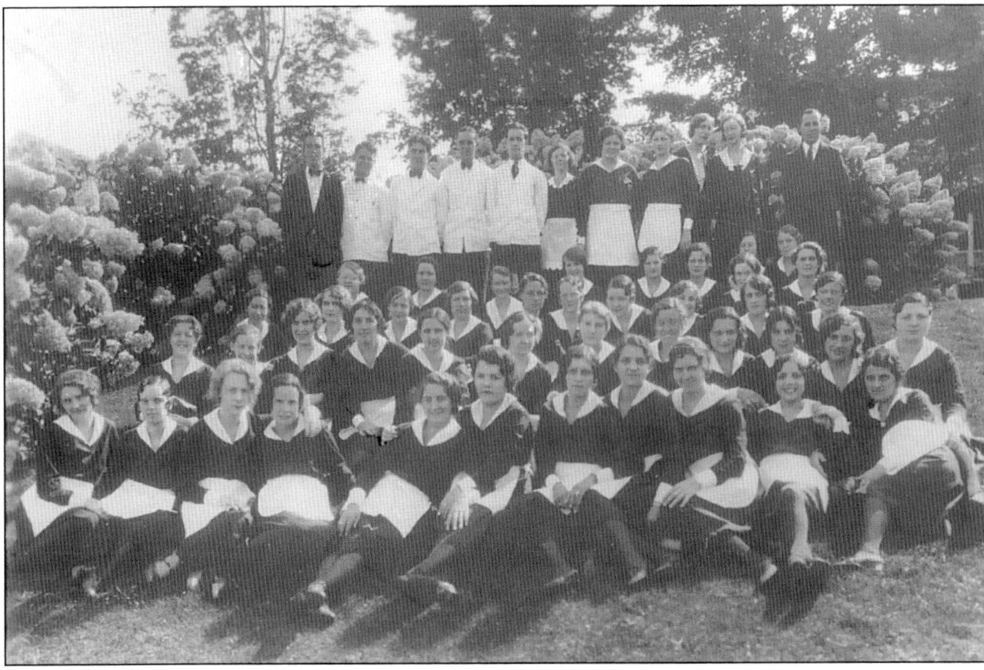

College students, local residents, and professional hotel workers made up the staff at the hotels. The professionals worked in Bethlehem and then headed to Florida or to Pinehurst, North Carolina, in the fall. Bethlehem hoteliers often owned or managed hotels in other locations, and they liked to keep a reliable staff. This *c.* 1930s photograph shows the Maplewood dining staff. (Bethlehem Heritage Museum.)

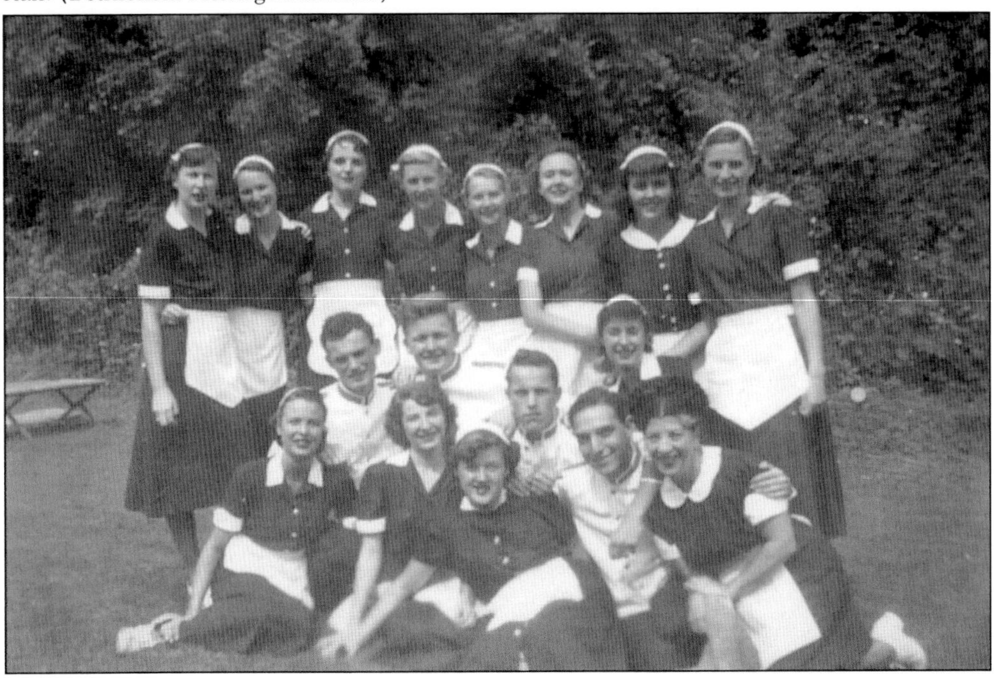

Former local girl Alice McCullock mailed this photograph of herself and her fellow employees at the Sinclair in 1950 or 1951. She is eighth from the left. (Alice McCullock.)

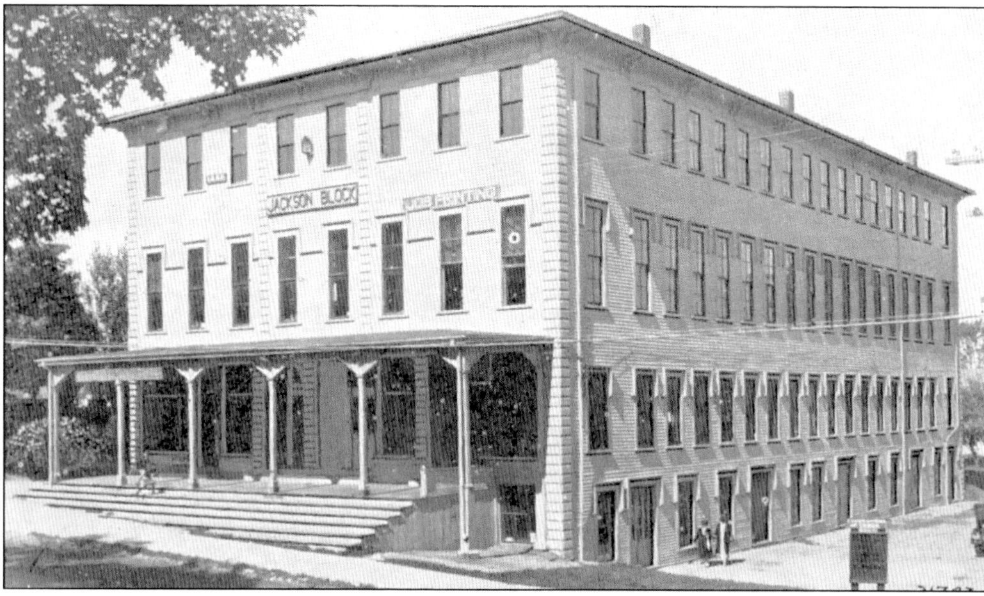

The Jackson Block was originally and once again is called the Cruft Block, named after the builder, Isaac Cruft, owner of the Maplewood. Luther Jackson and his son Myron Jackson operated a department store from 1911 to 1955. Sugar and flour were brought in by the train carload to supply the hotels, and several hotels stored their dry goods in the basement during the winter. Jackson's offered clothing, hardware, hats, shoes, canned goods, and fresh meat. Children enjoyed the candy counter and the bins offering 20 types of cookies. Locals favored the Jackson Dance Hall on the second floor, which had 50-cent weekend dances with live bands. Other businesses in the building included the post office, the Coos Telephone Company, and Bob Jellison's Bethlehem Press, which printed the famous *White Mountain Echo* newspaper and menus for various hotels. (Olive Jackson Whittier.)

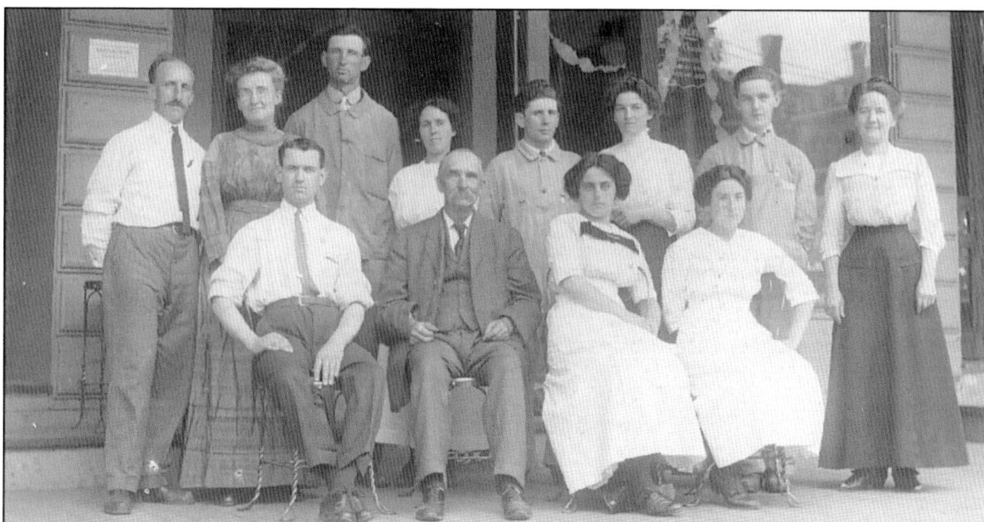

Employees of the Jackson Block pose on the porch. They are, from left to right, as follows: (front row) Willis Lyford, Luther Jackson, Inez Whitcomb Bodwell, and Alice Jobin; (back row) Myron Jackson, Elsie Jackson, Fred Harvey, Vina Trudeau, Joe Coney, Georgia Straw, George Seymore, and Sarah Drouin. (Paul Hudson.)

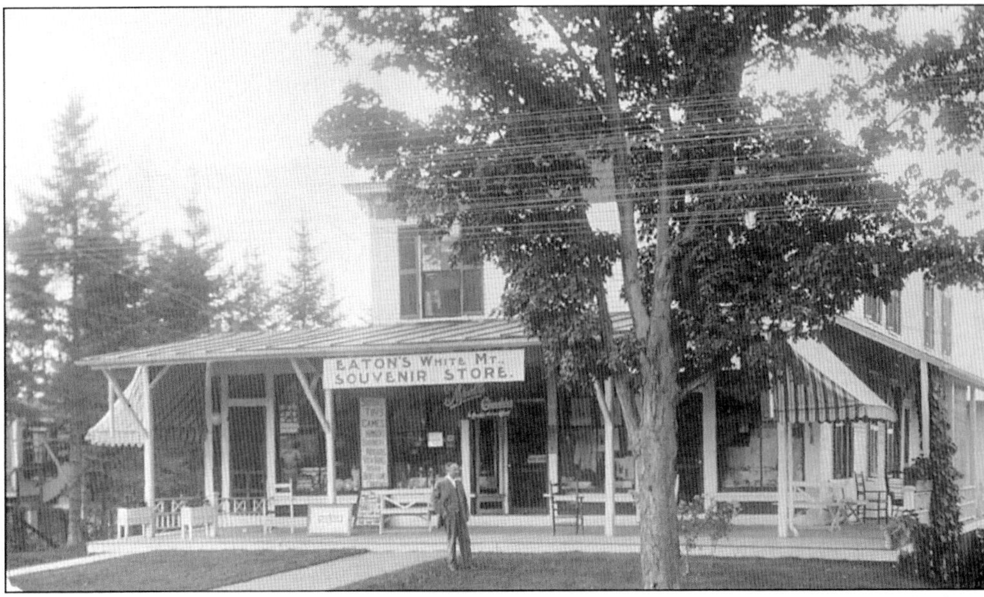

According to the 1913 *Bethlehem Outlook*, Eaton's offered souvenirs, china novelties, baskets, needlework, Utopia yarns, and D.M.C. cotton. The Eaton's building is now an antique shop. (Paul Hudson.)

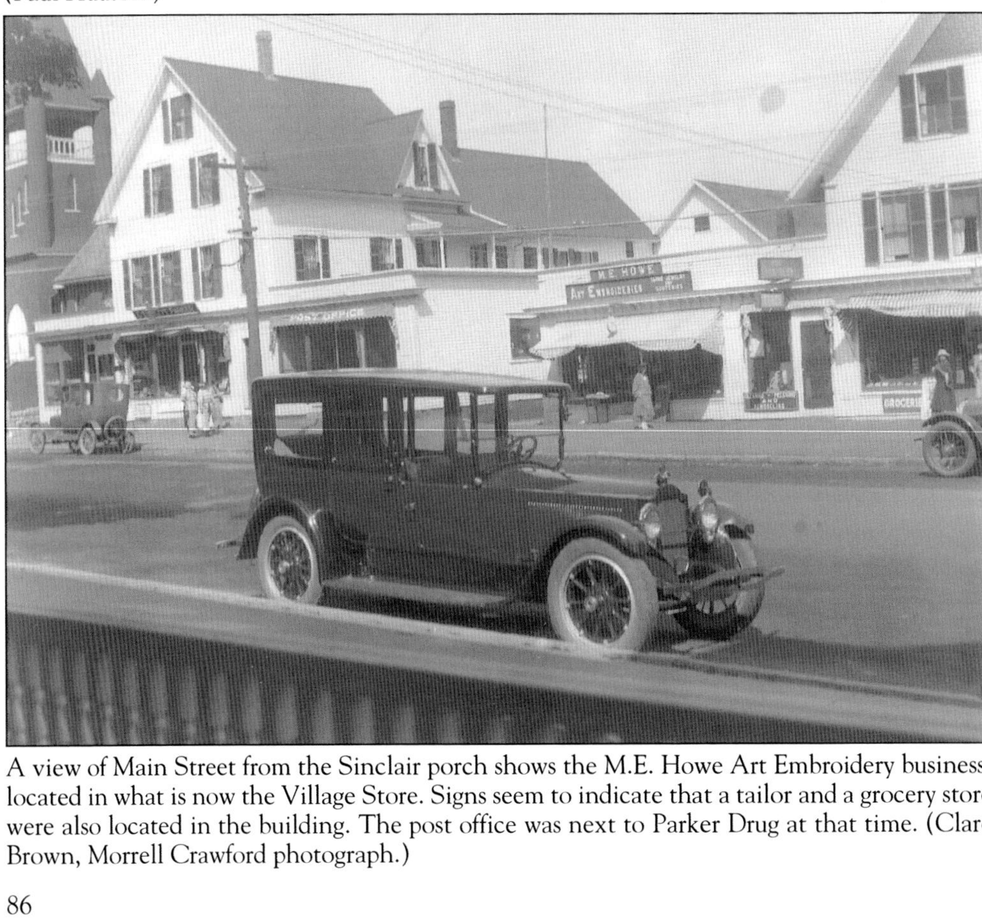

A view of Main Street from the Sinclair porch shows the M.E. Howe Art Embroidery business, located in what is now the Village Store. Signs seem to indicate that a tailor and a grocery store were also located in the building. The post office was next to Parker Drug at that time. (Clare Brown, Morrell Crawford photograph.)

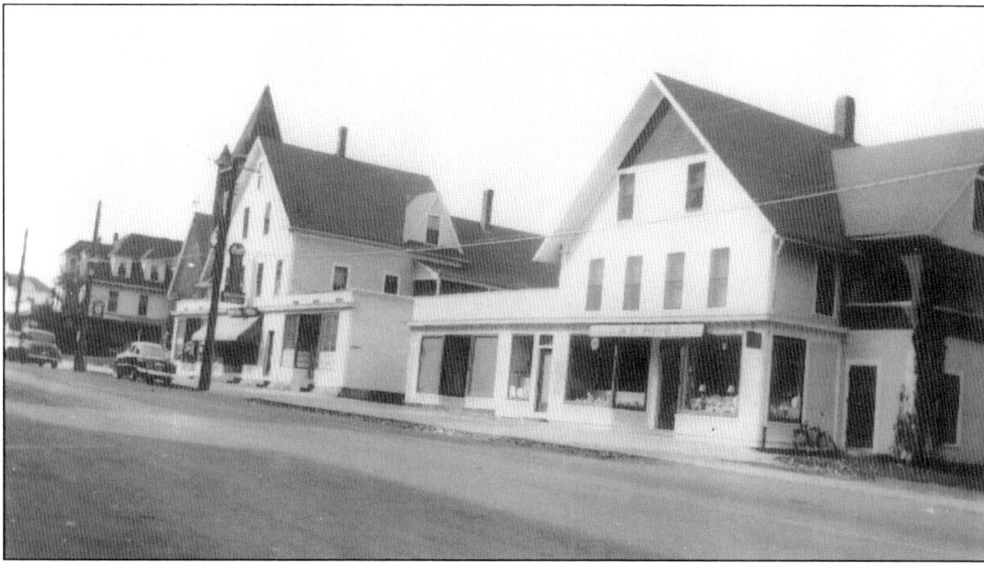

In 1946, Al Reid opened A.E. Reid Gas and Electric in the M.E. Howe building. His business offered electrical and gas appliances, hardware, and electrical contracting. He served the area from Lincoln to Groveton until his retirement in the 1970s. In the 1960s, he moved the business to the old American House, which is now owned by a flooring company. (Courtesy of Dartmouth College Library.)

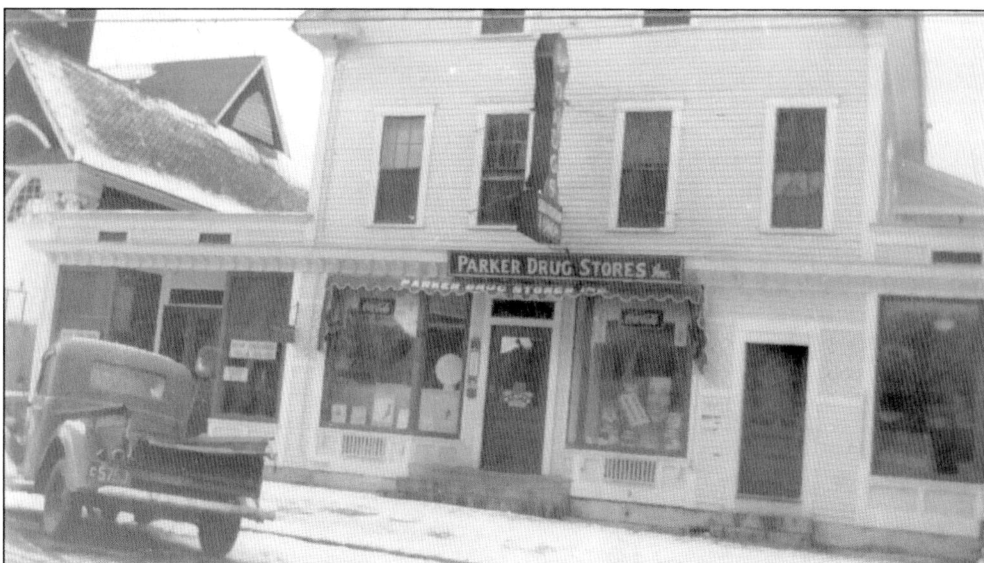

Another view of Parker Drug shows the store in the 1940s. The Bethlehem store was one of several owned by the Parker family. Other Parker drugstores were in Littleton, North Woodstock, and St. Johnsbury, Vermont, as well as one at the Maplewood hotel. In this photograph, New England Telephone occupies the left wing of the building, where it stayed until June 25, 1964, when the system went dial. Parker Drug is now Lloyd Hills Restaurant, and the telephone office is a laundromat. (Patsy Bonardi.)

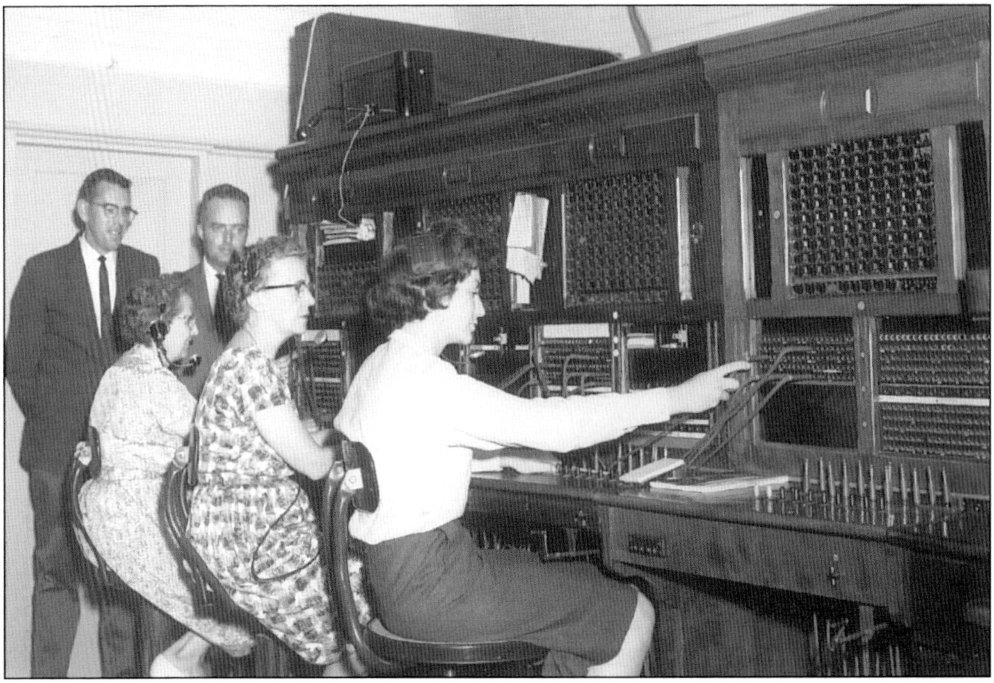

At the telephone office, 68 years of personal service come to an end as the Bethlehem operators take a few final calls on the old system. They are, from left to right, Howard Keach, Mr. Nickerson, Marjorie Wysocki, Olive Whittier, and Sharon (Nelson) Robie. (Bethlehem Heritage Museum.)

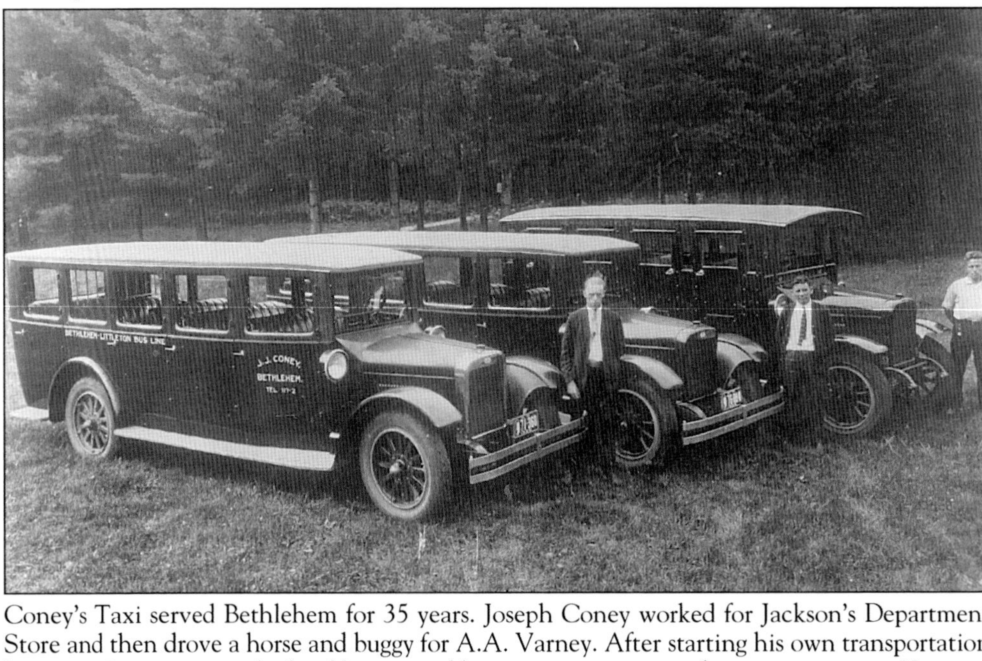

Coney's Taxi served Bethlehem for 35 years. Joseph Coney worked for Jackson's Department Store and then drove a horse and buggy for A.A. Varney. After starting his own transportation business, Coney operated school buses, mail buses, private taxis, and a touring service. He was a popular figure, known for his wealth of local knowledge. With Coney are Leon Garneau, on the left, and Mr. Dexter, on the right. (Bethlehem Heritage Museum.)

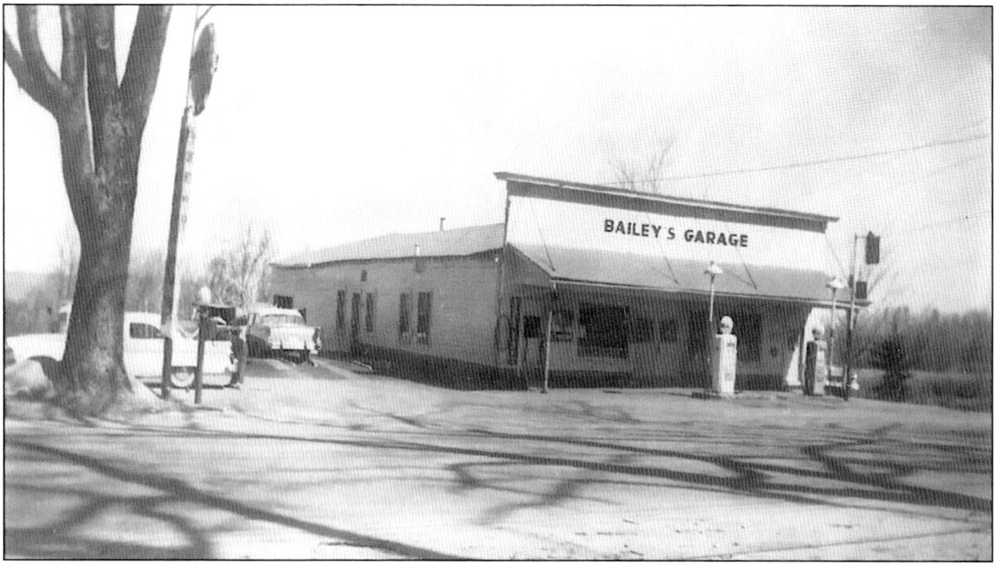

Frank A. Bailey's "stage auto" business is listed in the 1917 *White Mountain Directory*. Bailey also drove carriages for hire. Later on, he had an automobile garage. On one exciting day in 1930, garage employee Al Reid had the honor of working on Gen. John J. Pershing's car. This building also housed the first movie theater in town, opened in 1913 by Arthur Dexter. (Courtesy of Dartmouth College Library.)

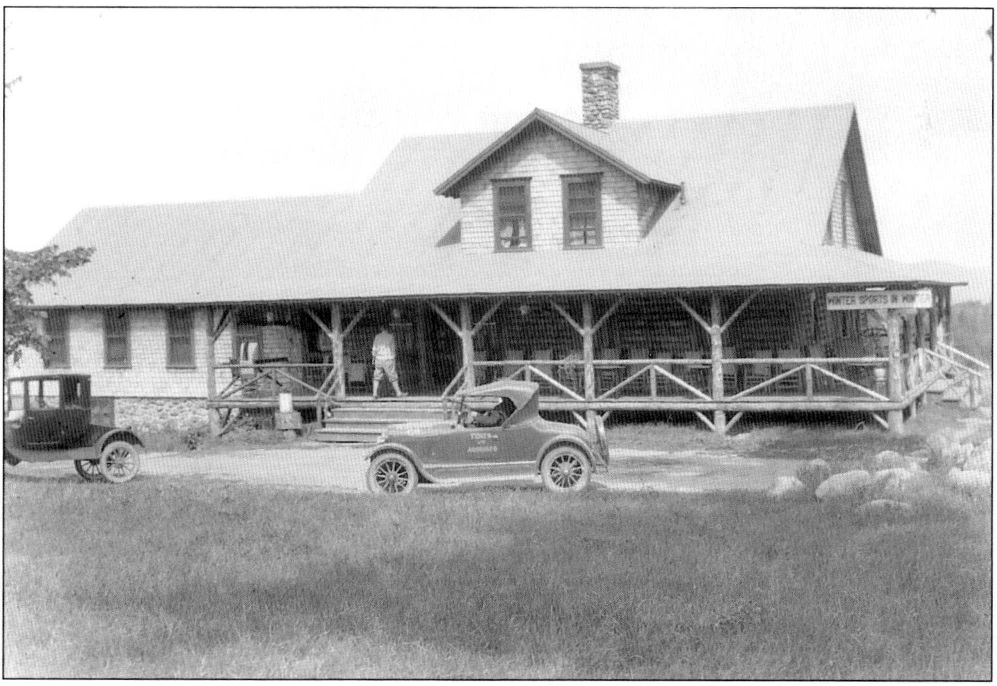

Harry Goodwin's Log Cabin was a lively spot in the 1920s and 1930s, offering morning and evening jazz and orchestra music, luncheon, tea, and dinner. The layout featured a large room for 75, with a fireplace, a dance floor for 150, and ten private dining rooms, each with its own window that, as rumor has it, served as an escape hatch during Prohibition-era raids. The Log Cabin is now a private home. (Clare Brown, Morrell Crawford photograph.)

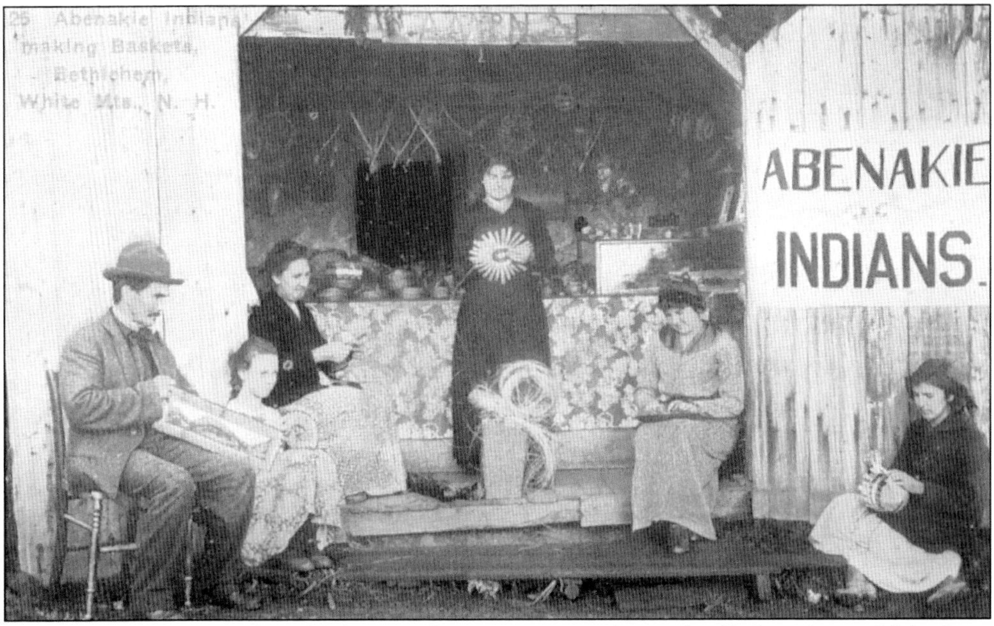

Abenaki Indians visited Bethlehem each summer to make and sell their beautiful baskets. They stayed in houses up on Strawberry Hill. Descendent and renowned basket maker Newton Washburn currently lives in Bethlehem. Several of his ash baskets are in the Smithsonian. (Paul Hudson.)

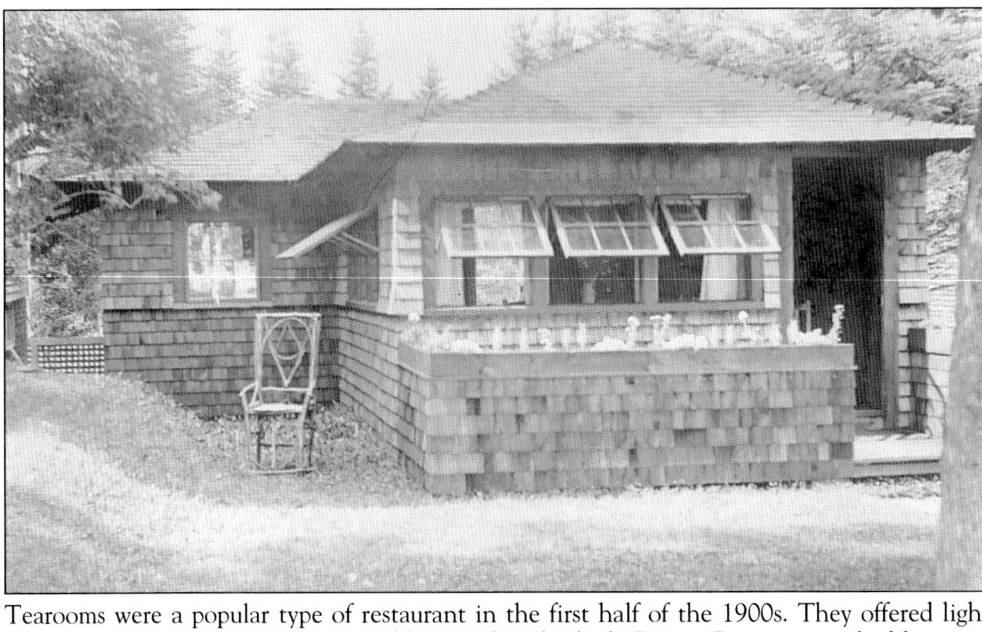

Tearooms were a popular type of restaurant in the first half of the 1900s. They offered light lunches, pastries, and coffee, tea, and lemonade. The little Brown Betty was tucked between Sunlight Cottage and Eaton's Souvenirs. This tearoom was well known for delicious waffles and hot chocolate. Tea was served daily from 3:00 to 6:00. (Paul Hudson.)

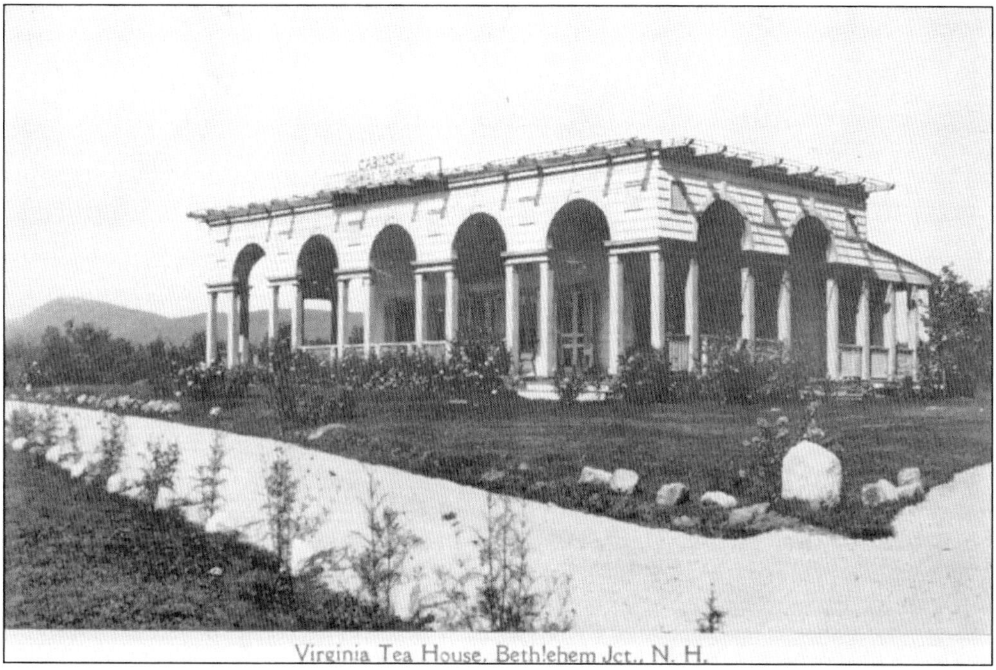

Virginia's operated during the 1920s and 1930s and was renowned for its beautiful décor and airy comfort. Virginia's also rented cabins, a common side business for many in the area. The tearoom is now a private home, and the arches are hidden in the walls. (Philip Bell.)

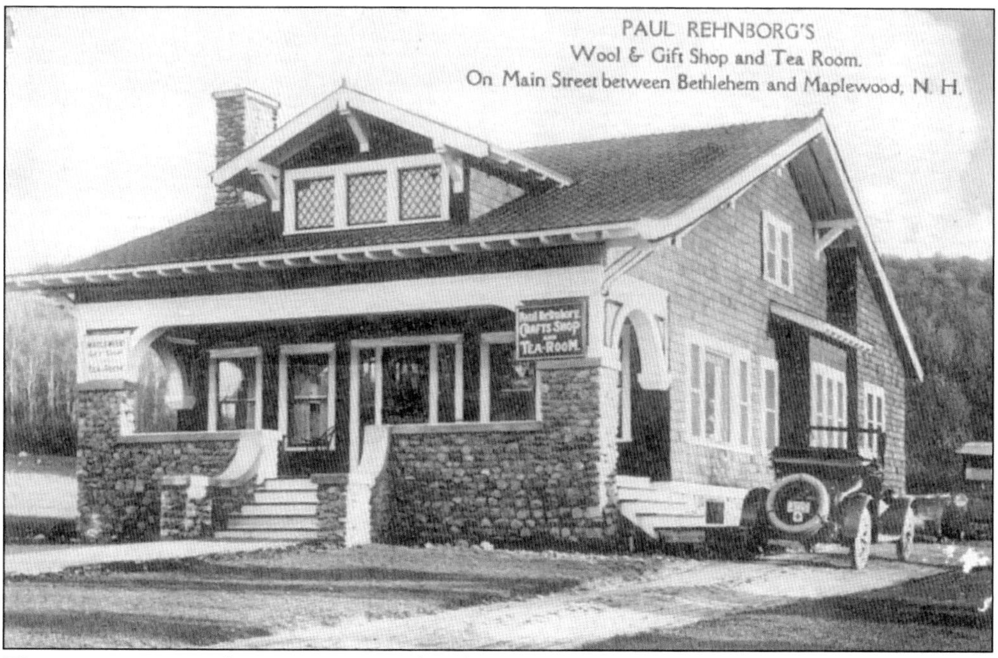

The cottage pictured is a nice example of a Craftsman-style bungalow. The gift shop and tearoom was one of Paul Rehnborg's many Bethlehem endeavors. He worked mostly in real estate: buying and selling land, renting summer homes, and brokering commercial properties. The cottage is now a private home. (Paul Hudson.)

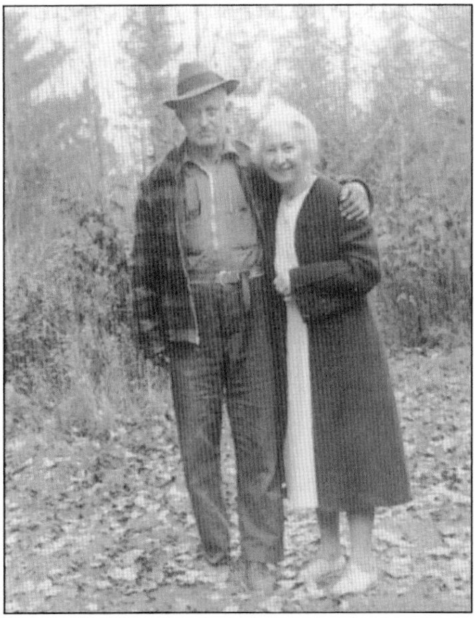

The boom in hotels and summer homes provided plenty of carpentry, plumbing, masonry, and electrical jobs. Some men worked independently; others, such as Bernard Harvey, built up quite large businesses. Harvey, shown with his wife, had construction jobs at the Adair, Tillagouri, the second Lemen cottage, McCullock's, the Annex and the dining room at the Agassiz, the Alpine's dining room, and an addition at the Central House. At one point, Harvey had 50 ditch diggers on his payroll. This was to his advantage, as during that period, many contractors were paid a salary and a percentage of their payroll. (Clare Brown.)

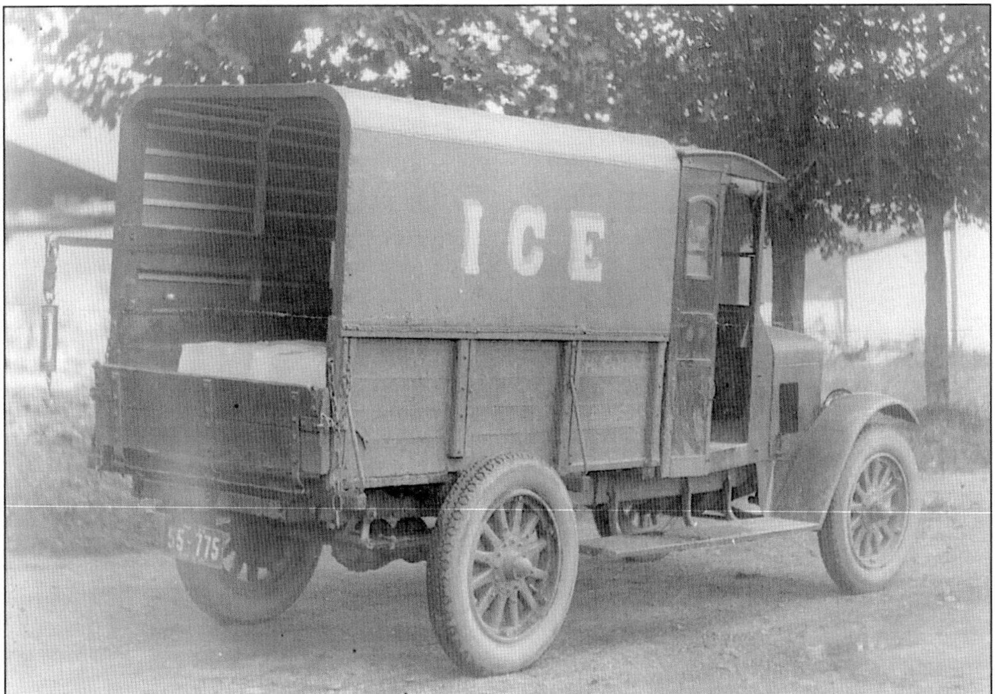

In the days before refrigerators were common, natural ice was a valuable commodity. It was cut in the winter and stored in sawdust in barns. Bethlehem ice was cut from a man-made pond at the base of Mount Agassiz. A.C. Atto was the original owner of the ice company and of the farm that went with the property. In fact, the Bethlehem Water Precinct signed a 99-year agreement with Atto to provide water for the pond in return for precinct residents' receiving ice at a reasonable price. In the late 1920s, Thomas Churchill bought the ice business and the farm. The Churchill family owned the ice company until the late 1940s. The pond is now named Churchill Pond. This photograph shows one of the company trucks. (Clare Brown.)

Iceman Bill Cere is shown delivering ice. Icemen would use large tongs to lift and carry blocks of ice into homes for insertion into the icebox. (Muriel Brown.)

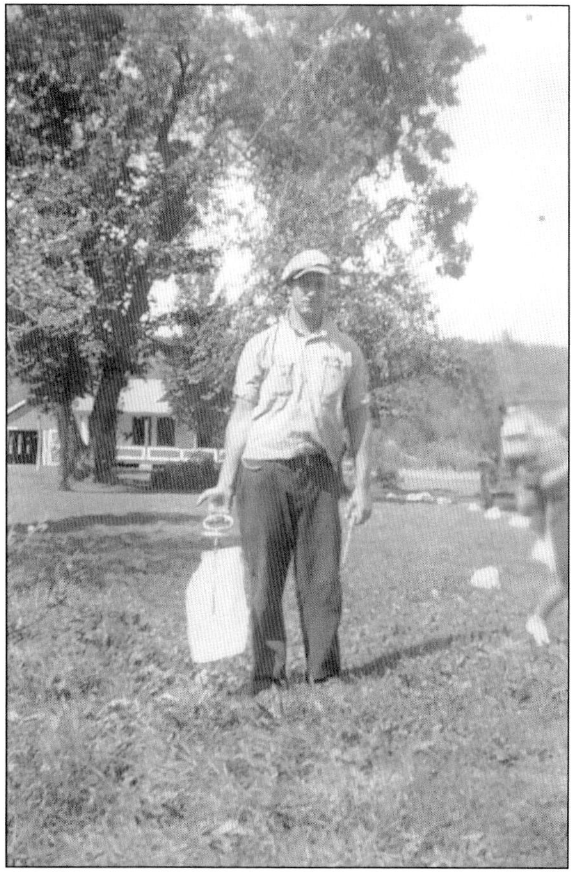

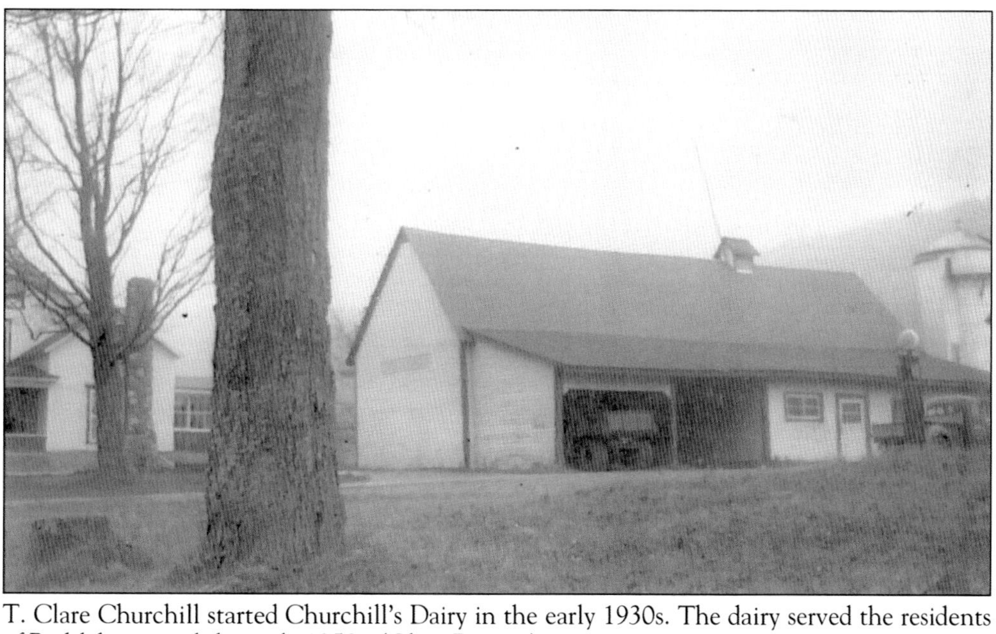

T. Clare Churchill started Churchill's Dairy in the early 1930s. The dairy served the residents of Bethlehem until the early 1950s. (Clare Brown.)

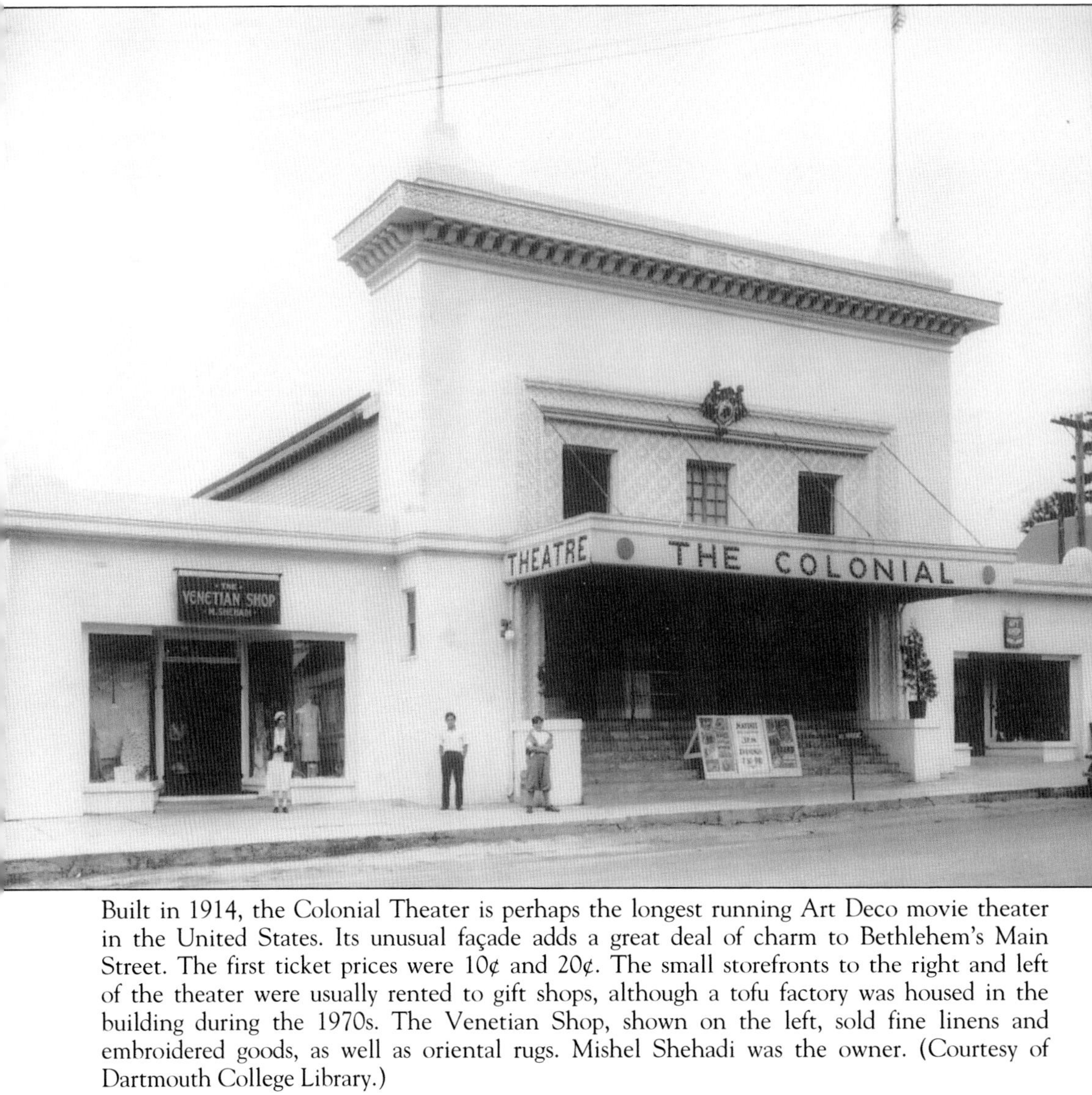

Built in 1914, the Colonial Theater is perhaps the longest running Art Deco movie theater in the United States. Its unusual façade adds a great deal of charm to Bethlehem's Main Street. The first ticket prices were 10¢ and 20¢. The small storefronts to the right and left of the theater were usually rented to gift shops, although a tofu factory was housed in the building during the 1970s. The Venetian Shop, shown on the left, sold fine linens and embroidered goods, as well as oriental rugs. Mishel Shehadi was the owner. (Courtesy of Dartmouth College Library.)

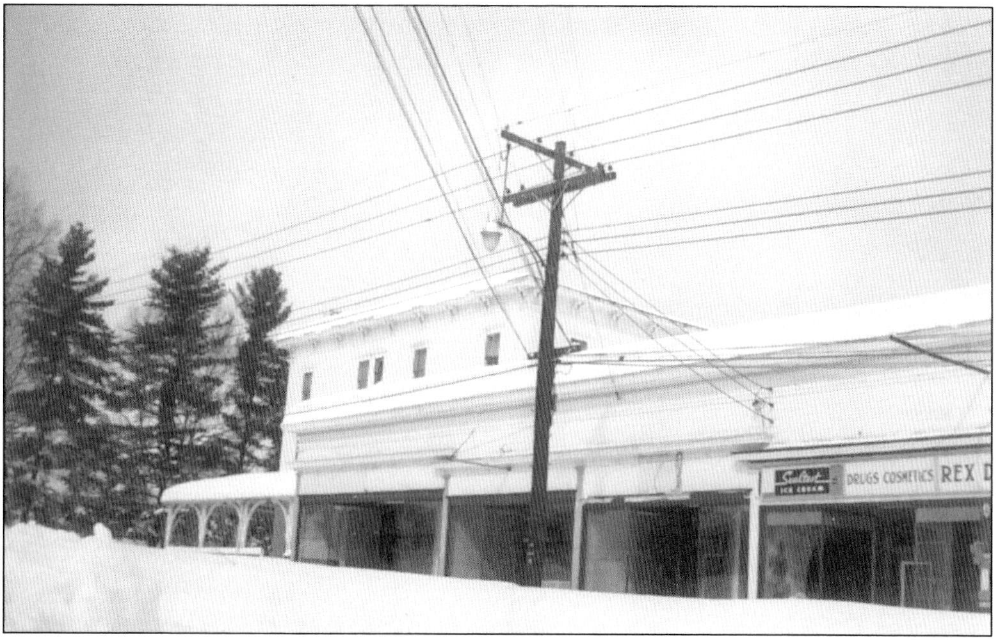

In the 1920s, Hyman Berman built the storefront block that later became known as the Martignetti Block. This photograph was taken in the winter of 1956. The Altamonte Hotel stands next to the block. Over the years, these storefronts have been home to drugstores, food stores, souvenir shops, restaurants, a dance studio, and antique stores. (Betty Glusky.)

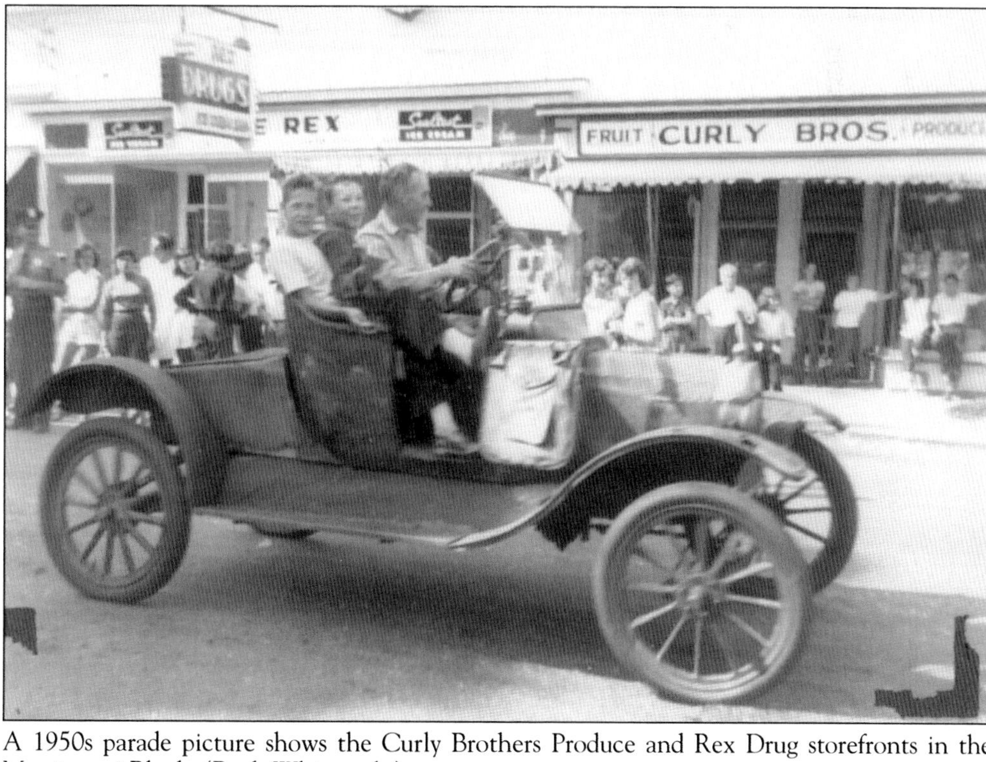

A 1950s parade picture shows the Curly Brothers Produce and Rex Drug storefronts in the Martignetti Block. (Ruth Whitcomb.)

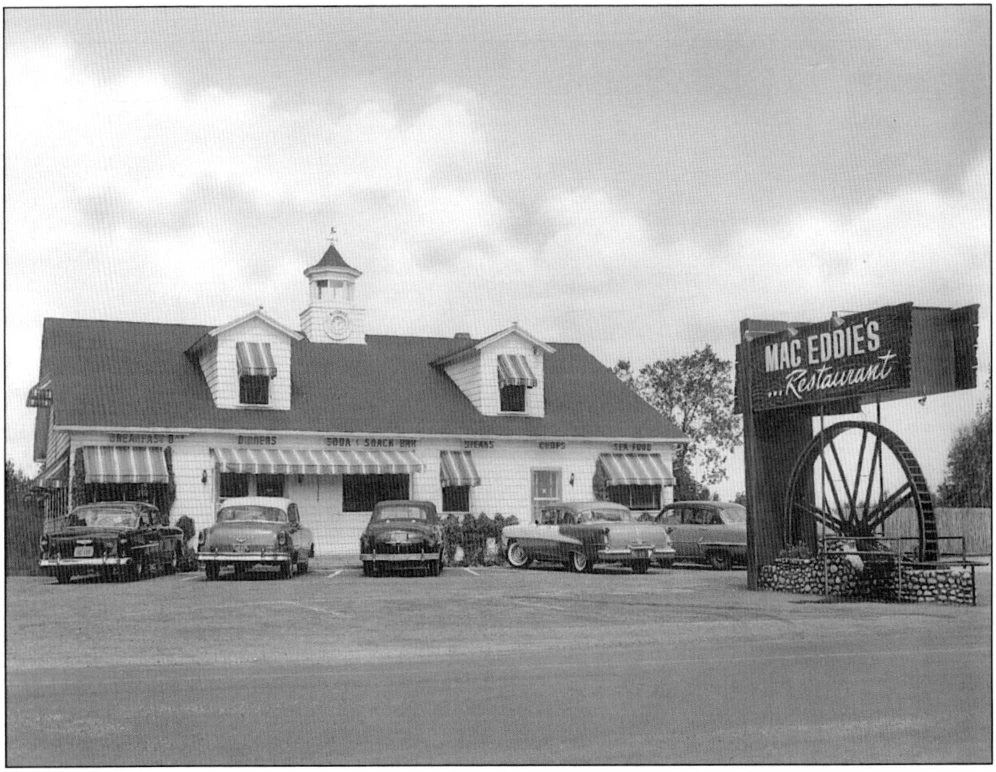

MacEddie's Restaurant was the partnership of Mac Stevenson and Eddie Wysocki. The waterwheel was an eye-catching landmark on Main Street for years. The building now houses the post office and a video store. (Bethlehem Heritage Museum.)

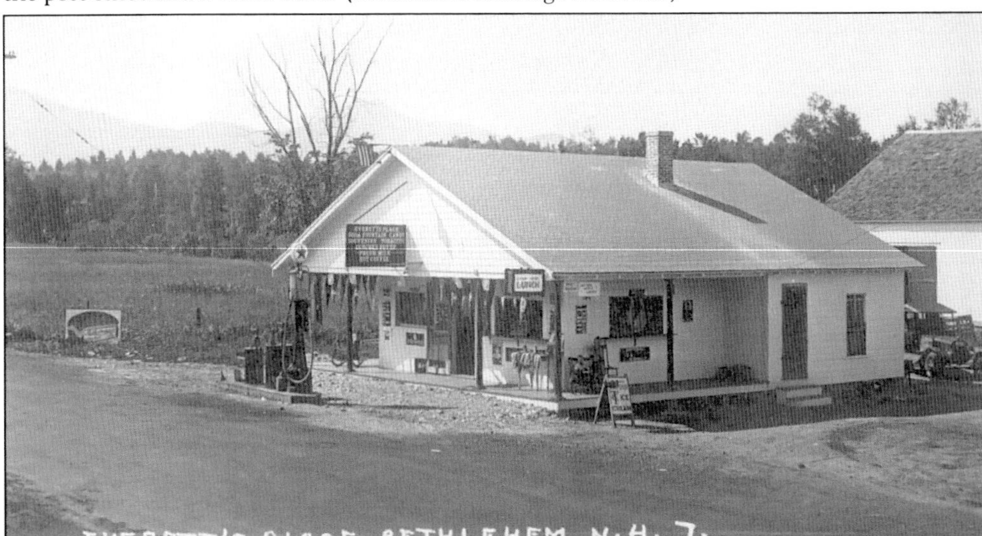

Everett's Place was a popular roadhouse located opposite the Pierce Bridge Station. The 1929 directory advertisement stated, "Good things to eat. Good music. Meals at all hours." Everett Stone was the owner for years. He later sold the place to Joseph Williamson. Everett's burned in 1941. (Paul Hudson.)

Five

A Close-knit Community

With the turning of the leaves, summer visitors and residents left for home and school. The hotels were closed up and readied for the winter, and the owners traveled south to their other operations in North Carolina or Florida. The suddenly deserted Bethlehem might have been as forlorn as a ballroom the morning after a magnificent party.

Not so. Relieved of responsibilities toward visitors, residents drew together during the winter. School and church and community organizations were the common interests around which they met. The cliché of small town life—everyone knew everybody (or was related to them)—was true.

It is still true today, to a large extent. Neighbors help each other. They watch each other's houses and look out for the kids. Volunteerism is strong, most notably in the fire department, which has always operated with volunteers. Volunteers help in the school, the library, the development association, the heritage society, the churches, as well as with community and youth programs. Despite differences that arise, Bethlehem has a strong sense of community.

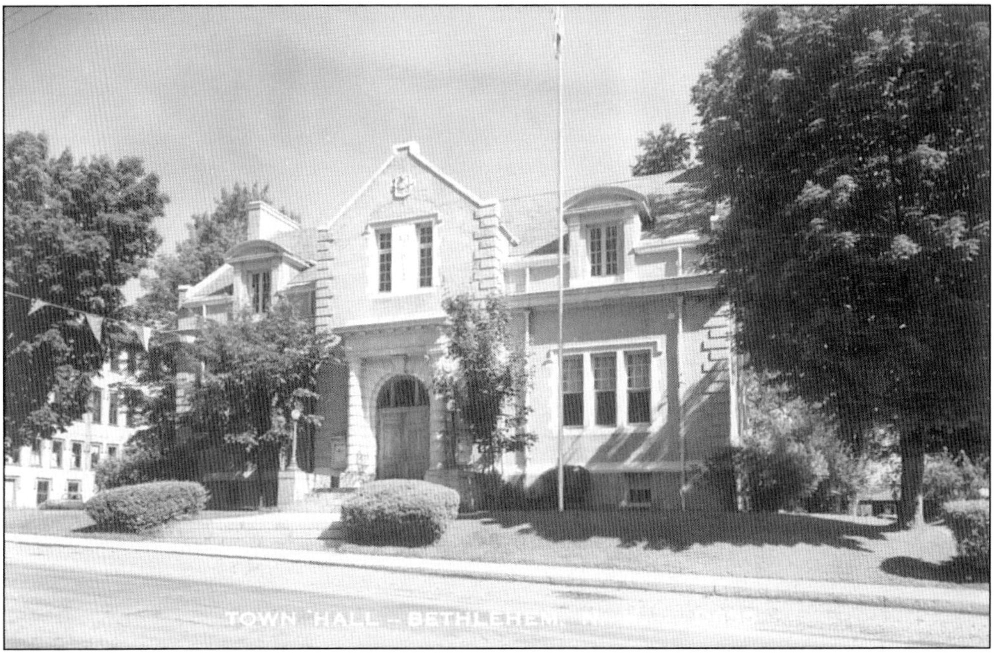

Bethlehem's town building is a beautiful landmark built in 1912. Isaac Cruft's nephew, Gen. George Cruft, gave the building to the town as a gift. The library, the fire and police stations, and the town offices are housed there. (David Olson.)

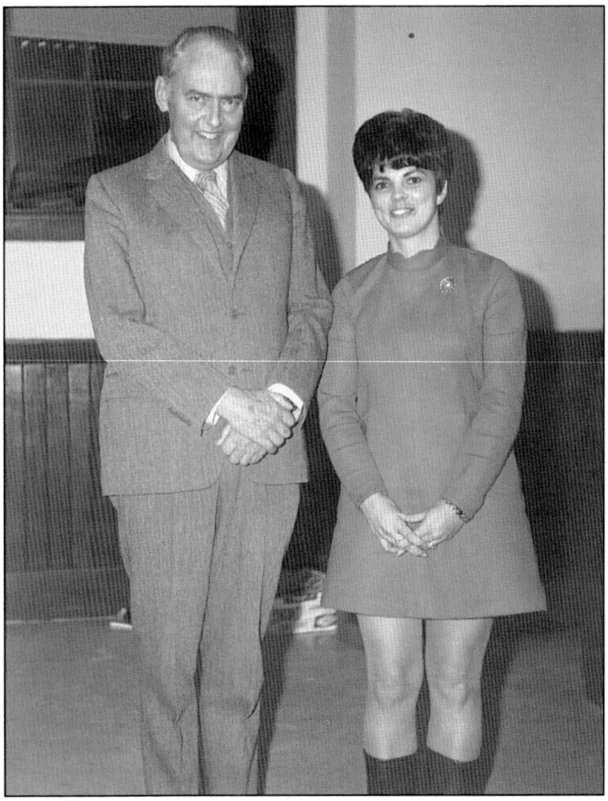

In 1971, George Noyes stepped down from 40 years as town clerk, and Myrtle Ledoux stepped in. (Marilyn Noyes Carmen, photograph by Al MacBain.)

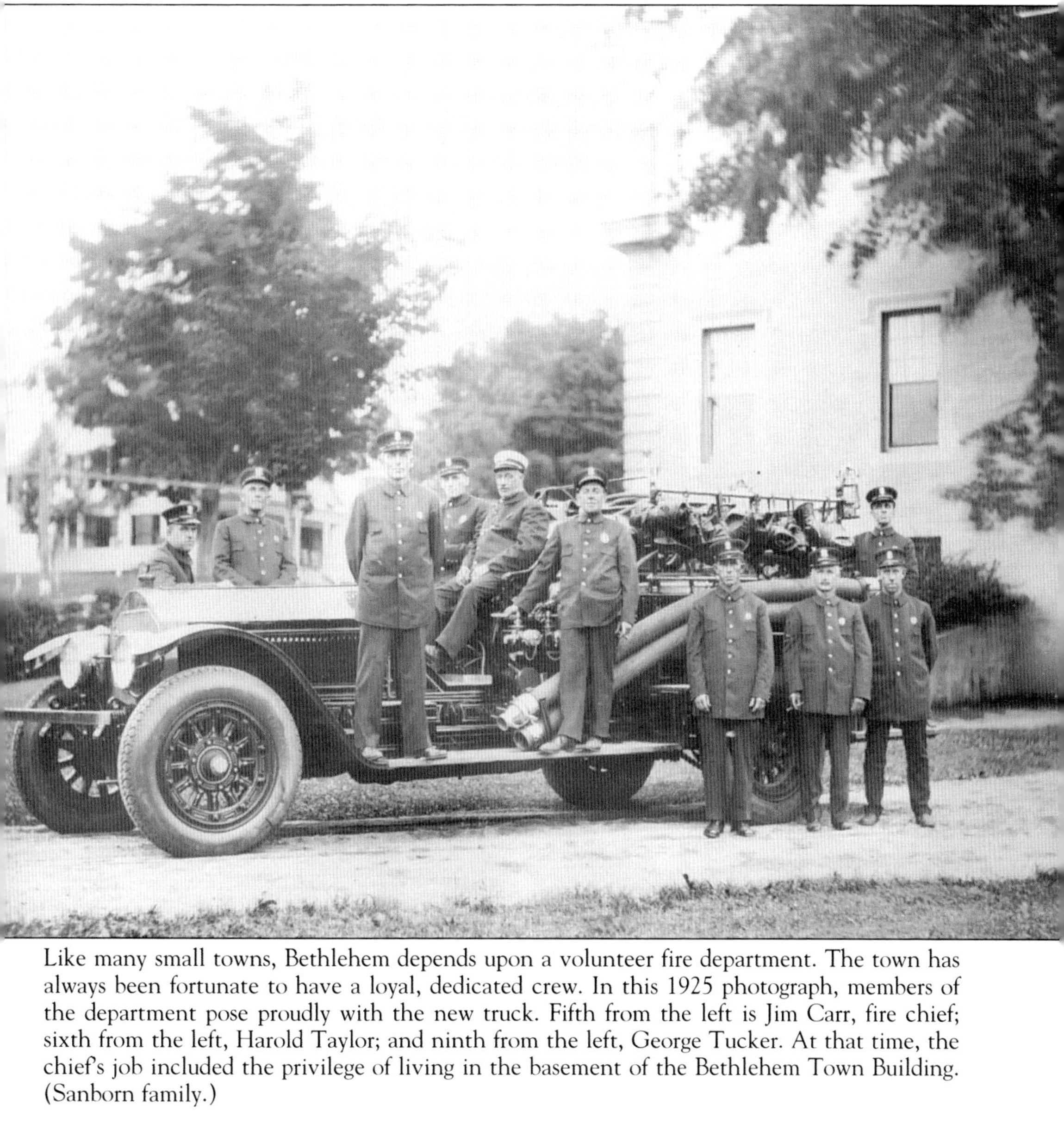

Like many small towns, Bethlehem depends upon a volunteer fire department. The town has always been fortunate to have a loyal, dedicated crew. In this 1925 photograph, members of the department pose proudly with the new truck. Fifth from the left is Jim Carr, fire chief; sixth from the left, Harold Taylor; and ninth from the left, George Tucker. At that time, the chief's job included the privilege of living in the basement of the Bethlehem Town Building. (Sanborn family.)

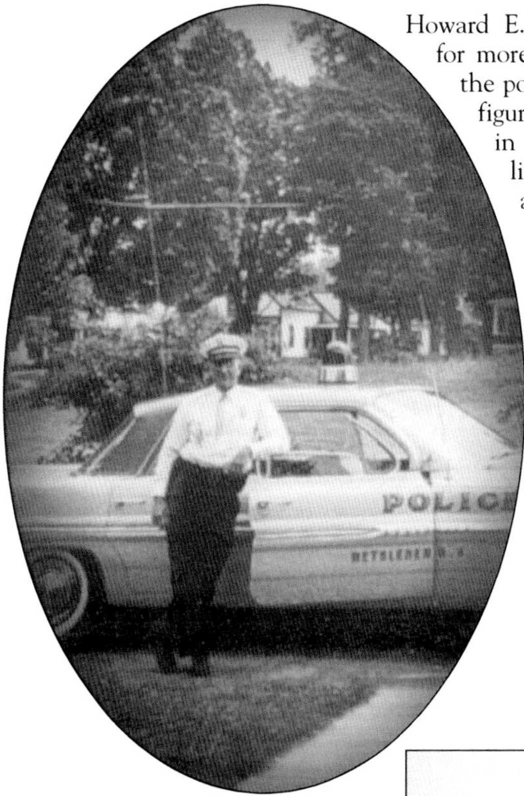

Howard E. Sanborn provided community leadership for more than 50 years in his dual role as chief of the police and fire departments. He was a familiar figure around town in his fedora hat or parked in his cruiser, keeping an eye on the town. A lifelong Bethlehem resident, he died at the age of 81 in 1996, while still in office. The fire station was renamed the Howard E. Sanborn Memorial Station in his honor. (Clare Brown.)

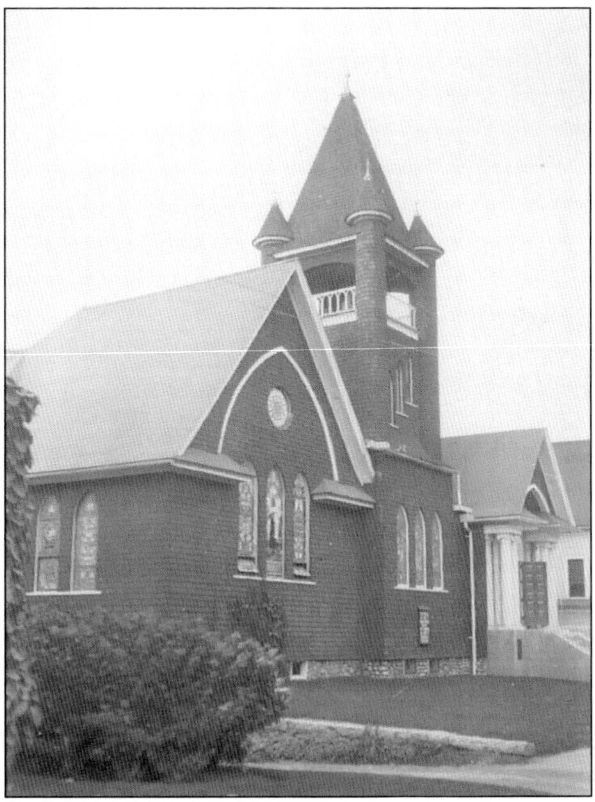

The Methodists built a church on Main Street in Bethlehem c. 1830. For 35 years, the Congregationalists shared the building, using it on alternate Sundays. In 1901, a new church was built on the site. Its unusual design and shingled siding reflect the eclectic architectural design used in Bethlehem during that period. The church has beautiful stained-glass windows, many of which were donated in memory of members' loved ones. The church holds services year-round. (Bethlehem Heritage Museum.)

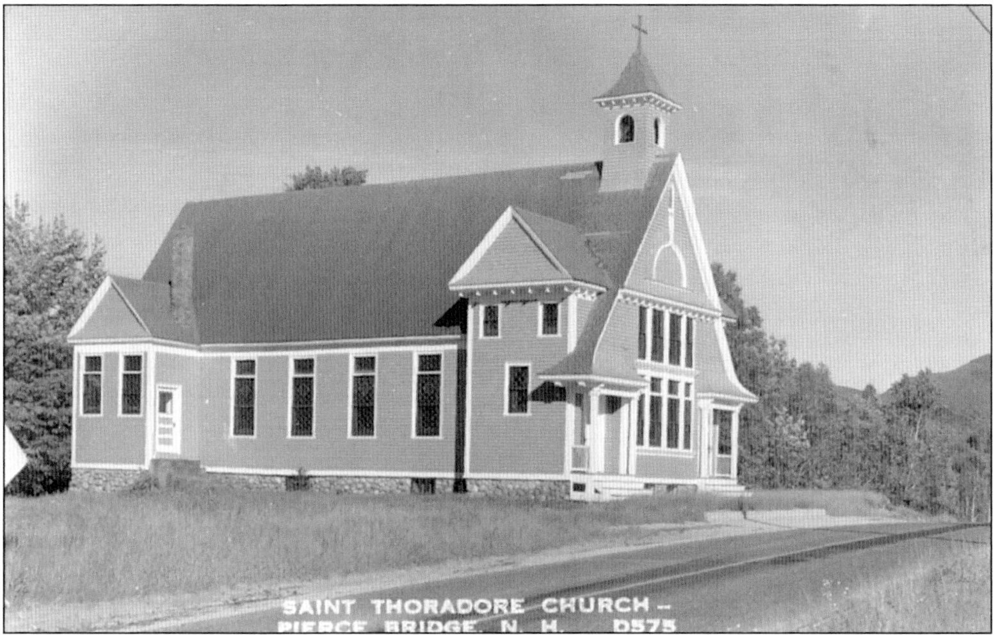

In 1895, St. Theodore's, the first Catholic church in town, opened at Pierce Bridge. (Olive Jackson Whittier.)

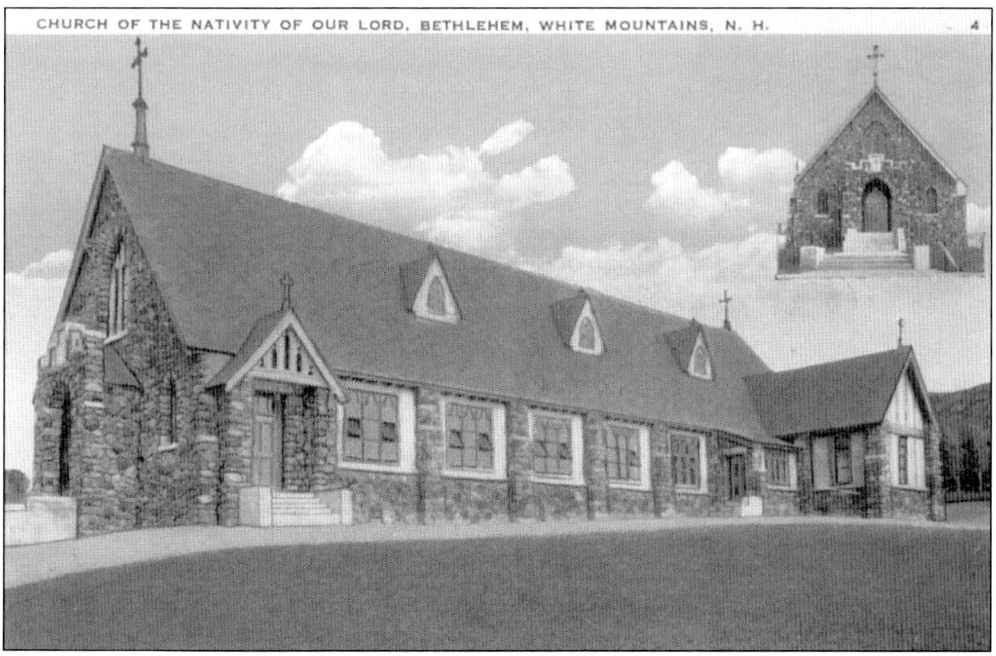

It is believed that wealthy Cuban visitors in the 1920s were influential in helping local Catholics build a permanent church. In 1928, Christ the King was built on the corner of Cottage Street. Interestingly, there are also Catholic churches built of local fieldstone in Littleton and Twin Mountain. Services are held at Christ the King in the summer. (Olive Jackson Whittier.)

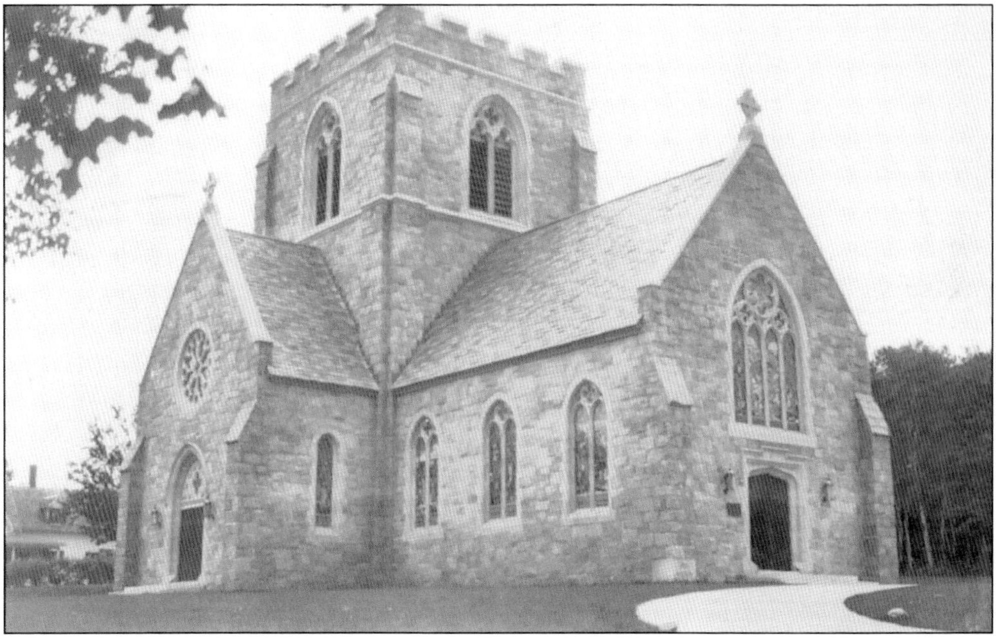

Alvin Ivie built the Ivie Memorial Chapel in 1930 as a memorial to his daughter, Florence Ivie Abbott. The style of the church is English Perpendicular Gothic, and its features include hand-carved pews, European stained-glass windows, and a pipe organ. Currently owned by the Episcopal Diocese, the church is used by the White Mountain School for special events. (Paul Hudson.)

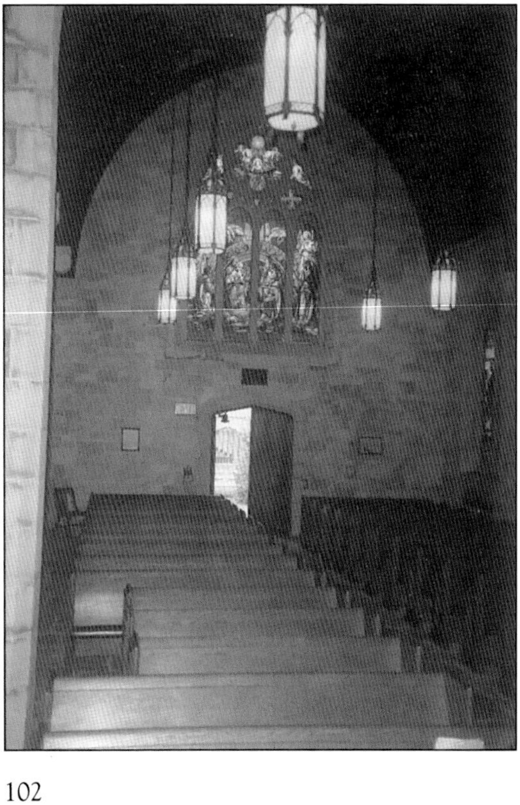

An interior view of the Ivie Memorial Chapel shows the hand-carved pews, stonework, and the elegant light fixtures. (Joyce Donadio.)

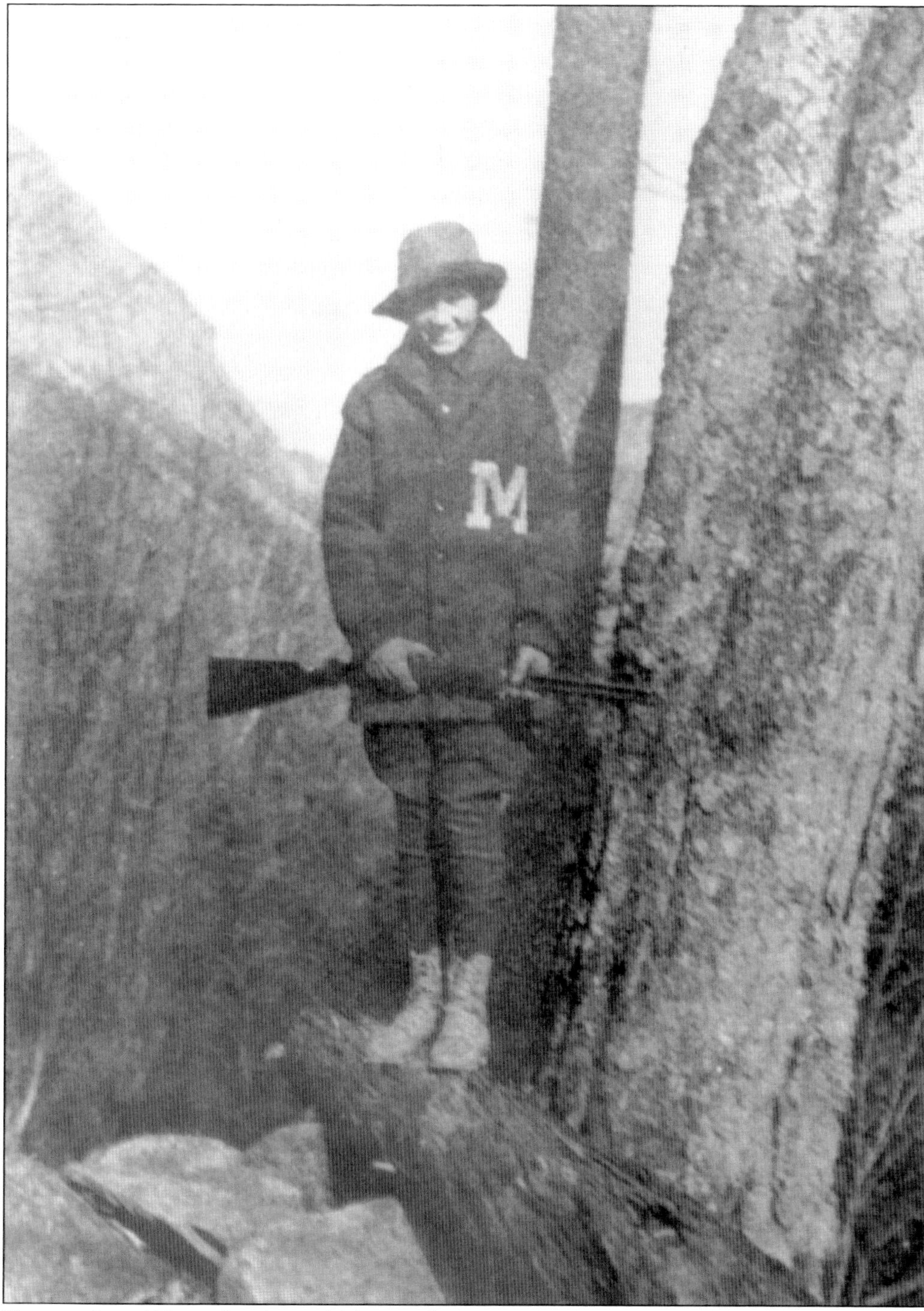

Florence Ivie Abbott, daughter of Alvin and Henrietta Ivie, was the wife of Karl Abbott, owner of the Upland Terrace. Married in 1918, she was the mother of two children: Frank Jr. and Gladys. Tragically, she died of complications from surgery on June 7, 1924. Pictures of her, such as this one on the way to Lonesome Lake, reveal both her beauty and her vibrant personality. (Bethlehem Heritage Museum.)

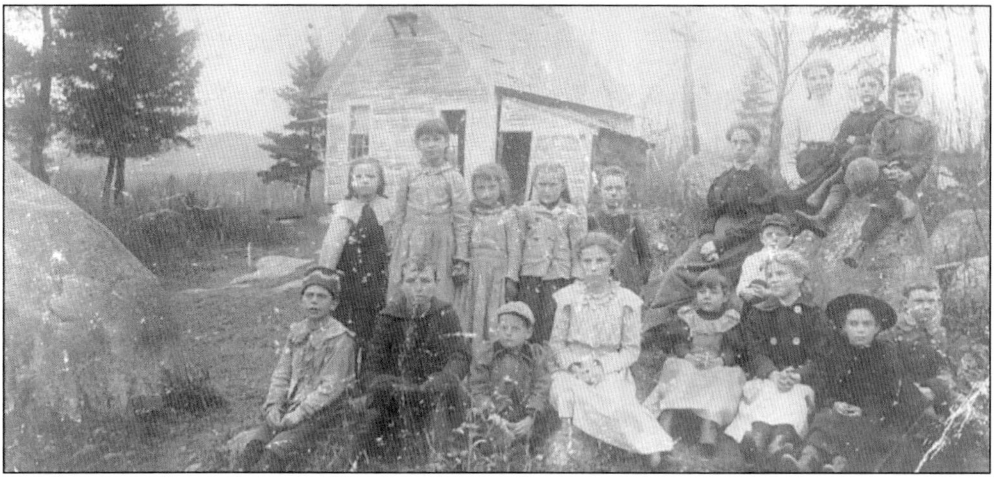

Alder Brook was a little community on the Whitefield Road in Bethlehem, with a train depot, logging operation, post office and one-room schoolhouse. No evidence of this community remains today. Posed outside the school, from left to right, are the following: (front row) Perry Plant, Elmer Plant, Daisy Eastman, Jean McIntire, unidentified, Leah McIntire, Mary Cotnoir, and Prosper Cotnoir; (middle row) Elmer Miller; (back row) Leona Cotnoir, Lettie Plant, Gertrude Plant, Jenny Donaghy, Fred Cotnoir, teacher Erma McIntire, Nola McIntire, Alfred Kay, and Ernest Johnson. (Wayne Miller.)

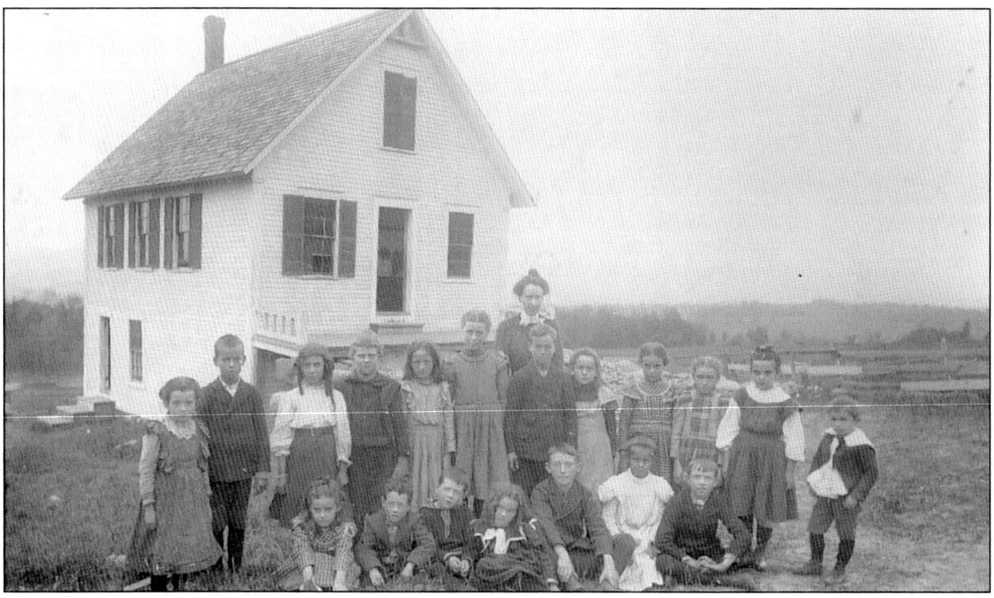

In 1885, Bethlehem had nine school districts with eleven common schools and one graded school. This one-room schoolhouse was on Lewis Hill Road. Hattie Whitcomb Taylor wrote about carrying her lunch in a tin pail, drinking from a communal water dipper, and making frequent trips to the "necessary" so as to sneak in a few extra slides down the hill on her milk pan. Shown, from left to right, are the following: (front row) unidentified, Fay Fitzgerald, unidentified, Marguerite Fitzgerald, Ray Fitzgerald, Molly Abby, and unidentified; (back row) unidentified, Verdi Whitcomb, Florence Johnson, Earl Howland, Geneva Drohen, Emma Howland, unidentified, Fannie Seymour, unidentified, Eva Guy, Inez Whitcomb, and Ray Guy. (Ruth Whitcomb.)

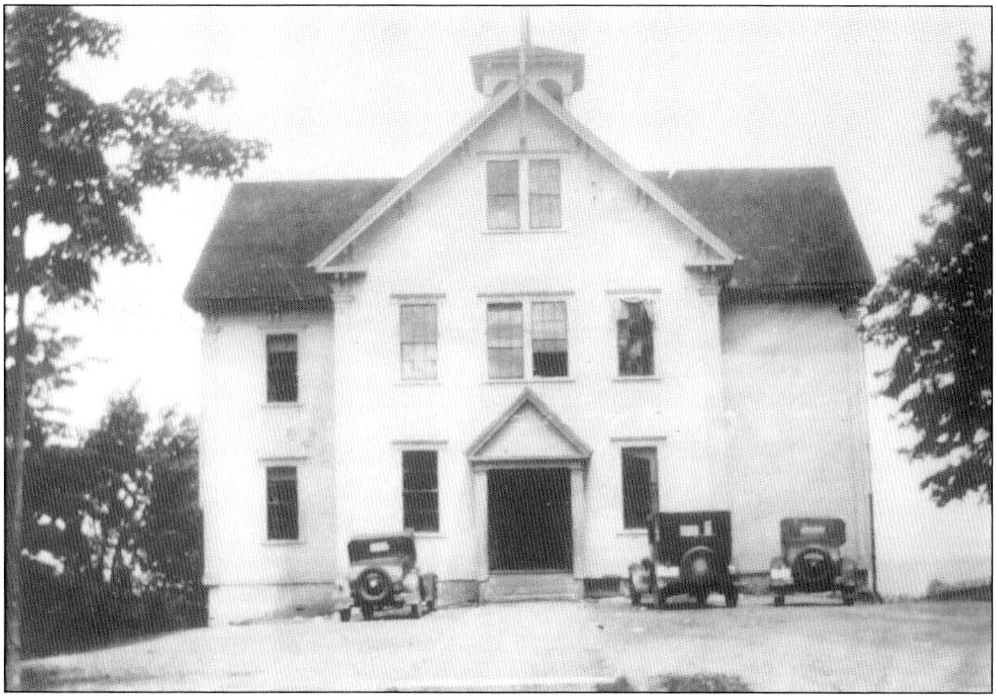

The original graded school was a wooden structure. High school students went here, too. (Bethlehem Heritage Museum.)

MUSIC,

ORCHESTRA.

PRAYER,

REV. W. P. TAYLOR.

QUARTETTE, - - - - - - Selected

G. D. PRICE, W. T. CARLETON,

M. D. BARROWS, W. E. MERRILL.

Dartmouth Quartette.

PRIZE SPEAKING,

(For Cruft Prizes.)

SELECTION,

DARTMOUTH QUARTETTE.

ESSAY, - - "The Sphere of the Drama."

VALEDICTORY,

MISS CLAUDIA M. THOMPSON.

SELECTION,

DARTMOUTH QUARTETTE.

AWARDING OF DIPLOMA AND PRIZES.

ORCHESTRA.

Prize Speaking

For two prizes given by Gen. G. T. Cruft.

First Prize $3. Second Prize $2.

THE POLISH BOY,

MISS MINNIE E. CRANE.

THE LEAK IN THE DYKE,

MISS SARA E. ROCKINGHAM.

MRS. CAUDLE ON "BUTTONS,"

MISS MAUD H. TUCKER.

JUSTICE IN LEADVILLE,

MISS MATTIE TUCKER.

DEATHBED OF BENEDICT ARNOLD.

BENSON P. WILKINS.

JUDGES.

DR. H. A. HILDRETH. W. H. PRESBY,

MRS. J. K. BARRETT.

The first high school graduation was held in 1889, with six graduates. Bethlehem took its graduations seriously and did not stint on ceremony no matter how small the class. This elaborate graduation event was held in 1891 for the benefit of one student, Claudia M. Thompson. (Bethlehem Heritage Museum.)

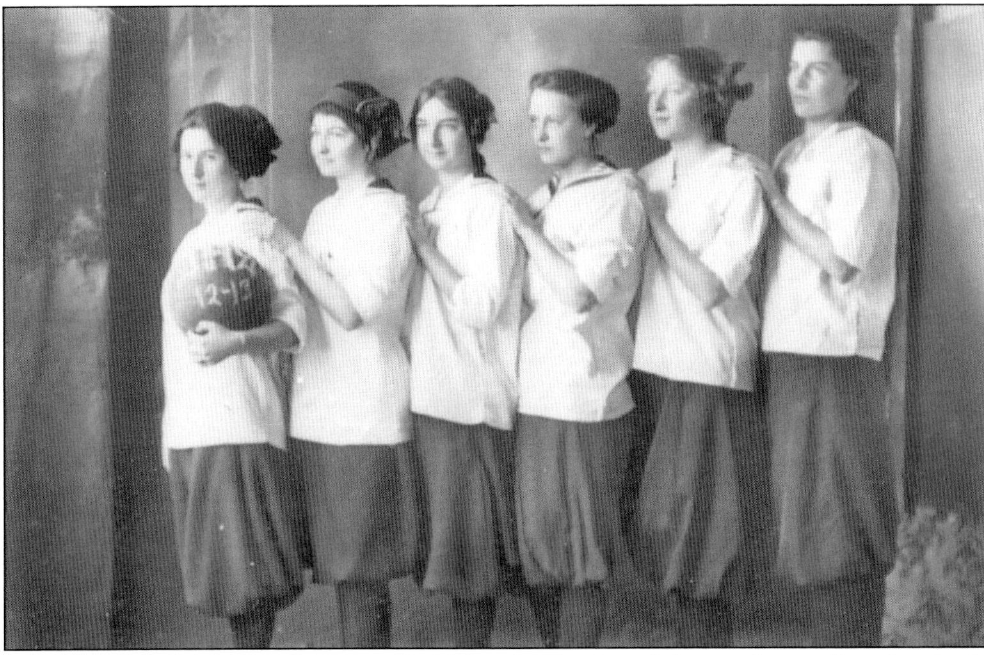

Sports have always been a priority in Bethlehem's schools and despite the small student body, teams have done well in basketball, soccer, skiing, and field hockey. Here, the 1911–1912 girls' basketball team poses for the camera. Girls from the 1959–1960 team remember playing against Orford High School. At that time, Orford's gym was in a barn; when the crowd got excited during a game, the cows would moo. A potbellied stove was placed under one hoop, which meant great care was needed when going for that basket. (Bethlehem Heritage Museum.)

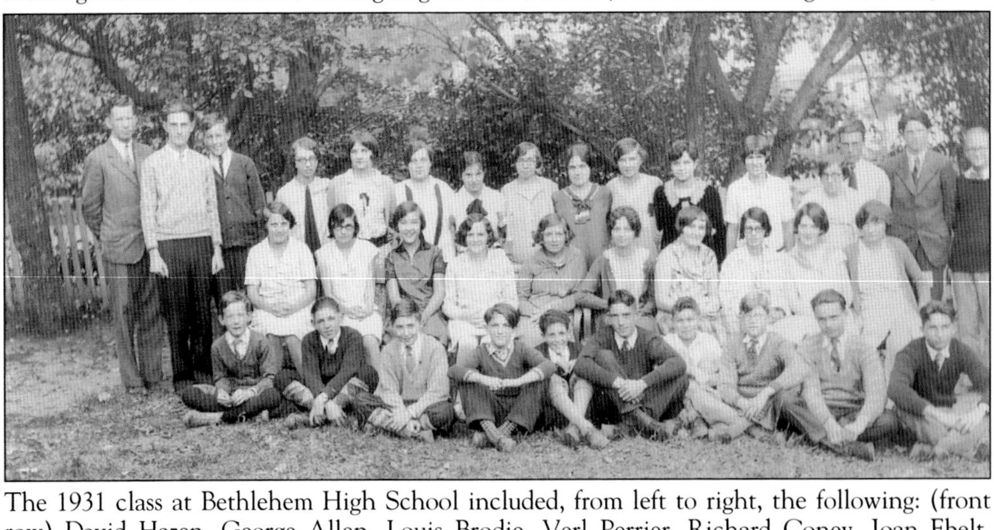

The 1931 class at Bethlehem High School included, from left to right, the following: (front row) David Hazen, George Allen, Louis Brodie, Verl Perrier, Richard Coney, Joan Ebelt, unidentified, Robert Turner, Victor Whitcomb, and Elvin Miller; (middle row) Olive Jackson, Dora Plante, Martha Bishop, Avis Buckler, Lillian Allen, Muriel Miller, Leona Sanborn, Edith Edgell, Pauline Hazen, and Marion Sanborn; (back row) Professor Cummings, Francis Beaton, Elvin Blaney, Alice Hoyt, Eleanor Jackson, Helen Kahler, Marjorie Blandin, Miss Crane, Miss Mann, Alice McDonnell, Charlotte Covell, Dorothy Reid, Katherine Seace, John Garneau, Wendall McLeor, and Henry Colby. (Clare Brown.)

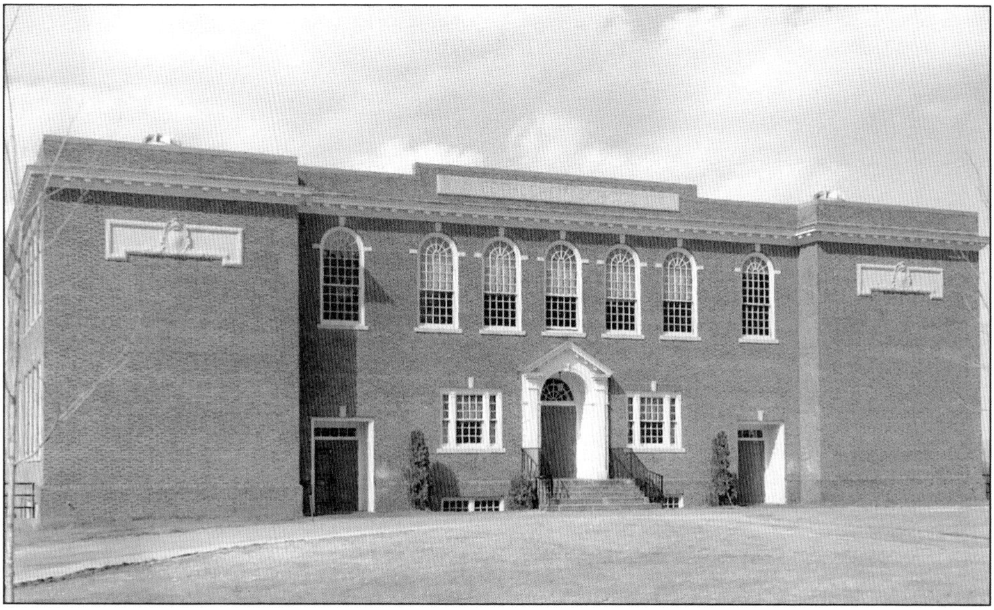

In 1931, a beautiful brick school was built and all the common schools were consolidated. Today, this school houses kindergarten through grade six. The junior and high school students go to Profile School, along with children from Sugar Hill, Easton, and Franconia. (Bethlehem Heritage Museum.)

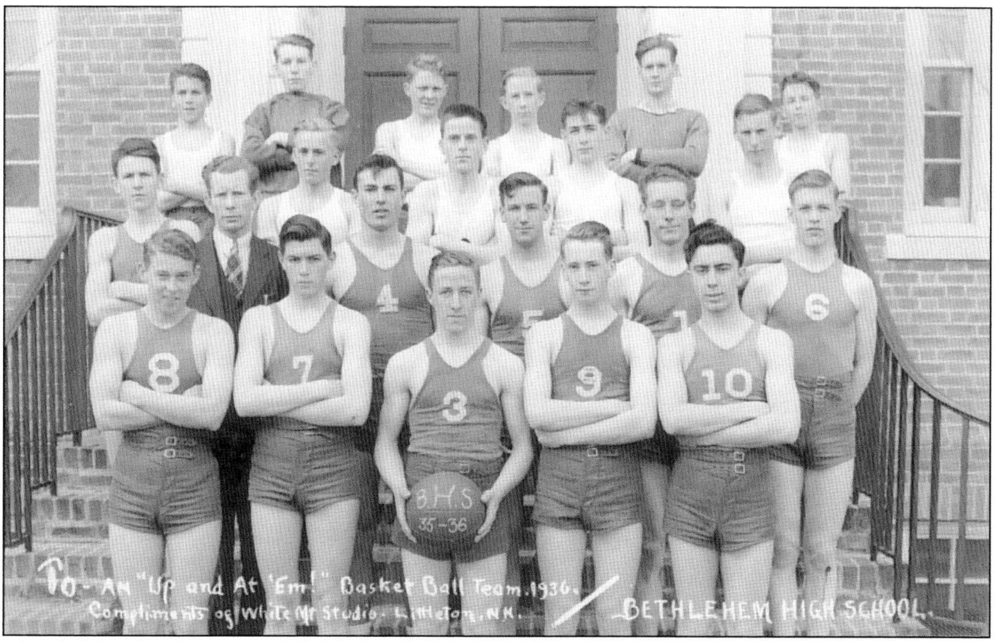

The 1936 boys' basketball team poses on the front steps of the school. Team members are, from left to right, the following: (first row) Harold Brown, Linwood Roy, Walter Drohen, Steve Currie, and William Roy; (second row) George Reid, Leslie Cummings, Fred Winterbottom, Arthur Blaney, George Tucker, and Tom Garneau; (third row) Donald Johnson, Ward Gardner, Gerald Wolcott, and James Newcombe; (fourth row) Henry Marcotte, Millard Clark, David Stone, Arthur Jobin, Douglas Cole, and ? Hatch. (Paul Hudson.)

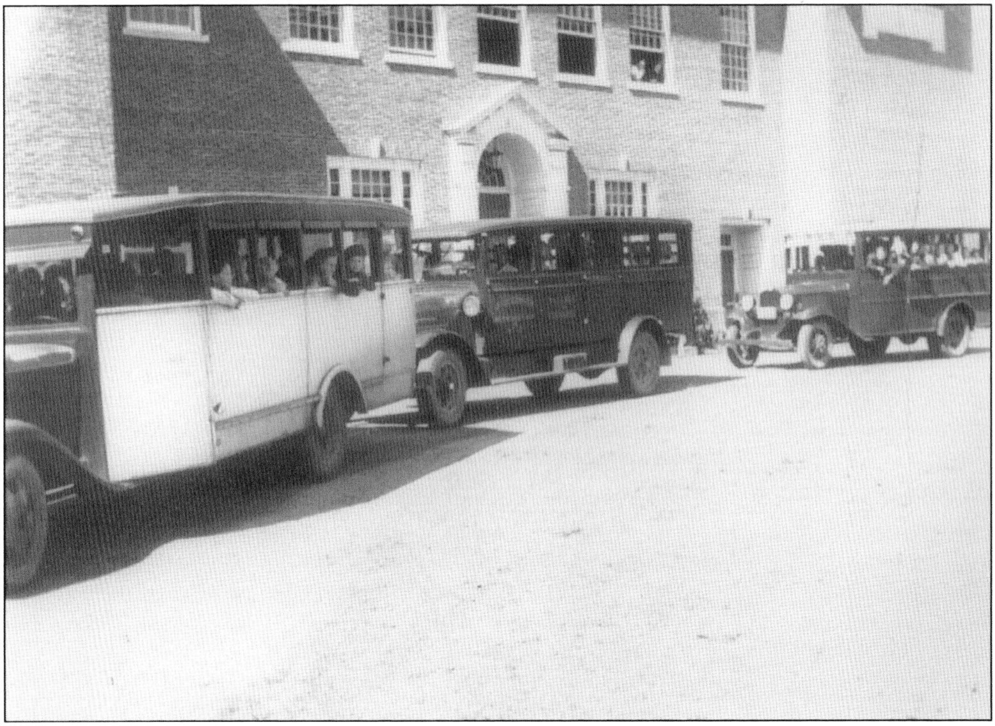

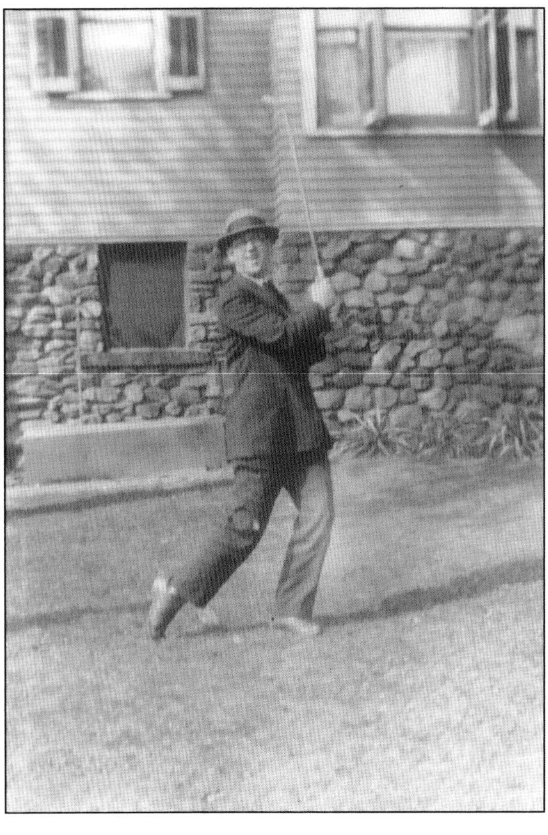

Quaint school buses line up at the Bethlehem School. The one on the left is headed for Kimball Hill, and the one on the right is the Pierce Bridge bus. (Muriel Brown.)

Hundreds of Bethlehem children have been able to go to college due to the generosity of Jason Somerville. Jason Somerville first came to Bethlehem as a small child. His family lived on the Beck Farm on West Farm Road, and he later owned a cottage on Pinewood Avenue. He supported himself through landscaping and odd jobs, and frequently performed as a musician in the hotels. In later life, Somerville was reclusive and extremely frugal, so when he set up a scholarship fund in 1954, many people were surprised. Now the fund is worth over $1 million, and each year the interest is distributed. In 1972, Somerville died at the age of 81. (Clare Brown, Morrell Crawford photograph.)

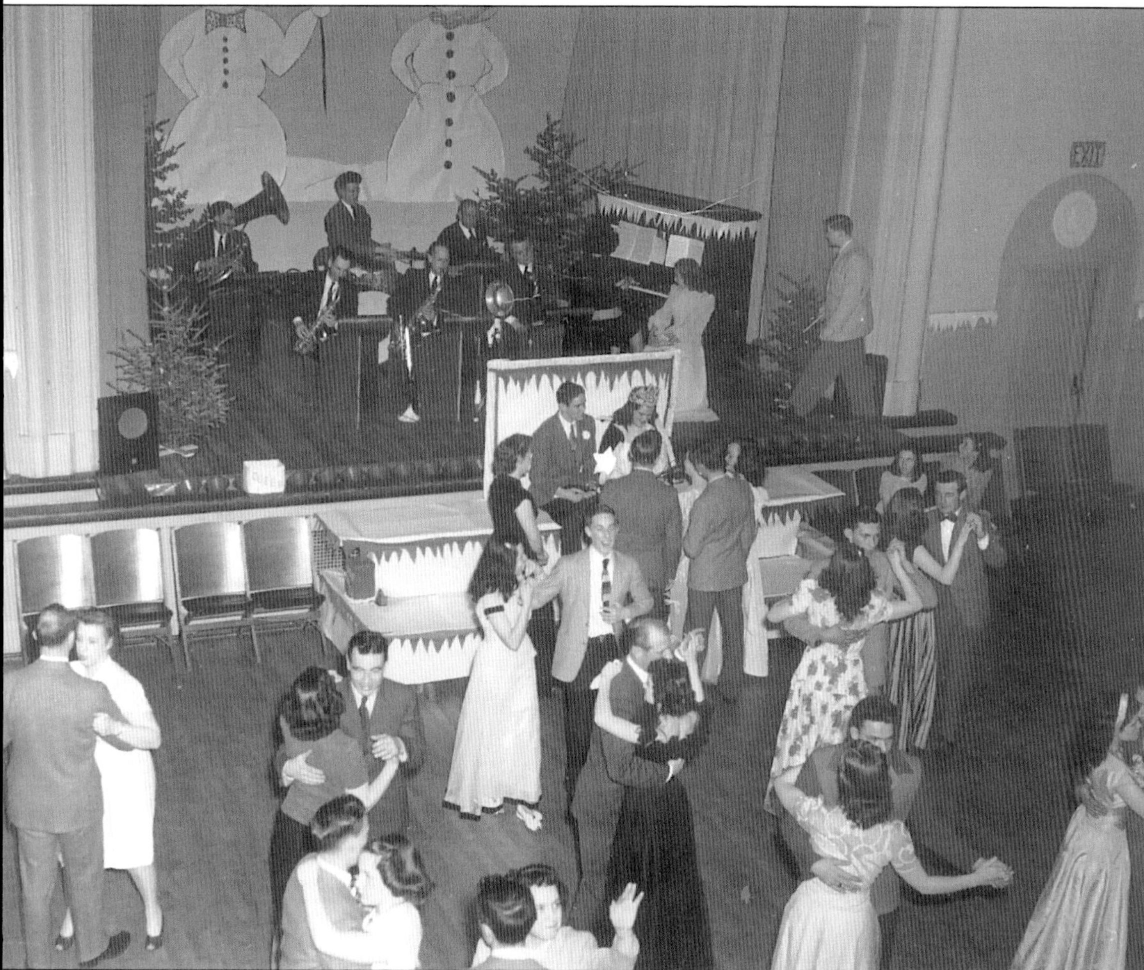

Bethlehem High School students enjoy the culmination of the 1948 Winter Carnival—the Winter Carnival Dance complete with a queen, Patsy Bonardi. (Bethlehem Heritage Museum.)

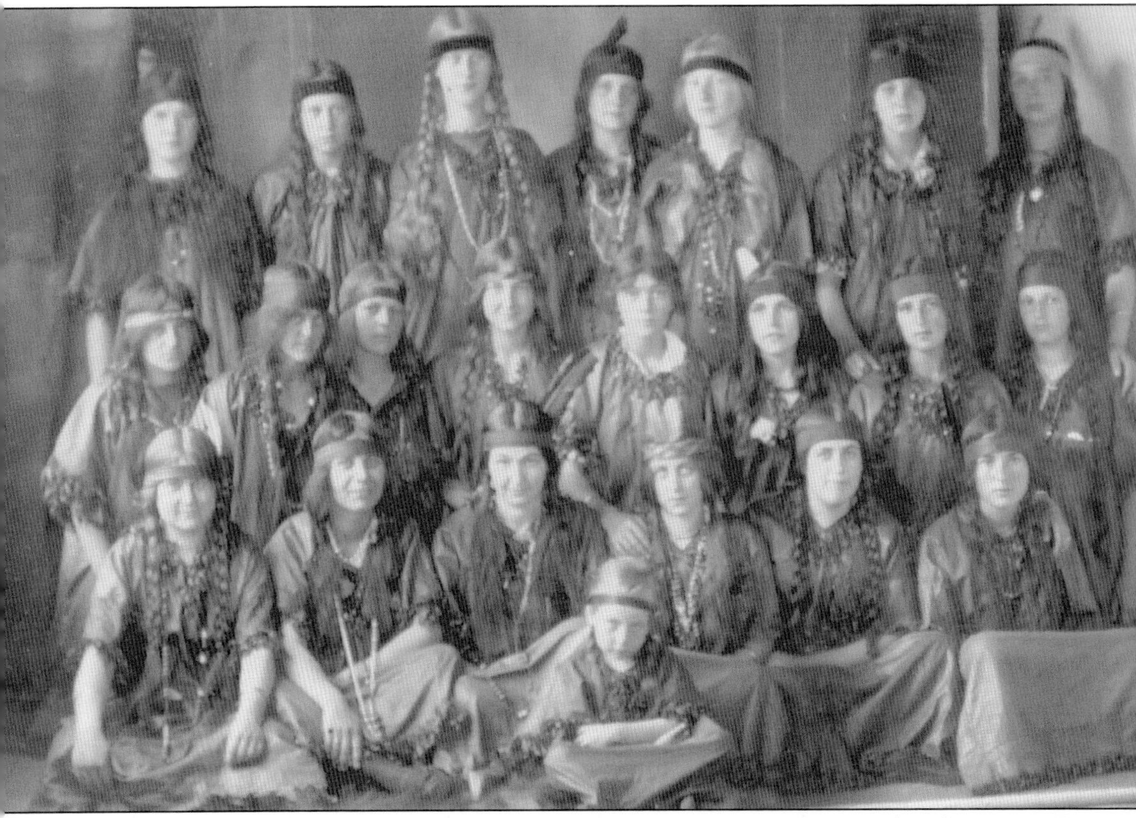

The local chapter of the Camp Fire Girls poses in this 1913 photograph. The Camp Fire Girls learned useful and interesting skills under the categories of Nature Lore, Camp Craft, Indian Craft, Wood Craft, Home Craft, and Hand Craft. Each summer they spent a week at nearby Forest Lake, camping, swimming, boating, and practicing their new skills. (Bethlehem Heritage Museum.)

Verdi Whitcomb was one of 53 Bethlehem men and women who served in World War I. His family has lived on Whitcomb Hill, at the top of Lewis Hill, since the early 1800s and had a farm there until after World War II. Whitcomb wrote a song in 1917 called "The Girl and the Country That I Loved," and registered it with the Library of Congress. He was also a gifted amateur photographer, and the Heritage Museum is fortunate to have a small album of his 1913 photographs. Whitcomb married Helen Hay, who succumbed to tuberculosis shortly after giving birth to their son, Victor Whitcomb. Whitcomb survived the war but fell victim to the flu epidemic that followed shortly afterward. (Ruth Whitcomb.)

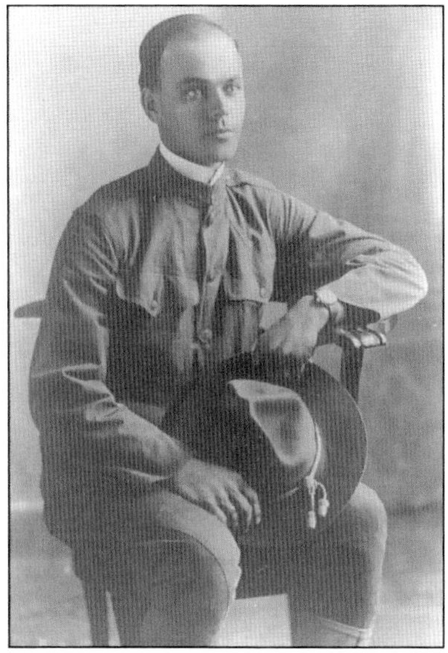

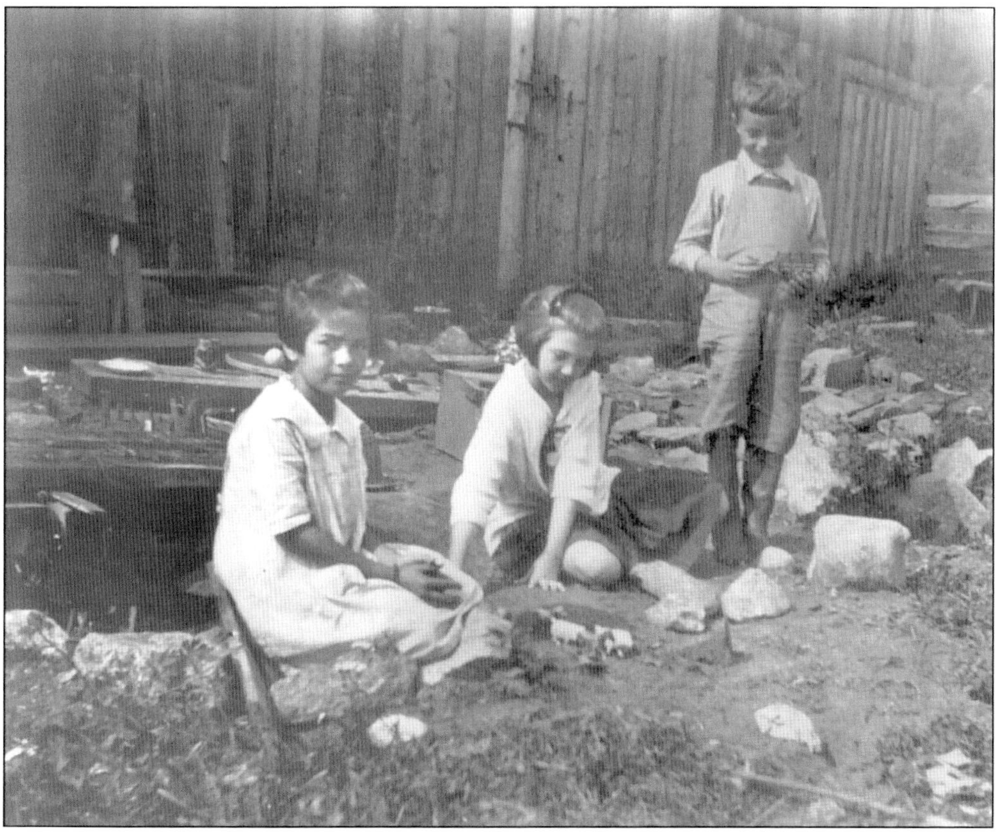

Victor Whitcomb, son of Verdi and Helen Whitcomb, had a chicken farm with 700 New Hampshire Reds until World War II. He sold eggs as far away as Faneuil Hall in Boston. After the war, he worked in various occupations, serving as Bethlehem road agent for a time. He and his wife, Ruth Whitcomb, were musicians and played with local bands. In this 1918 photograph, Whitcomb, Persis Johnson, and a cousin play some music on a sunny day. (Marilyn Johnson.)

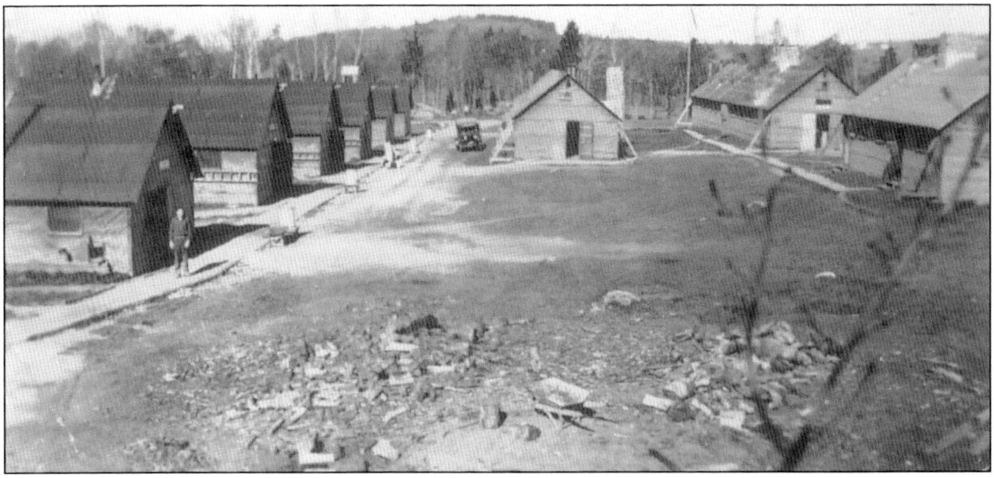

Located off Muchmore Road, Civilian Conservation Corps Camp No. 153, Pierce Bridge or Gale River Camp, was one of 17 camps operating in the White Mountains during the period from 1933 to 1942. Men enrolling in the camps received $30 per month, plus food, board, medical care, and clothing. Pierce Bridge projects included bridge and campground building, moving telephone poles up to Cherry Mountain and Garfield Lookout, forest improvement in the White Mountain National Forest, and road building. One memorable break in the hard work was a visit from actress Bette Davis, who stayed for supper and visited with the men for several hours afterward. The camp's foundations are still visible in the woods. (Bethlehem Heritage Museum.)

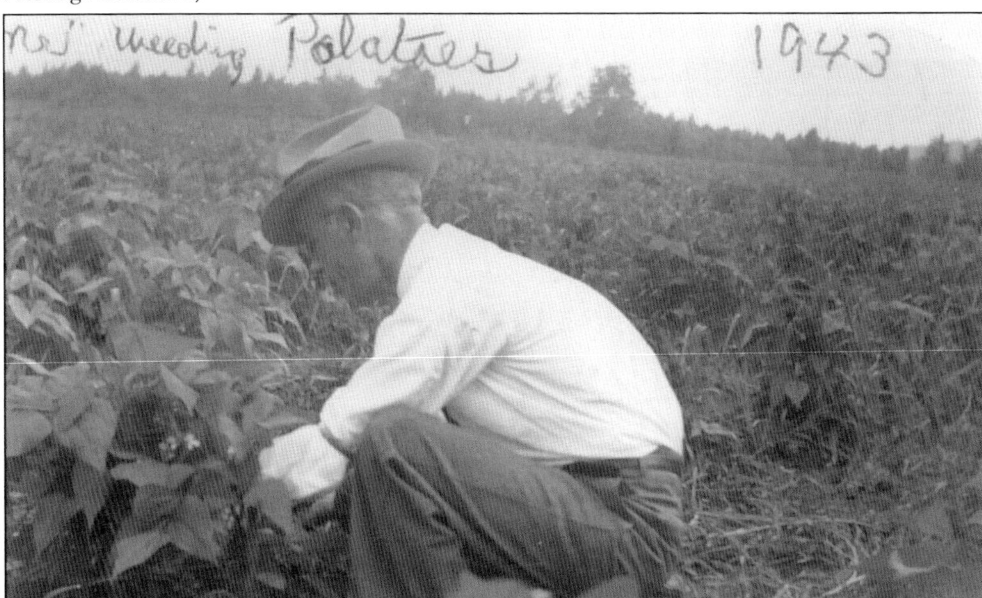

In 1943, the Maplewood closed for the war and the caddies worked in victory gardens instead of carrying golf clubs. In this photograph, camp director Norman Franzeim takes a turn at weeding. In 1943, the camp raised 550,000 pounds of potatoes. In 1942, the hotel dedicated 10 percent of its gross receipts to the purchase of war bonds and stamps. All 140 employees donated 10 percent of their wages for the same. Manager Howard Dalton gave the employees a 10 percent bonus, which also went for bonds and stamps. (Helen Cunningham.)

A total of 125 Bethlehem servicemen and two nurses served in World War II. On the home front, business was good, as travel restrictions made long hotel stays attractive. Bethlehem participated in the war effort with scrap drives, a Defense Committee, and United Service Organizations (USO) fund drives, which received generous donations from wealthy residents. (Muriel Brown.)

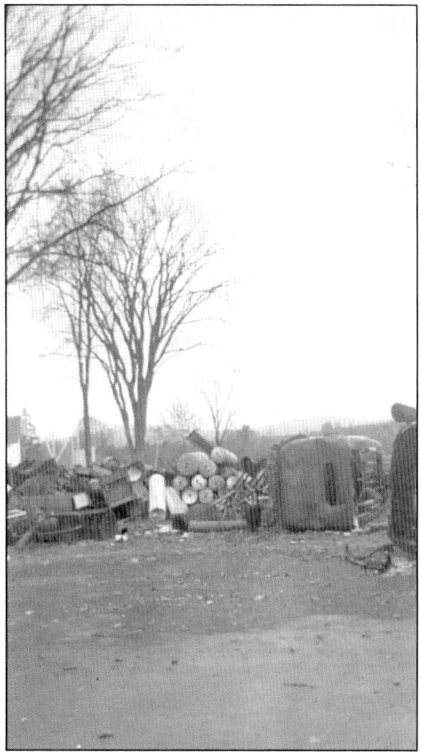

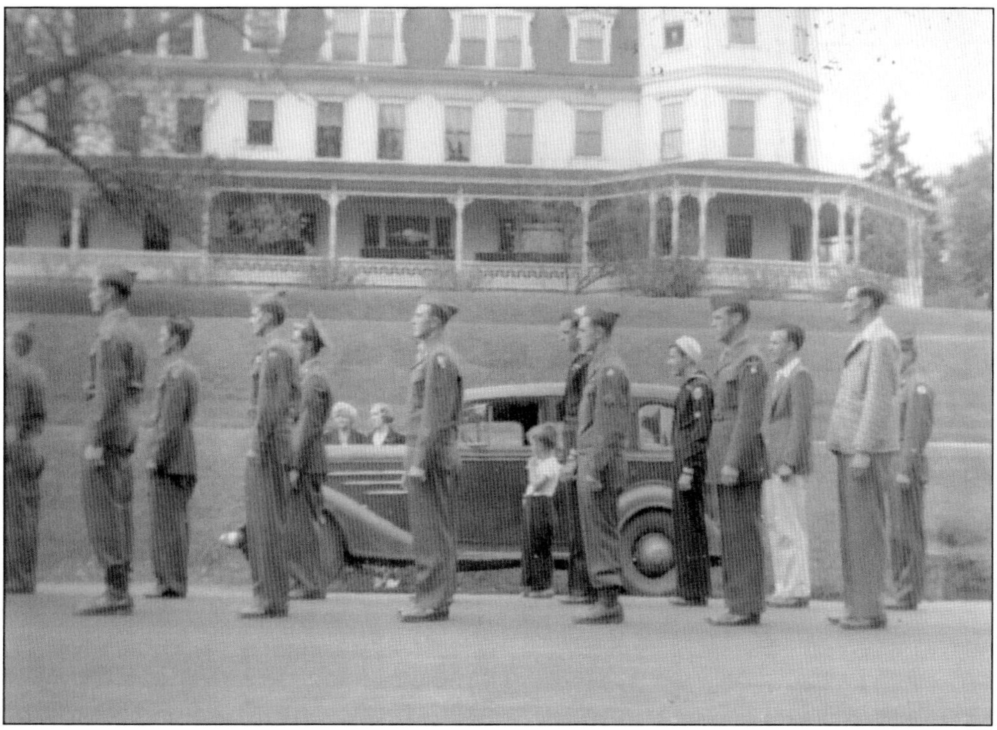

The 1947 Memorial Day parade pauses in front of the Upland Terrace. Bethlehem lost five soldiers in the war. (Bethlehem Heritage Museum.)

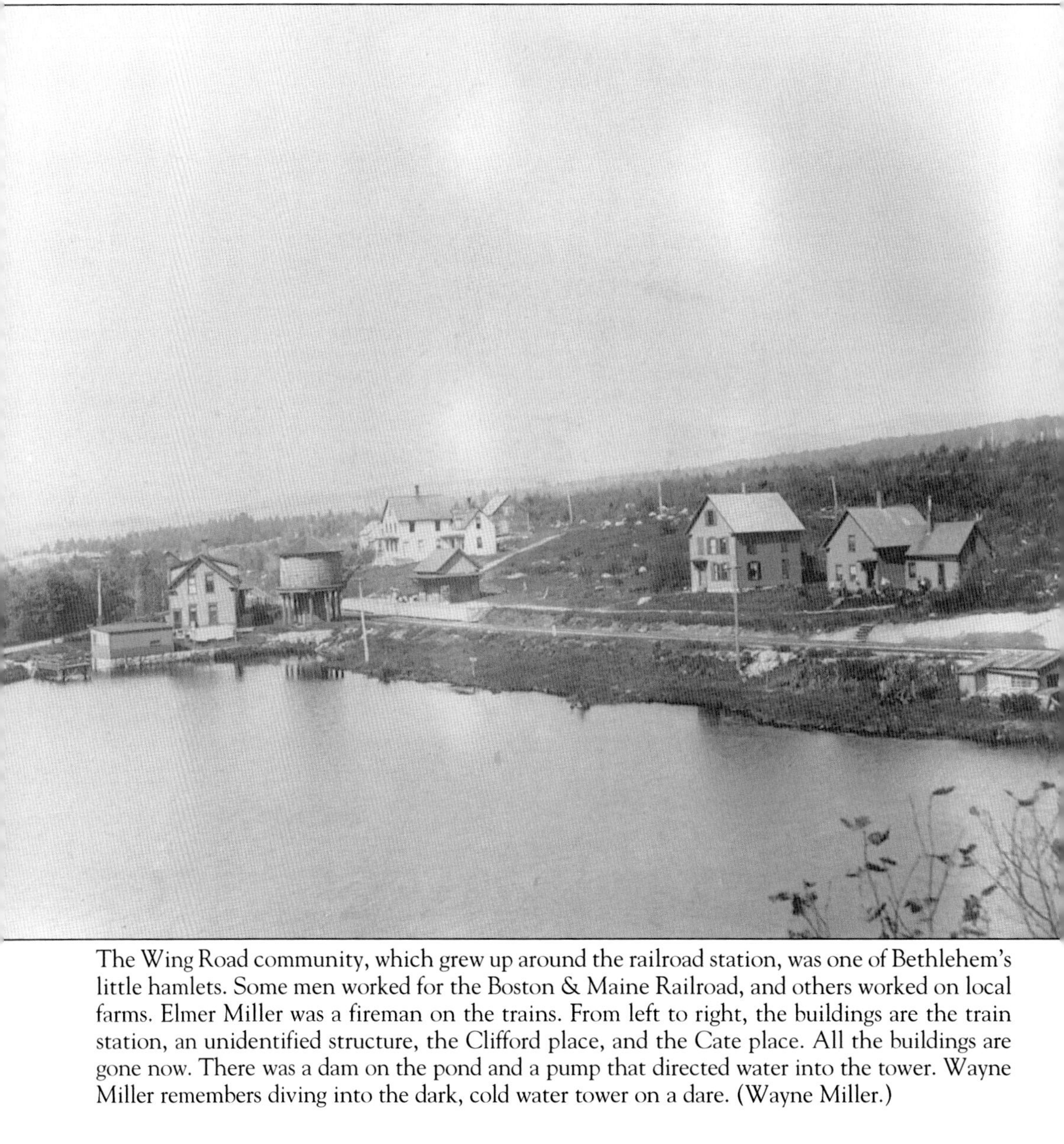

The Wing Road community, which grew up around the railroad station, was one of Bethlehem's little hamlets. Some men worked for the Boston & Maine Railroad, and others worked on local farms. Elmer Miller was a fireman on the trains. From left to right, the buildings are the train station, an unidentified structure, the Clifford place, and the Cate place. All the buildings are gone now. There was a dam on the pond and a pump that directed water into the tower. Wayne Miller remembers diving into the dark, cold water tower on a dare. (Wayne Miller.)

Six

Jewish Guests and Neighbors

In 1916, Isidor Lusher bought the Altamont Hotel. Quietly and without fanfare, Bethlehem was set on a course that would bring prosperity to the town through the Depression, the war, and the general decline of the hotel trade.

Hay fever relief was the key. Bethlehem's climate provided what thousands of Jewish New Yorkers needed. They began to arrive in droves. By 1923, five of the smaller hotels catered to the Jewish trade. By 1956, that number had risen to more than one dozen and included the major hotels—the Sinclair and the Maplewood. Jewish people bought summer homes in Bethlehem. Some became permanent residents and retired here. The Hay Fever Relief Association and the Sisterhood of the Bethlehem Congregation did many good works.

This era wound down in the late 1950s, with the advent of antihistamines, air-conditioning, other travel options, and the demise of the hotel vacation. In the late 1960s, another group, the Hassidim, began coming to Bethlehem. They bought the Alpine, the Highland, the Park View, and the Arlington. Only the Arlington is still operating.

The Bethlehem Jewish community is small now, but what remains is strong. The Bethlehem Hebrew Congregation is active year-round. And the Arlington is still thronged with cars and guests on August nights.

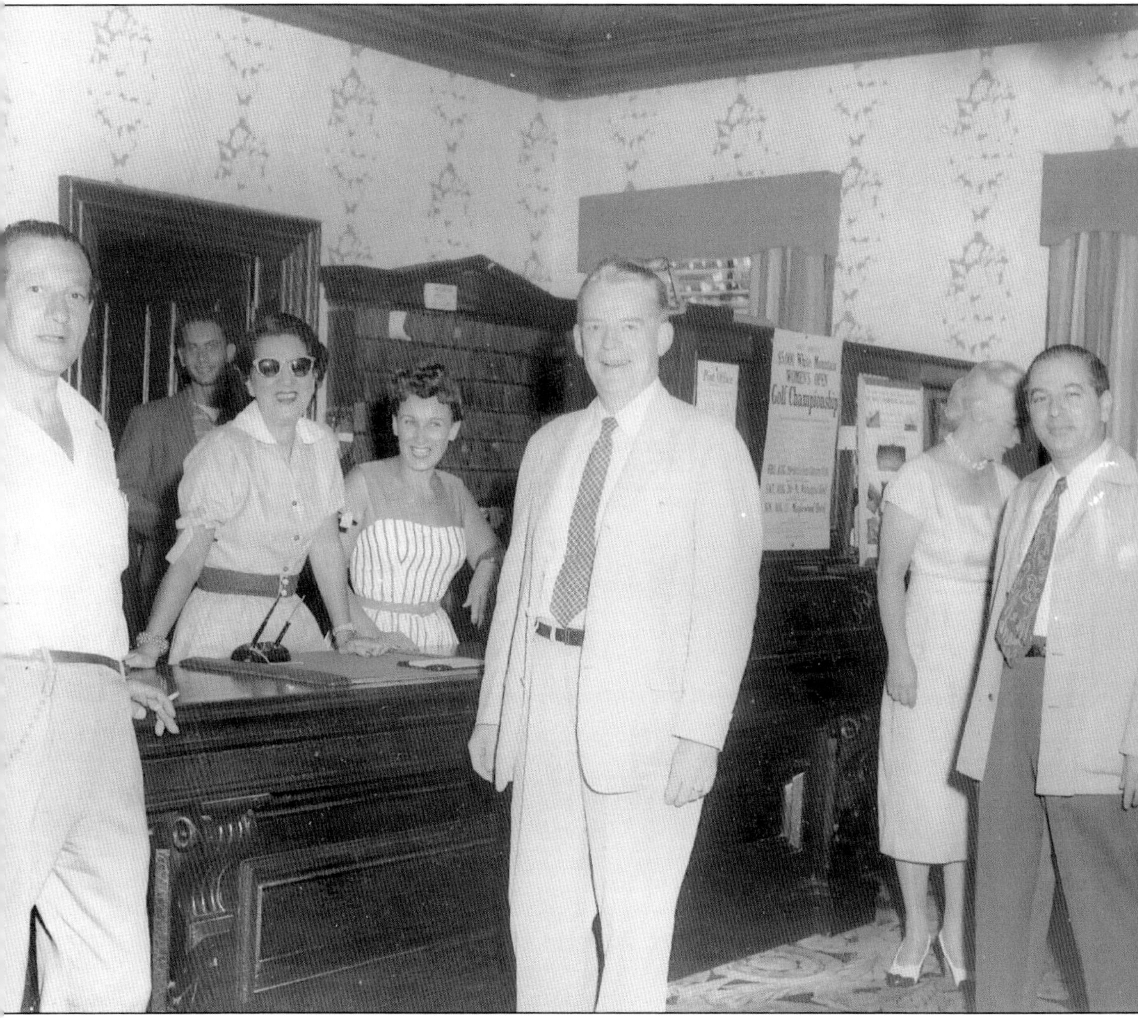

In the 1950s, the Sinclair was under the ownership of David Spiwack and Myron Herrman; the New Agassiz was also under their management. The Sinclair brochure promised "Days of Play . . . Nights of Romance." Pictured in 1951, from left to right, are Marcy Leondar, Pauline Leondar, social director Jerry ?, Dorothy Herrman, Gov. Lane Dwinell, Mrs. Dwinell, and Myron Herrman. (Bethlehem Heritage Museum.)

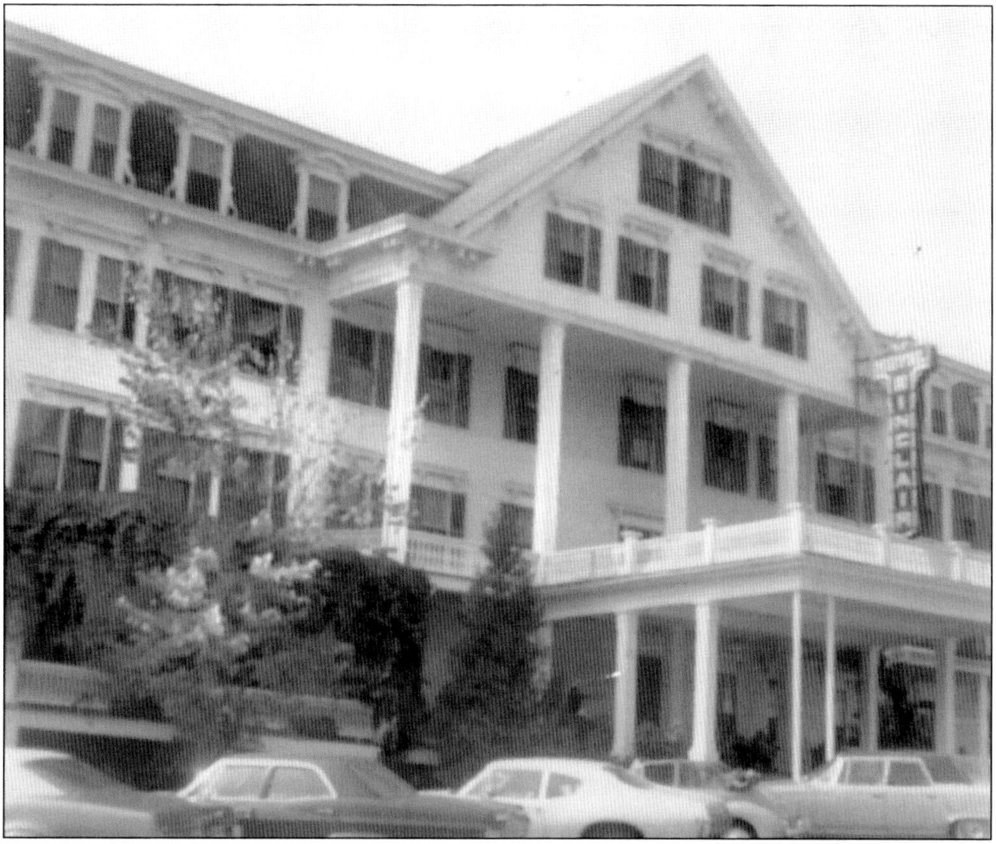

Most hotels had photographers on staff to provide souvenir photographs to guests. These photographs were printed on postcard stock and could be mailed to friends or relatives. (Bethlehem Heritage Museum.)

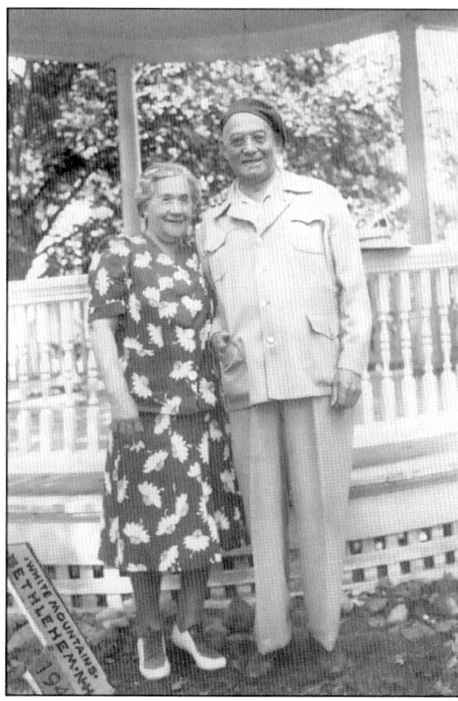

The Sinclair in 1970 was entering its last years of operation. (Bethlehem Heritage Museum.)

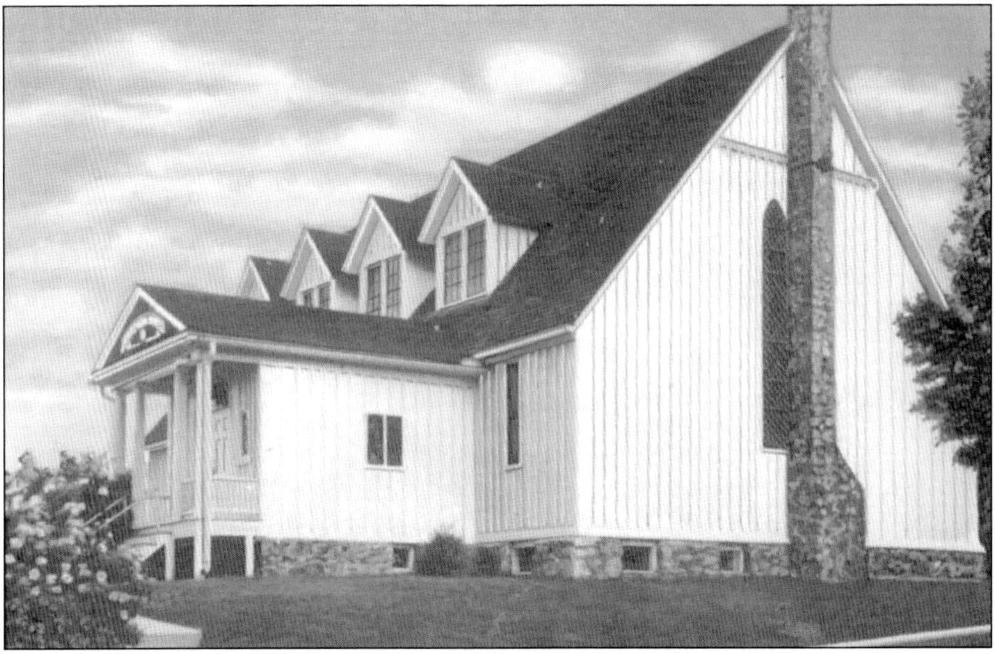

The first Jewish visitors to Bethlehem gathered in storefronts or homes for worship services. A document from 1920 lists 77 individuals who donated money for the purchase of a Torah. Eventually, the Jewish community grew large enough that a permanent place of worship was needed, and a former Episcopal church on Strawberry Hill was purchased. Called the Bethlehem Hebrew Congregation, this synagogue serves both summer visitors and a small year-round population. (Bethlehem Heritage Museum.)

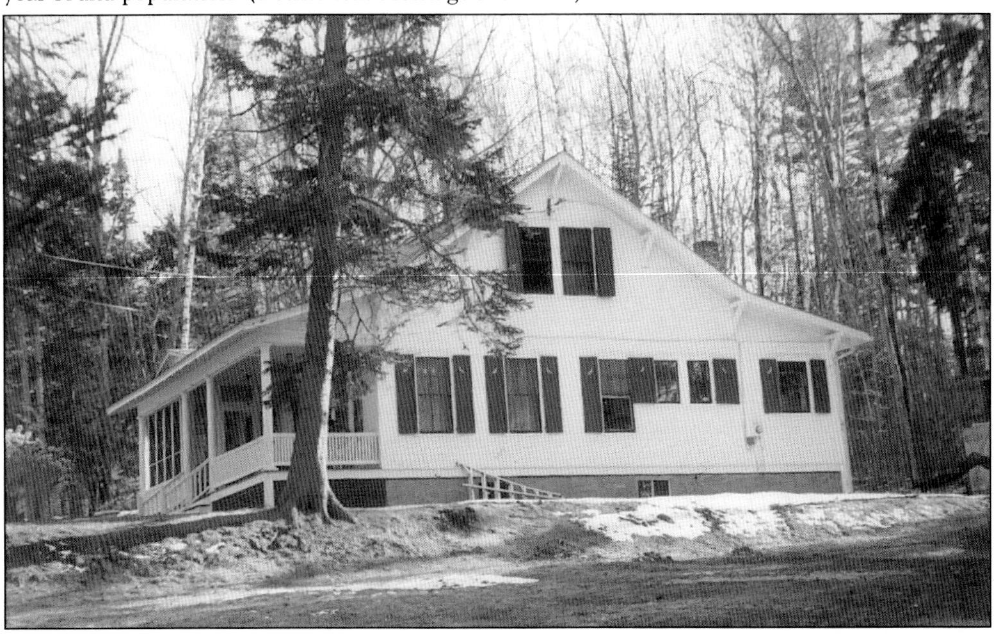

Well-known attorney and writer Louis Nizer donated his parents' summer cottage for use of the Bethlehem Hebrew Congregation's rabbis. The cottage is located on Strawberry Hill a short distance from the synagogue. Lately it has been sold and is now a private home. (Elizabeth Ward.)

The Bethlehem Hebrew Congregation actively celebrates the holy days of Jewish life. Sukkot, also known as the Festival of Tabernacles or Booths, is celebrated for eight days at the end of the harvest period in the autumn. Part of the festival ceremony involves building sukkahs, temporary tabernacles or shelters. Here, a couple stands outside a sukkah on the grounds of the synagogue. (Adele Fisch.)

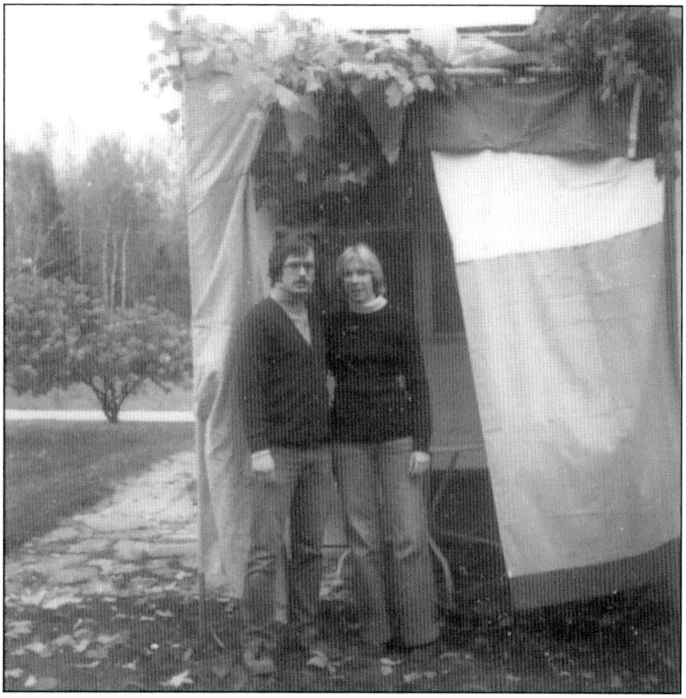

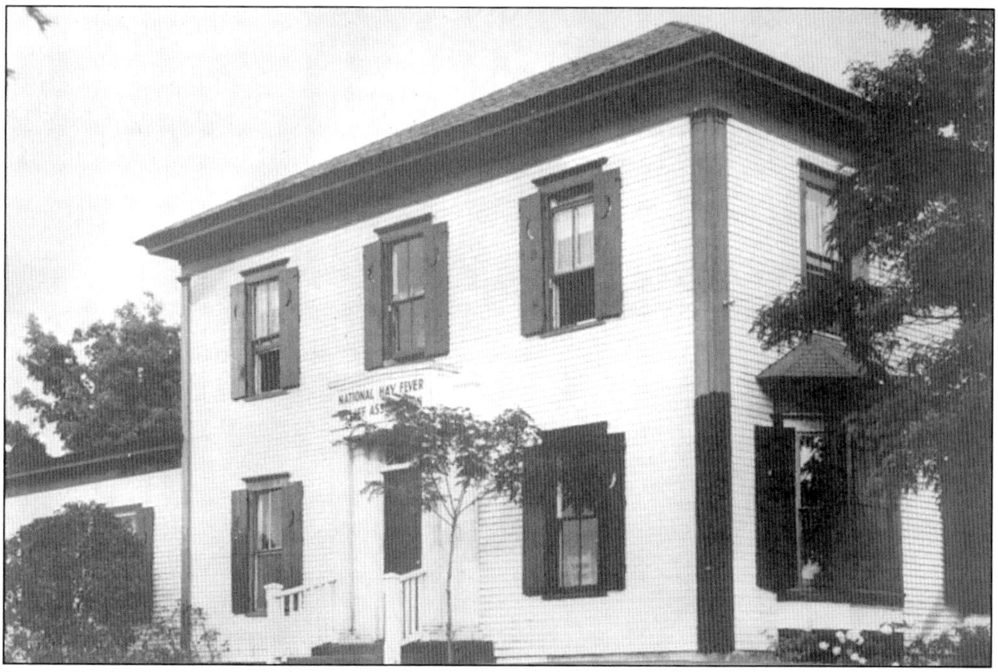

From the late 1920s into the 1970s, the Hay Fever Relief Association maintained a summer camp just outside of town on the northbound side of Route 142. Busloads of hay fever and asthma sufferers came up from New York to enjoy Bethlehem's pollen-free air. In order to ensure air quality, teams of men went around Bethlehem pulling up ragweed. Dr. Herbert Blum, public relations director of the camp, performed important scientific experiments regarding pollen counts. (Bethlehem Heritage Society.)

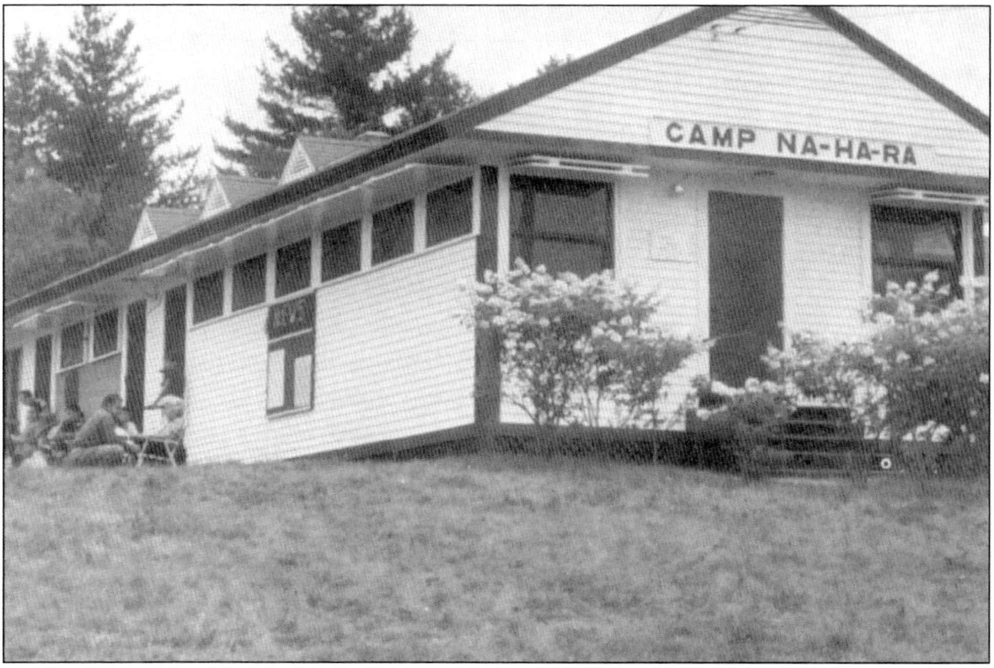

The Na Ha Ra camp for children specialized in providing instruction and amusement for children suffering from hay fever and asthma. (Bethlehem Heritage Society.)

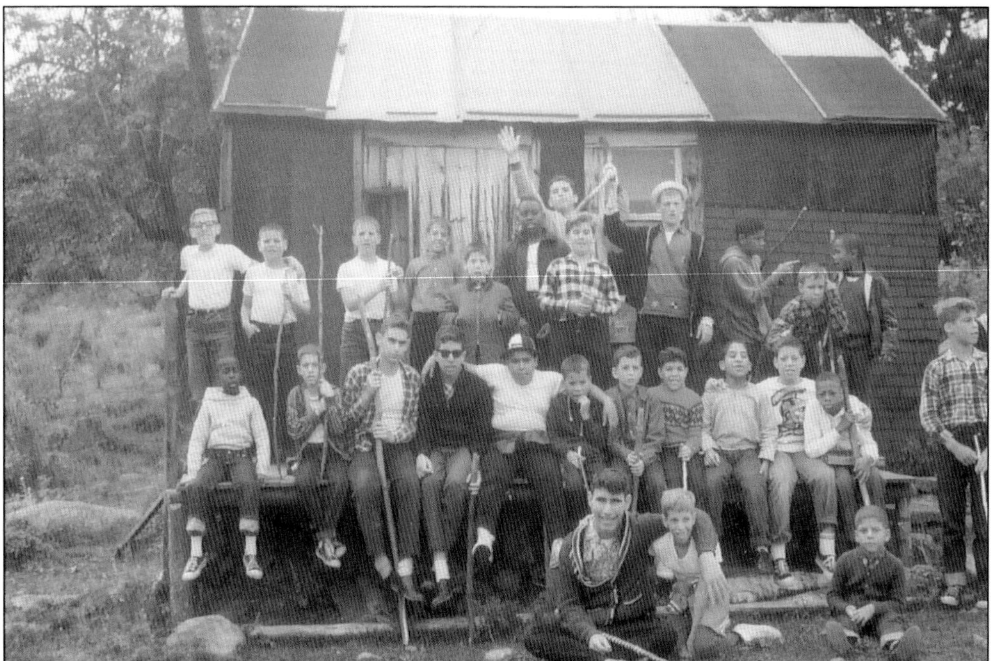

A group of children poses at the Na Ha Ra camp. (Bethlehem Heritage Museum.)

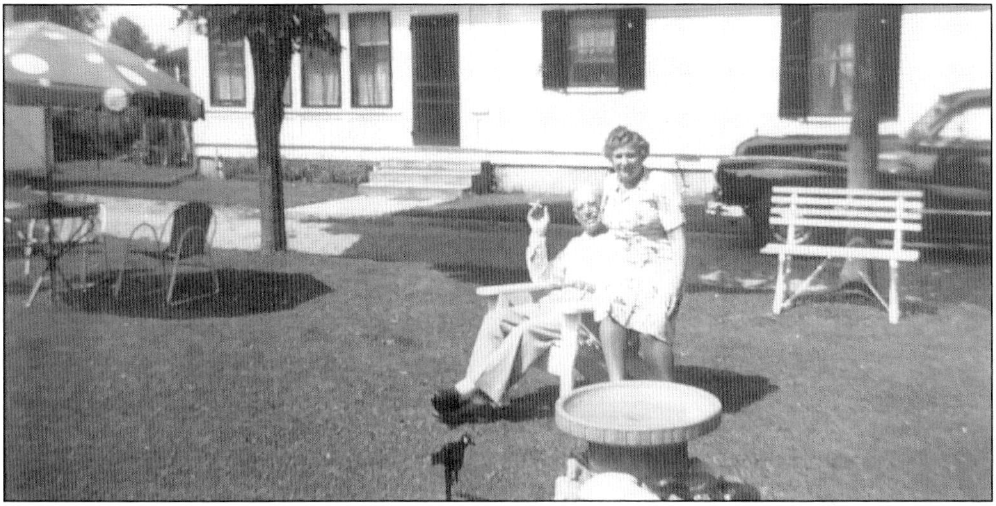

Hyman Berman and his wife enjoy their summer lodgings at 36 Church Street. The family still summers there. Berman built a nine-hole golf course for Jewish visitors on the south side of Mount Agassiz during the 1920s. He also built the storefront block known as the Martignetti Block on Main Street. (Betty Glusky.)

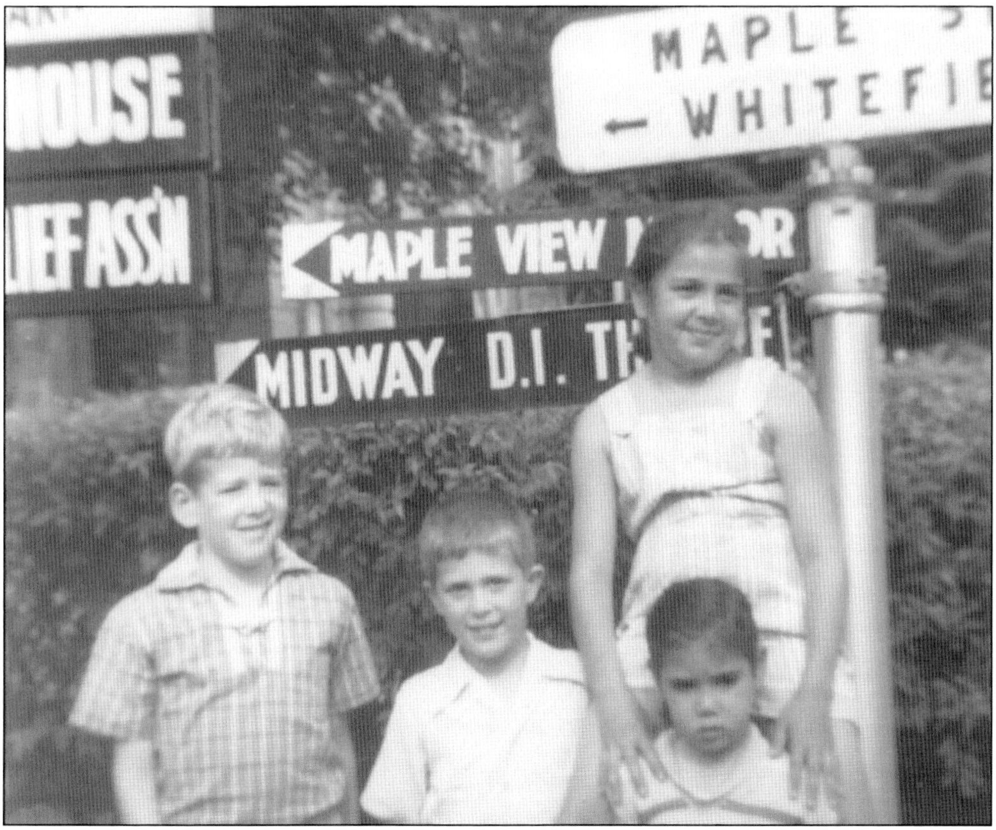

Hyman Berman's grandchildren, Janice and Howard Glusky and Steven and Michelle Barrett, stand in front of the Maple Street sign in 1957. Note the hedge and the signs for the Hay Fever Relief Association, a drive-in theater, and the Maple View. (Betty Glusky.)

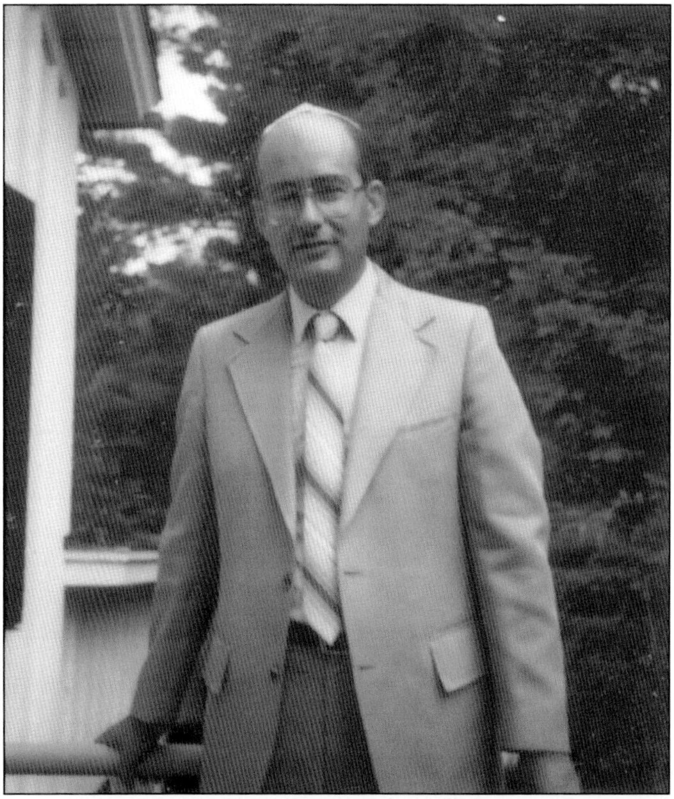

Israel Consul Arthur Avnon visited the Bethlehem Hebrew Congregation on August 5, 1984. (Adele Fisch.)

Dr. Mortimer Fisch confers with a scholar at the Bethlehem Hebrew Congregation. Fisch, a former educator, was president of the congregation and also served as a Bethlehem Library trustee. He and his wife, Adele Fisch, also an educator, retired to Bethlehem in the 1970s. (Adele Fisch.)

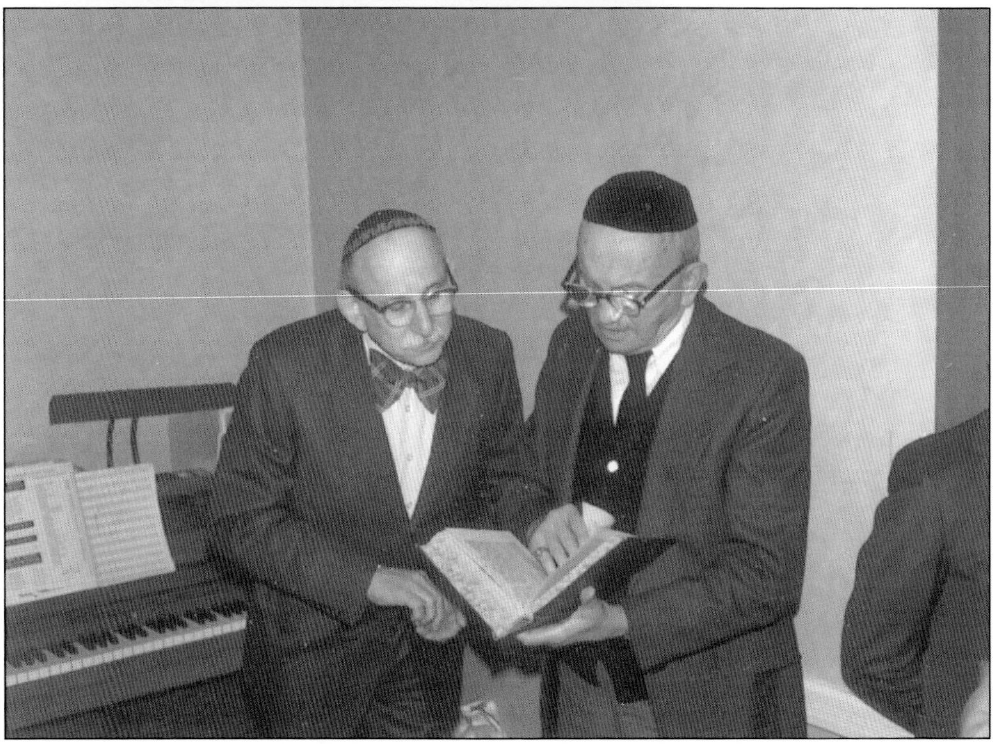

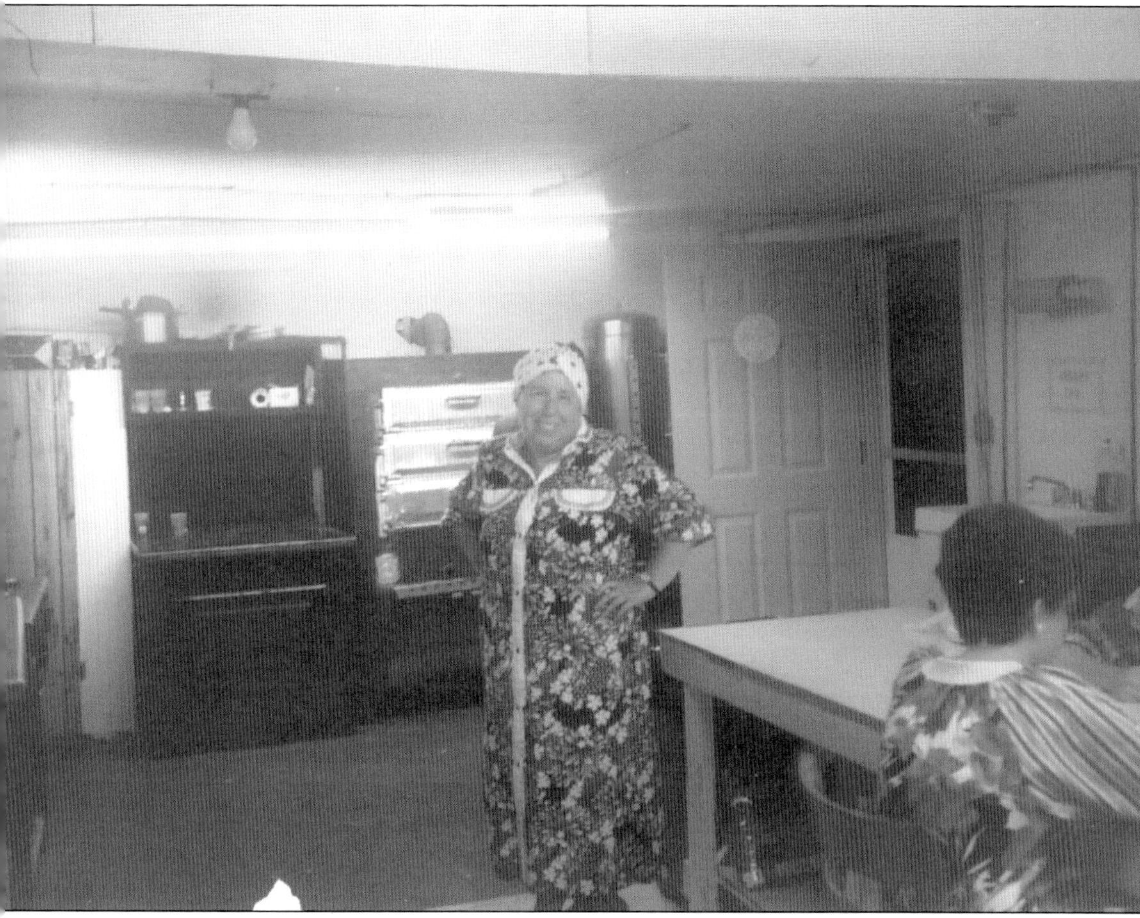

Owner of the New Arlington Hotel since 1969, Jolan Strulovic stands in the dairy kitchen of the hotel, which offers a strictly kosher kitchen and takeout service as well as a mikvah, the ceremonial bath used by Jewish women. In kosher kitchens, meat and dairy products are handled separately. The Arlington has been kosher since the 1940s, when Mr. and Mrs. Gross from Washington, D.C., purchased it. (Solomon Fleischman.)

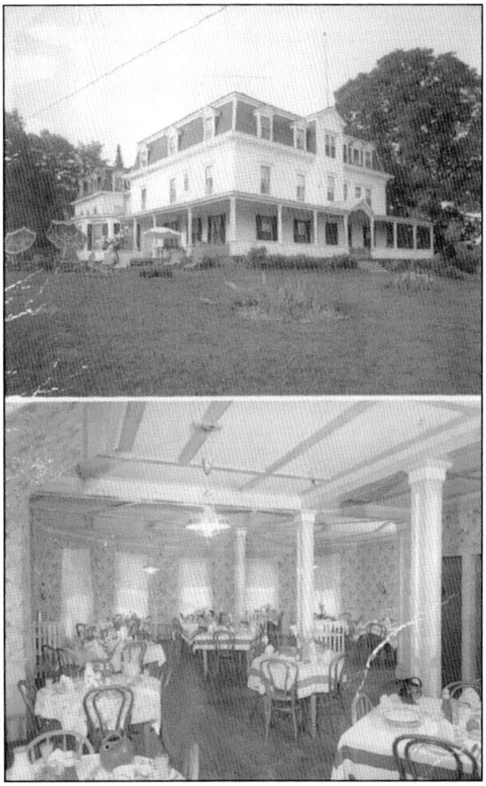

A postcard shows the Arlington Hotel and its dining room in the 1960s. (Solomon Fleischman.)

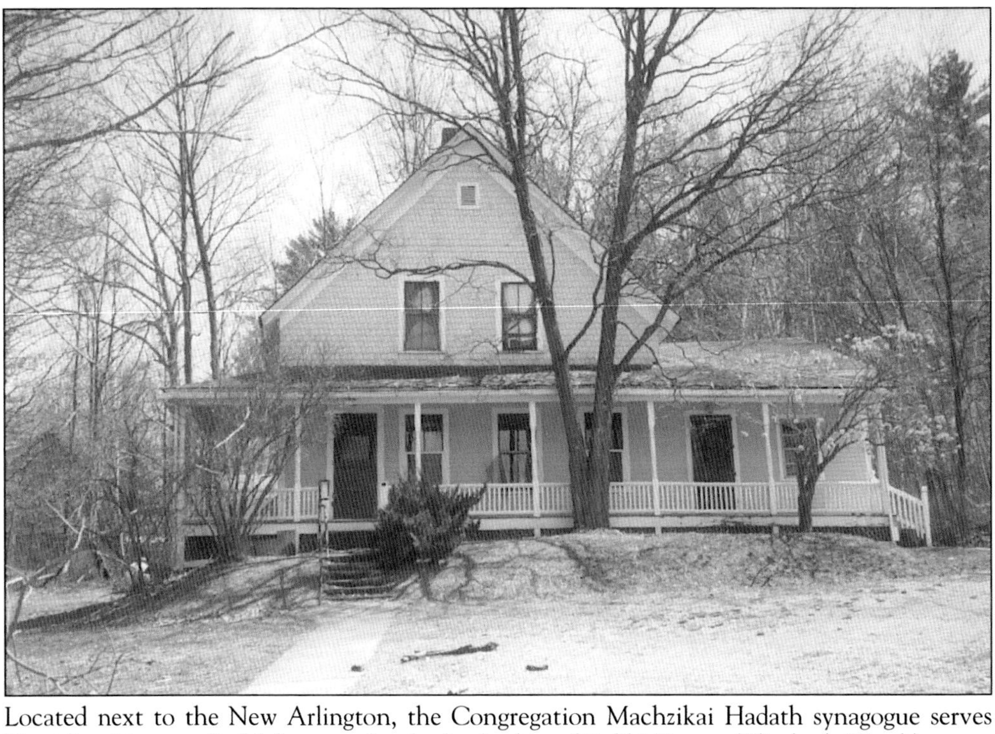

Located next to the New Arlington, the Congregation Machzikai Hadath synagogue serves Hassidic visitors to Bethlehem, under the leadership of Rabbi Hauer. (Elizabeth Ward.)

Relaxing and knitting on the grounds of the New Arlington is a favorite pastime for Mrs. J. Weisz and Sara Fleischman. Although Hassidic families tour the mountains and participate in activities, they spend much time socializing and relaxing at their lodgings. (Solomon Fleischman.)

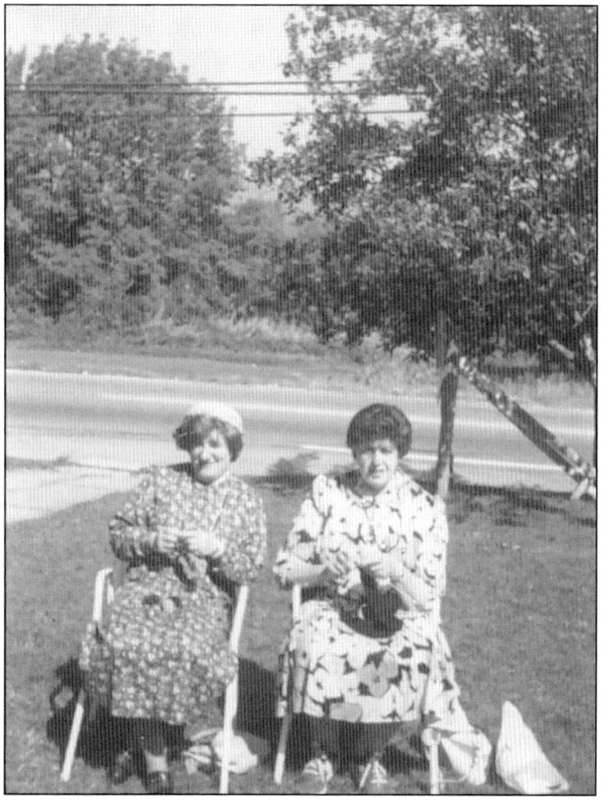

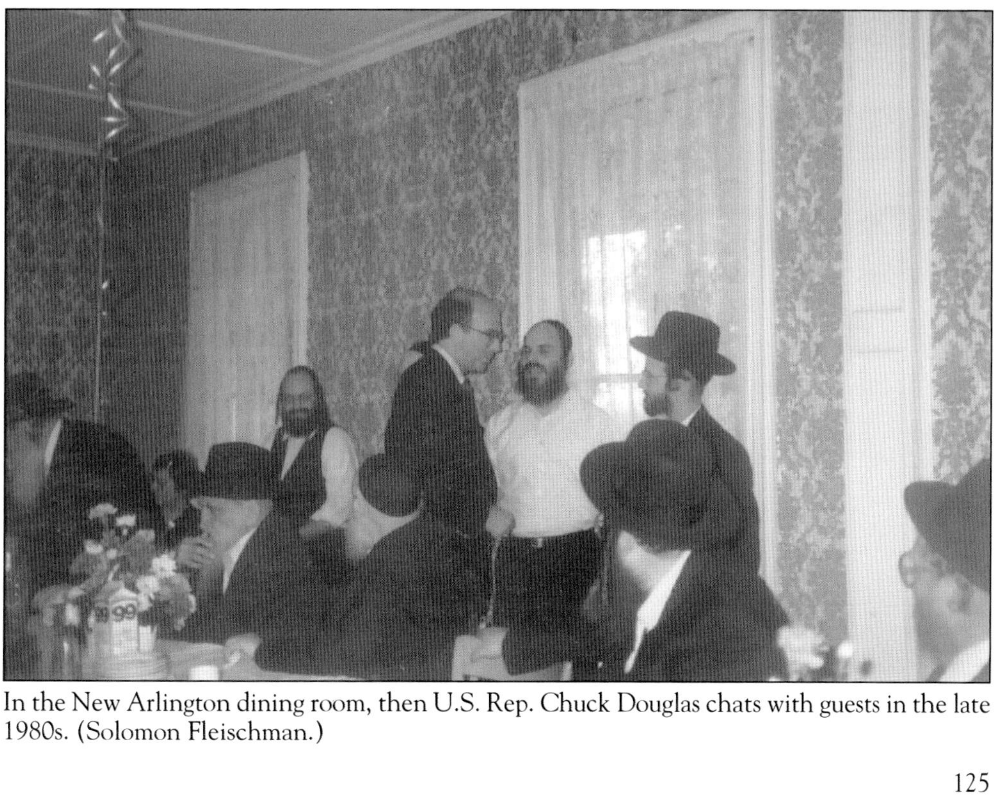

In the New Arlington dining room, then U.S. Rep. Chuck Douglas chats with guests in the late 1980s. (Solomon Fleischman.)

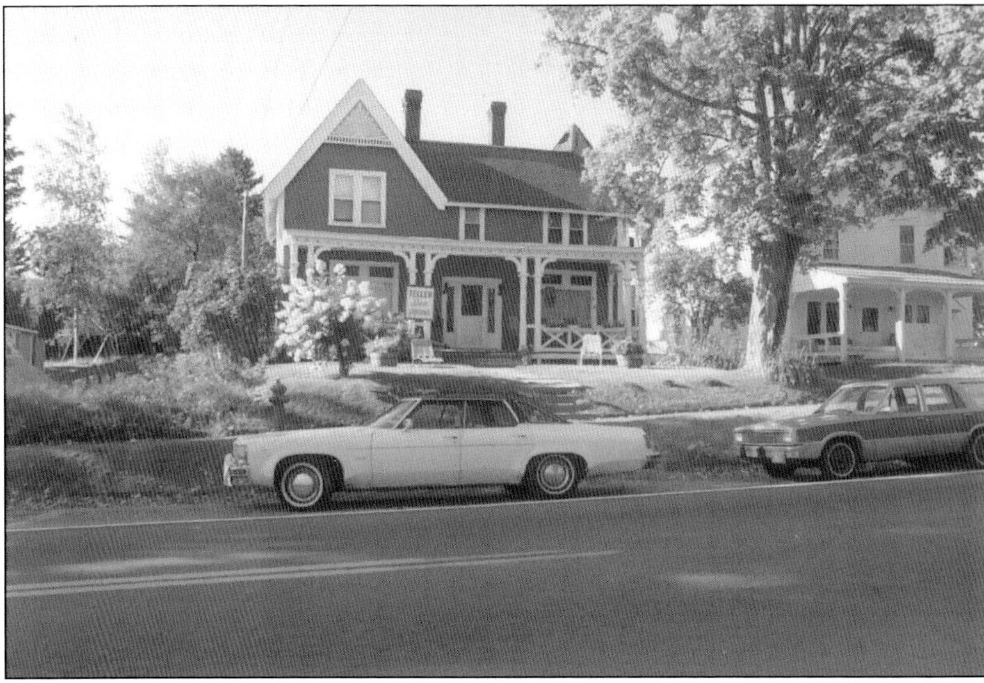

The Teller Inn on Main Street next to the Sherman Inn catered to the Hassidic visitors until the 1990s. (Solomon Fleischman.)

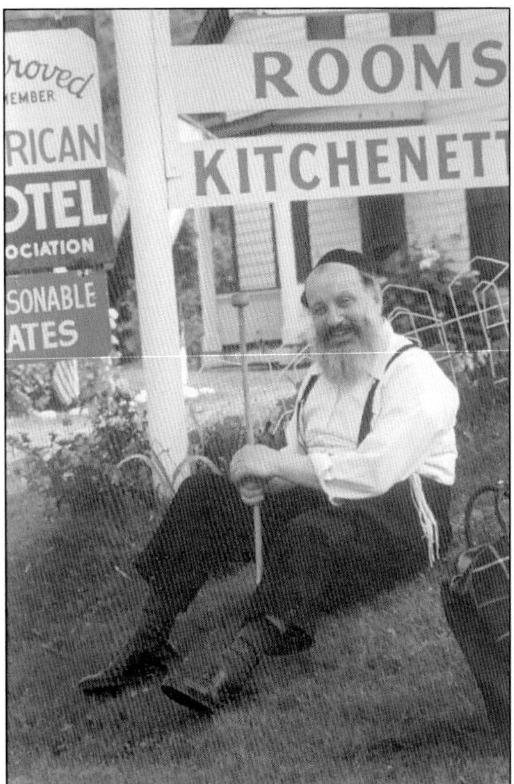

Joseph Katz rests near the Pinewood Motel on Route 302 in 1977. He was a frequent guest at the Park View. (Solomon Fleischman.)

Moses Gruen and his wife pose on the grounds of the Sherman Inn. (Solomon Fleischman.)

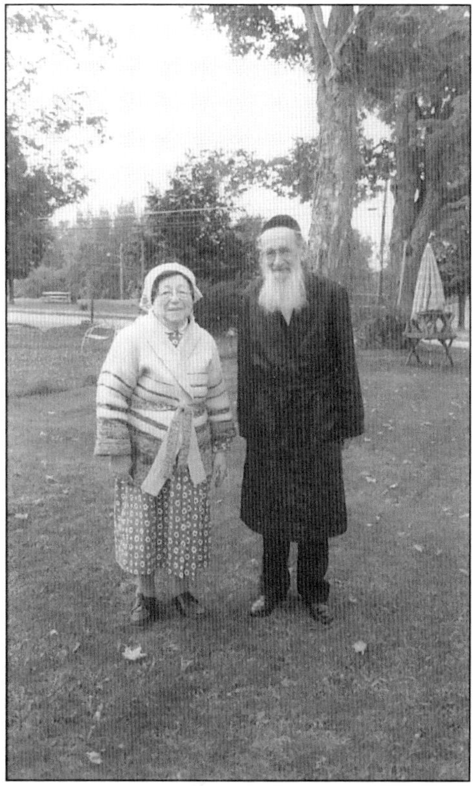

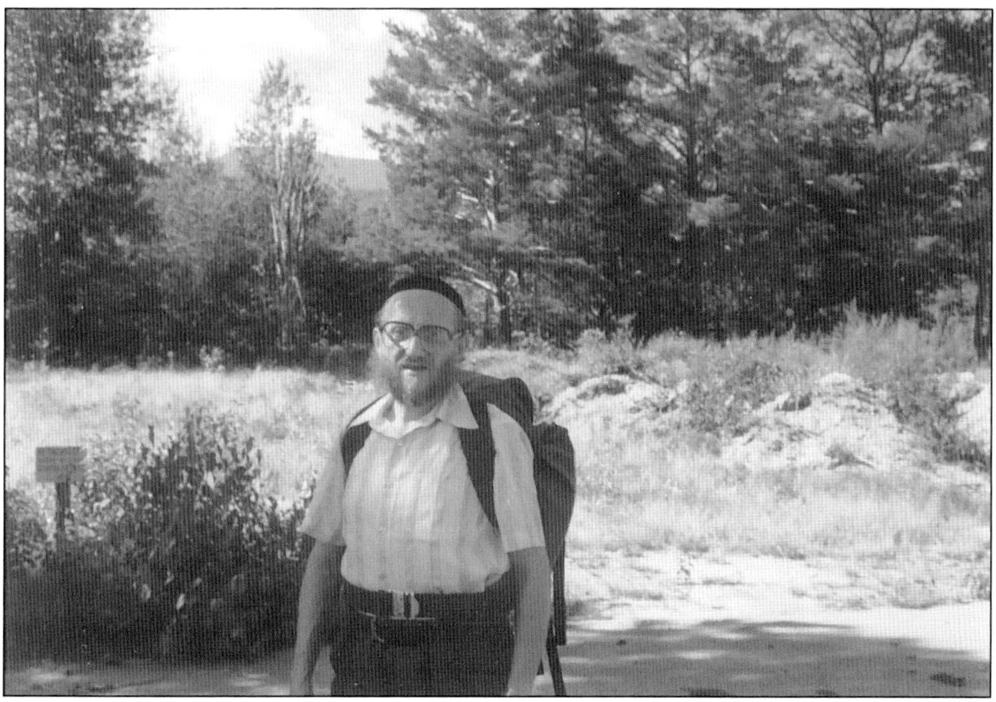

On the grounds of the Park View, Solomon Fleischman prepares for a hike in the White Mountains. (Josef Flein.)

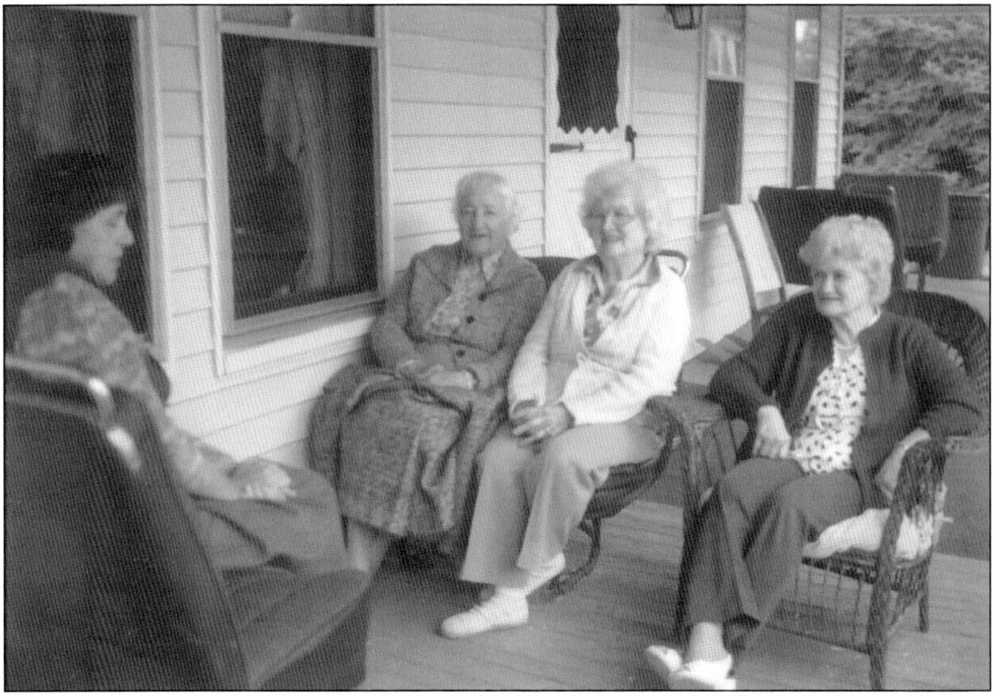

Several inns catering to the Hassidim are owned and operated by non-Jewish innkeepers. Pictured, from left to right, are guests Sara Fleischman and Pauline Lieberson with former owners of the Dew Drop Inn, Gay Lafond and her sister, Irene. (Solomon Fleischman.)

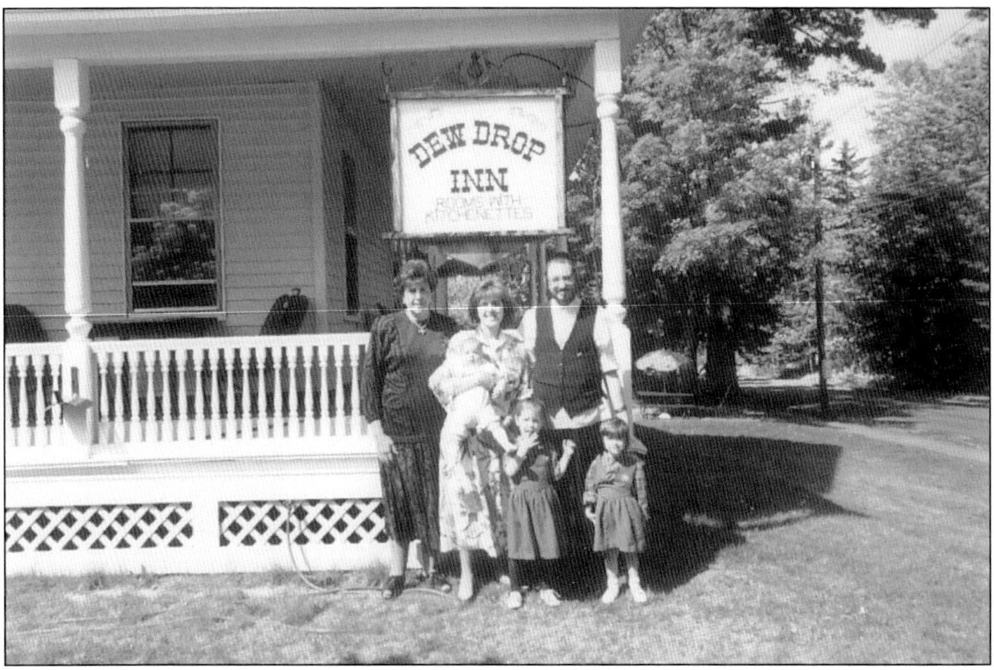

A new generation is coming to Bethlehem. From left to right are Sara Fleischman with her daughter Chana Rosenthal, her son-in-law Aaron Rosenthal, and her grandchildren Rachel, Rivka, and Reizy Rosenthal. (Solomon Fleischman.)